SINGING OUT

SINGING OUT

An Oral History of America's
Folk Music Revivals

DAVID KING DUNAWAY

MOLLY BEER

OXFORD
UNIVERSITY PRESS
2010

Oxford University Press, Inc., publishes works that further
Oxford University's objective of excellence
in research, scholarship, and education.

Oxford   New York
Auckland   Cape Town   Dar es Salaam   Hong Kong   Karachi
Kuala Lumpur   Madrid   Melbourne   Mexico City   Nairobi
New Delhi   Shanghai   Taipei   Toronto

With offices in
Argentina   Austria   Brazil   Chile   Czech Republic   France   Greece
Guatemala   Hungary   Italy   Japan   Poland   Portugal   Singapore
South Korea   Switzerland   Thailand   Turkey   Ukraine   Vietnam

Published by Oxford University Press, Inc.
198 Madison Avenue, New York, NY 10016

www.oup.com

Oxford is a registered trademark of Oxford University Press

Library of Congress Cataloging-in-Publication Data
Dunaway, David King.
Singing out : an oral history of America's folk music revivals
/ David King Dunaway, Molly Beer.
     p.   cm.
Includes bibliographical references and index.
ISBN 978-0-19-537834-4
1. Folk music—United States—History and criticism.
2. Folk songs, English—United States—History and criticism.
3. Oral tradition—United States. I. Beer, Molly. II. Title.
ML3551.D83 2010
781.62'13009—dc22
2009034127

9 8 7 6 5 4 3 2 1
Printed in the United States of America
on acid-free paper

Frontispiece: Collector Anne Warner records Frank Proffitt, source of the Kingston Trio's
first hit song, "Tom Dooley," in Pick Britches Valley, North Carolina, 1941.
Photo by Frank Warner, courtesy of the Frank and Anne Warner Collection

*This book is dedicated to all those who have heard a good old song,
found its lyrics, and sung it to themselves or anyone else.*

Contents

Foreword *by Pete Seeger* ix
Introduction *by David King Dunaway* 1

1 I NEVER HEARD A HORSE SING IT! Defining Folk Music 7

2 EARLY COLLECTORS 17

3 MUSIC FOR THE MASSES 29

4 GREENWICH VILLAGE: 1940s 49

5 AM I IN AMERICA? The Red Scare 76

6 FOLK BOOM 107

7 MOVEMENT MUSIC 137

8 FOLK-ROCK 151

9 NU FOLK: The Music Changes, but the Beat Goes On 168

10 THE POWER OF MUSIC 189

Notes on the Interviews 199
Biographies of Interviewees 202
Notes 211
Bibliography 226
Discography 231
Index 243

Foreword
Pete Seeger

Singing Out is a story of the links in what I think of as one of the world's most important chains, namely the chain of people's singers. I'm proud to be one of these links; I hope there are many more links to come. I'm glad there's a book about such links.

People give me too much credit because they've heard me. They don't know about people like Alan Lomax, or Woody Guthrie, and a whole lot of other people. Not to speak of Francis Child, or Cecil Sharp, and so on. And my father. I just happen to be the link that they've heard of, so they think I'm the daddy of it all. Of course this is not true. I look upon Woody Guthrie and Lead Belly, and Phil Ochs, and Bob Dylan, and countless lesser known people as more links in this chain. I look upon poet Taras Shevchenko of the Ukraine, and that fellow in Paris back in the thirteenth century—the Romantic poet, who lived with the lowlifes of Paris, with the cutthroats, and thieves—François Villon. We're all part of this chain. People who use poems and songs to help turn people's heads around. In one way or another. I'm still working on it in a thousand ways, and I hope this book can be a contribution to it. I think that songwriting and singing as an art form have generally been looked down on more than they should be.

People think, well the symphony's on a high plane; the novel's on a high plane; but I quote Béla Bartók, who said, "A song is just a short form that's on just as high a plane of art as anything else." And I'd like to encourage more people to be songwriters. I'd like it if everybody in the world thought of singing and songwriting as part of their life, just as much as cooking or eating, or tossing a baseball, or swimming. It's something creative you do with words and tunes and friends.

I decided I would be a musician in 1940, when I came back from that summer having supported myself singing in saloons. I'd spent the whole summer. I'd hitchhiked around, came back in good health. I hadn't had to write home for money, or to telephone home from jail. (Slept in a couple of jails.) I decided Alan Lomax was right: maybe I'd better stick with music. I was really enjoying it. I knew I'd never starve as long as I could pick a banjo. It was quite a victory.

Music became a device for me to get to meet people. I couldn't have gone into a saloon and ordered a glass of beer and started talking to people; I was too shy. But if I went into a saloon with a banjo in front of me, and they asked me to play, and I got started talking that way, that was fine.

I remember I got Woody Guthrie to teach me five or six of the songs which would get me by.

I said, "Woody, what kind of songs will get me some coins if I sing them?"

"Well," he says, "Try 'Makes No Difference Now,' and 'Be Nobody's Darling but Mine'; and a few Jimmie Rodgers's blues can't go wrong."

So I learned half a dozen songs from him, Gene Autry songs, and other ones, and armed with these, I walked into my first saloon, just like he told me.

He said: "Now don't start singing right away. Just keep that banjo slung on your back. Nurse a nickel beer as long as you can. Sooner or later someone's gonna say, 'Kid, can you play that thing?'

"And don't be too eager. Say, 'Well, just a bit.'

"Keep on sipping your beer.

"Sooner or later someone will say, 'Kid, I got a quarter for you if you'll pick us a tune.'

"Now you play your best piece."

When it comes to folk music revivals, I have had my doubts. Take a revival song like "Michael Row Your Boat Ashore." Here was a song I sang only half well. When you think of how truly magnificent it must have been when done by a bunch of sweating black people rowing ashore from Sullivan's Island, from those islands to the mainland, 150 years ago. It must have been an absolutely magnificent thing. The raw voices in the formal sense—but superbly trained voices in the sense that they'd been singing all their lives. Making up new verses and laughing as they think of a new verse to it. Who is Michael? Is it the Archangel Michael? The Michael at the oar? It's full of fluid ambiguity. The sunlight beating down, and the original situation probably would be something unforgettable.

In 1867, Charles Pickard Ware grabbed his pencil and paper and said, "I must get this down." And he wrote down as much as he could and then afterward he went around to the singers and said, "What verse was that you were singing?"

They said, "You mean you're writing this down? Wow, well here's what I was singing."

So then his book *Slave Songs of the United States* comes out and sits on that shelf. Ninety years later Tony Saletan goes through the book page by page. He shrewdly selects three verses out of fifteen or twenty. He teaches the song to me, and I teach it to the Weavers. We went to Carnegie Hall singing it.

Now it comes back to me from numerous schools and summer camps, such a pale wishy-washy piece of music compared to what it was once. And I realize that my own singing of it is kind of pale and wishy-washy, compared to what it was once. It makes me wonder, is it possible to revive folk music? Well, I finally came to the conclusion: yes, it is possible. We can try. All you can do in this world is try. And a good attempt at trying is sure better than never having tried.

Do you remember the man, Edward FitzGerald, who did the translation of Omar Khayyám saying "Better a live sparrow than a stuffed eagle?" They said, "Your translation is nowhere near as good as the original." He said, "But the original is sitting there on a piece of paper, with no one to read it. It's dead."

So, better a live sparrow.

I believe songs have a purpose, obviously, or else I wouldn't be doing what I'm doing. And occasionally I've come across well-known people who say something similar. John L. Lewis talked about the union songs, and Martin Luther King, Jr., talked about the civil rights songs. Historians have talked about the Irish song "Lillibullero" having cost King James his throne, and Anatole France has said songs have overthrown kings and emperors. I think you can overstate the case, because quite often songs try to, but they don't. But, if there's a human race still here a hundred years from now, I believe historians will agree that songs are one of the reasons.

Songs have proved a wonderful, flexible art form, going from one person to the other. It doesn't have to be written down; it can be memorized. And whereas mural painters need walls, dancers need floors, sculptors need warehouses, novelists need printers, and composers need symphonies—songwriters are lucky.

Acknowledgments

Books are cooperative undertaking, as writers often point out when they thank those who inspired and sustained their labors. For this coauthored book, this has been the case to an even greater extent. Our first and greatest debt is to the musicians, scholars, and other experts whose voices make up this volume. Over the years they have willingly shared their stories, some of them multiple times. We want to thank each of the sixty-five people whose interviews have been included here (each is listed individually in the biographies at the end of the book).

We would also like to thank the scholars of folk music whose insights have contributed greatly to the volume, particularly Ronald Cohen, Richard Reuss, Neil Rosenberg, Dick Weissman, Thomas Gruning, Benjamin Filene, and, of course, Pete and Charles Seeger. Though our intent with this book is to showcase the breadth of thinking on folk music revival, we build on the firm foundations laid by these writers.

Others who have helped in the creation of this book include these associates: Felicia Karas, Michael Russom, Steve Mayer, Todd Harvey of the American Folklife Center of the Library of Congress, the Ralph Rinzler Folklife Archives, the Woody Guthrie Archive, and our colleagues at the University of New Mexico and San Francisco State University. Thank you also to our editor at Oxford University Press, Nancy Toff, and all those who labor anonymously to perpetuate the world of books.

Finally we would like to thank our friends and families for their patience and support (and babysitting), especially Nina and Alexei, Sam and Lucia, Steven and Avery.

SINGING OUT

INTRODUCTION David King Dunaway

A "romantic mist" has long surrounded the study of folk culture.[1] Many collectors and enthusiasts of folk music have been romantics and, often, patriots. This is because folk music's common nobility of spirit is rooted in its origins in the peoples of a country and its landscape. The songs are carved from the contours of the land and the primordial experiences of communities.

Folk music has inspired some of our best-loved composers in the West: Liszt, Mussorgsky, Bartók, and Ives, among many. And no wonder. It's inevitable that the faintly heard pipe across the river valley would catch the composer's ear. And folk music is a river, always flowing, steady and heedless. It has always been the underground stream of American musical culture: the rhythms of daily life, the tune and lyrics of unspoken eloquence. From this river of folk musics has sprung three overlapping American folk music revivals, each with its own direction, personalities, and practice.

Only when we feel ourselves losing the old ways do we begin to think about preserving and reviving them. Thus, the folk music revivals of the twentieth century had their origin in the Romantic belief in human possibility. It is Jean-Jacques Rousseau teaching songs to the schoolboy Emile under a tree. It is Walt Whitman baying at the sea, and the high lonesome twang of a homemade banjo in the distance. Folk music is lighthearted, tragic and bloody, sad and glad, bawdy and blue.

It's best said in the beginning that there's no reviving what never died. Folk music is always with us. It is in the tap of the hammer to the music on the radio in the workshop or, in older days, to the workers' own singing. It is the rhythmic push of the cabinetmaker's saw, the scan across the checkout station to the beat of songs inside the checker's head.

The United States was founded by such workers and protesters—in particular, religious ones—drawn (or torn) from distant shores. In the baggage of these folk was their music, their instruments sometimes their only possessions. And if they had no instruments, they quickly found them in the New World's sticks and hides: banjos were made from raccoons, pipes carved from bone. And no sooner did they get together and sing the old songs than they started to hybridize them to fit their new circumstances.

From the first, Americans were addicted to revivals—of the old country's ways, of its holidays and ceremonies; and to revivals of faith, as in the Great Awakening (1730–60) or in the rise in religious fundamentalism since the 1980s. All depended on music as a social glue of community.

In the twentieth century, the first folk revival was led by researchers, thinkers, and collectors inspired by nineteenth-century Romantics, such as, in Germany, the brothers Grimm, Herder, Hauptmann, even Goethe. In sound recordings, the revivals' origins might date from the 1890s, with the first ethnographic recordings of the people of North America's first nations. Preservationists of stories, jokes, or tunes visited libraries; they drove or hiked across damp and dusty byways to find a local storyteller, or that "fiddler in the woods," only to be told: "But you should have seen his uncle—he was *really* good."

Out of these collectors' efforts, a folk music revival movement was born. In the winter of 1940 in Arlington, Virginia, John Lomax's son, Alan, was briefly the roommate of Charles Seeger's son, Peter. Together they would help make folk music respectable and fun, bringing it to millions of folks aching for the sounds of home. But the Lomax-Seeger cultural axis sought something different from what the earlier folk music antiquarians had sought: they wanted to sing their way to action, to build labor unions, to remind people the world over that they were brothers and sisters. With coast-to-coast radio available for the tuning in, a new audience was born. Out of this collector-based revival, beginning with the publication of *Cowboy Songs* and ending with the disbanding of the Weavers (1910–53), would eventually come a nation of singers and pickers. Yet it was not as simple as a critic for the *San Francisco Chronicle* wrote "The Seegers take mainly from Lomaxes and the Lomaxes take mainly from God."[2]

The early collectors, notably Cecil Sharp and Olive Dame Campbell, John and Alan Lomax, and Carl Sandburg, among many, published songbooks. Later, professional musicians found their work and sang it to urban audiences. In the ensuing years, a wave of folksingers descended on Greenwich Village. Woody Guthrie, Lead Belly, and others appeared at the first hootenannies hosted there by the Almanac Singers in 1940. Greenwich Village already had a bohemian reputation dating back to before World War I, but out of those twisting streets—that the old bourgeoisie of Manhattan Island passed over when they set up the city's grid—came unionizing songs of the 1930s and 1940s, the Henry Wallace presidential campaign of 1948, and the Weavers, who rehearsed on MacDougal Street in the Village and there achieved fantastic success with folk-styled songs like "Goodnight Irene" and "So Long (It's Been Good to Know Yuh)."

At this point, in the 1950s, the story of American folk music became more entwined with political history. In its domestic incarnation, the

Cold War had the FBI and the CIA chasing folksingers up and down the block. That era had its rats and its heroes, its songsters and its politicos— the two occasionally meeting at a hootenanny or rally. By the fifties, the only job a musician such as Pete Seeger or Earl Robinson could get was teaching folk music in schools, where a younger generation began to sing the songs. In that second revival, a folk music boom reverberated across America, from Washington Square Park in Greenwich Village to the Gate of Horn in Chicago, spreading west to the coffeehouses of California.

Regardless of blacklists, folk music was now flowing in America. By the 1960s, tens of thousands of boys and girls would think about buying a banjo or a guitar, learning a few chords, and winning friends (and dates) by strumming songs they remembered. The revival seeded some young-sters so profoundly that they centered their lives on making music and collecting folklore; in a few, these passions became a profession. And this second folk music revival mingled great new songs of the civil rights and antiwar movements with old ones, as African-American spirituals were recreated on the front line of protests.

As the popularity of folk music peaked in the mid-sixties, a schism emerged between folk music traditionalists and folk-rockers. For some, rock and roll—itself a revival of earlier rhythm-and-blues traditions— seemed to wipe out the sweeter, softer echoes of folk music sing-alongs. The later emergence of punk, rap, hip-hop, and other musical genres would occasionally bow in the direction of folk roots; but the sixties' countercul-ture seemed to toll the end of the folk music revival.

Yet out of the seeds scattered from Johnny Appleseed's musical bag, a third folk music boomlet was born. This third revival is today based on a world of influences. It might be said to have begun in 1989 with the founding of the Folk Alliance, which sought to represent musicians, educators, festival planners, and other stakeholders in folk-related com-merce. The third revival is more technocentric than earlier ones. Video and audio fidelity revives older recordings of the folk masters, and the Internet catapults them out to musicians everywhere. A vast new wave of amateur and professional documentaries, blogs, and other portable pub-lic media is emerging. The revivalists of today might well be asked what traditions they are keeping alive; they would answer: "All!" or "A dozen or so." There are folk-rockers like The Oysterband, banging away at old ballads like "Hard Times Of Old England," and harpists like Alan Stivell, syncopating hymns into jazz. There are modern-day griots, such as Kim and Reggie Harris, teaching the power of song across time. Their sources are global, fast-traveling yet individual; contemporary revivalists bring to these choices their personal starting points—their family and commu-nity's musical traditions, what they learned in school or choir, or at a campfire.

In this third revival, the grandchildren of Woody Guthrie and Pete Seeger—the Sarah Lee or Abe Guthries or Tao Rodriguez-Seegers and the thousands more who are their children by influence—are making their musical imprint. They are pulling out songbooks or warped records from their parents' folk revival, learning to play an instrument or two, and then performing for their MySpace friends or the virtual audience in what *Rolling Stone* called in 2007 the "YouTube Folk Revival." If they perform on a physical stage, in front of a live audience, it might be at one of the hundreds of folk music summer camps or coffeehouses, or one of the numerous festivals held each year across America.

It's friends who get together and sing on Friday nights instead of going out to concerts; maybe it's parents getting together for a pancake breakfast and teaching their kids old songs; maybe it's a bonfire, where revelers sit together and sing a few songs they all know.

That is the lesson of folk music revivals: that *we* are the ones being revived, not the songs, tales, and sayings that the revivalists uncovered and published. It is the oldest discovery: that we all have roots, and they are the source of what makes us each musically distinctive. Sometimes the urge to revive starts in someone's living room, over tea or beer. Sometimes it begins in the library stacks where a musician or scholar has poked his or her head. Sometimes it starts with large-scale American collecting efforts, such as those of the Library of Congress. Eventually, it rises up singing.

THE INTERVIEWS

For more than thirty years (1975–2009), I've been conducting detailed interviews on topics related to folk music; many are now archived at the American Folklife Center of the Library of Congress, in the David Dunaway Collection. The resulting material—thousands upon thousands of pages of transcripts, crates of recordings—may be accessed there by scholars and the public. (See the note on the interviews at the end of the book.) My research priorities—like those of any researcher—were shaped by my origins. I grew up in a dyed-in-the-wool bohemian family in Greenwich Village during the frightened fifties, between the end of the first folk revival and the flowering of the second. My parents (an editor and a dramaturge) were as politically engaged and as hounded by the FBI as many of those speaking here. But as a teenager wandering the crooked streets of the Village and ducking down into the basement folk clubs, the politics of folk music were less compelling than its community of high-spirited freethinkers and dynamic cultural exploration.

My fascination with the Village's fusion of music and politics ultimately led me to Berkeley, and its first Ph.D. in American studies. I conducted my first group of interviews then, from the perspective of a doctoral candidate at Berkeley. Charles Seeger, patriarch of the Seeger clan and preeminent ethnomusicologist, was eighty-nine on the April day in 1976 when I wrote the following field notes after conducting a series of interviews with him.

> I arrived each day at around 10:30. Pulling over an old wooden chair with a rope seat, I would set up a stereo cassette recorder, and two high-quality microphones. There was a patrician manner about Charlie, a tall, upright man dressed in casual slacks, a jacket and vest, and an ascot of silk that screened his hearing aid. His hair was thinned, revealing a broad brow with even furrows that spread back from his crown. In his Yankee dialect, he pronounced "calm" more closely to "come," and rang the final syllable in "Peter" as if admonishing a slow-learning composition student. Reclining on a couch covered with a wooly throw of South American Indian origin, he would close his eyes, resting those arching eyebrows and reminisce, occasionally pausing to hold his ear like the old ballad singers do, to still the resonance of his own voice. Throughout, there was a feeling of a still, ordered world, where family, personal character, the right way of doing things—all were predetermined; no discussion on such matters was necessary.
>
> "Oh, when Peter plays in Bridgewater, [Connecticut,]" Charlie laughed, "he would never sing anything that might offend the friends of old Aunt Elsie, who grew up there."

ORGANIZATION AND METHOD

This book explores the origin, characters, and situation of folk music revivals, via contextualized interviews. For those interested in the lively field of folk music as it is in the world (as opposed to its dusty archives) it is intended to be a lively, readable collection. Each chapter is framed around a major folk music topic and provides historical background. Though the chapters are roughly chronological, our story is not linear. Just as the river meanders, so do accounts of folk music and topical song—like a ballad of eighteen verses that over time is reduced to a half dozen, folk music by definition changes. Parts are left out, new material added. The application of a song shifts with the times, yet what Tristram Potter Coffin called "the emotional core" of the song remains the same.[3] True to the oral tradition of folk music, this book's story is told by the voices of those who shaped revivals of folk music: ethnomusicologists, political theorists, writers, producers, and, of course, the singers and composers themselves. At the beginning of this story, collectors, or "songcatchers," rummaged through America's musical attic. Later, composers with a new way of singing things transformed the collected songs for topical, political ends. Later yet, it took an Aunt Molly Jackson, a midwife from Kentucky coal country and union activist, to confront a scholar like Charles Seeger with the weight of his country's musical past.

Rather than attempting to capture and compartmentalize folk music revivals in a definitive and analytical work, this book seeks to balance oral testimony and historical narrative. The oral history segments (edited for print, and excluding the interviewer's questions) that make up this collection represent two categories of oral historiography: oral biography[4] and oral literary history.[5] The primary value of this volume may be in how oral history allows multiple voices to piece history together collectively.

Over the course of this book, many folk music figures will become familiar to the reader, as their voices recur from chapter to chapter. These interviewees represent a cross-section of revival scholars, performers, and onlookers from across the past century; some are obscure, others internationally known; and the cast of speakers is far from comprehensive. They grapple with questions about the nature of folk music in terms of tradition, commercialism, and musicality. They offer no definitive answers. Nor do we.

As folk music has passed from old-timers to scholars to performers to fans, and then on to their children, and those children's children, it has broadened into something new—timeless, worldly, and essentially democratic. The speakers in this volume are all a part of that process; here we have seated them together to let them tell their collective story.

1

"I NEVER HEARD A HORSE SING IT"

Defining Folk Music

In the beginning, there were the folk, and they sang songs. They did not sing folk songs; they did not know that term. They sang songs. Along comes the collector, who collects the song and calls it a folk song.
—Joe Hickerson

WHAT IS FOLK MUSIC? Anglo-Saxon sailors' songs? Calypso? Kentucky bluegrass? Flamenco? Cajun and zydeco? Rap!? And who, by the way, are "folk"? These are simple questions for which there have never been simple answers; they lead to a string of dichotomies: us and them, old and new, authentic and imitation, "low" culture and "high." The following efforts to define (or simply describe) folk music demonstrate the sheer range of opinion.[1]

Composer Earl Robinson, on the essential nature of folk music: Ah, the folk song is close to the people. It's the average person's way of expressing themselves without hassle, or in the middle of hassle. It's almost a natural way, like you can spend time writing words, but when you add music to it, it adds this other dimension that sometimes you don't need the words, even. But it expresses a deep—psychic, if you like—part of human beings, which we must express; we must express whenever we can.[2]

Editor Mark Moss, on the public conception of folk music: It's a little bit easier if you talk about how the public defines folk music; they define it in a much more rigid way than I would. The public actually does not define it as traditional music. They define it as the contemporary singer-songwriter: white guy, white girl with a guitar singing original songs.[3]

Musician John Cohen, on perceptions of folk music: I've talked to a lot of people about the perception of traditional music in the thirties and forties. I did a lot of research. One of the things I did was ask everybody what their perception of traditional music was. Everyone said the same: Woody Guthrie, Josh White, Lead Belly. It came up over and over again. That, for people in the folk song movement, represented all traditional music.

It's interesting because that excluded all of these incredible recordings. People could see these four or five trees and said that they represented the whole forest. If you want to trace that issue you'll find a huge split between those who came from the Woody/Lead Belly tradition, and those who know about all the other things. Political differences, social differences, maybe even economic differences.[4]

Musician Mike Seeger, on defining folk music: One of the best things about folk music is that you can say just about anything; you're supposed to talk about everything that's happening—groundhogs to lords and ladies—from three hundred years ago to what happened yesterday on the picket line. I specialize in the sounds of the music and the representation of the music.

How about [Aunt Molly Jackson's] "Come All You Coal Miners"? It ends with:

Let's sink this capitalist system
In the darkest pits of hell.

You wouldn't really call it a folk song, but it is. Except that it hasn't lived on in the traditional means.[5]

Mark Moss, on defining folk music: Folk music is folk music foremost because of its connection to the community and because of how it's made and how it's used. The interesting question is, which is more folk music, Doc Watson singing an old Appalachian ballad on the stage of Carnegie Hall for people who have paid $75 a ticket and they're all wearing tuxes; or a guy singing a Beatles song to his baby in his kitchen while they're waiting for Mom to make dinner? I say the latter....Celine Dion [singing "If I Had a Hammer"] doesn't make it folk music.

[Some critics] don't understand what folk music is, what traditional music is. Francis Child, when he was going around and collecting ballads from people, people were also singing to him all these bawdy songs and ballads that they knew. And because he was a proper English gentleman he didn't count those. Doc Watson, when Ralph Rinzler first found him, was playing along with the traditional music that was his family music; while he was earning a living playing rockabilly in a bar. Doc incorporates a wide array of that stuff. [Alan] Lomax would go and record these older singers. And similarly, they would be singing this old ballad and then they would sing, a cappella, this Rudy Vallee song or other pop music of the day.…

I think the concept of folk music is about a living tradition, and that it's about all this stuff that is happening around you.[6]

Folksinger Arlo Guthrie, on defining folk music: If people want to get back to playing homegrown music, it's probably because they've discovered it's just more fun, more creative, and it's their music; which is something that I grew up learning. So I'm not newly interested or necessarily involved in things that have just happened. I've always tried to make those connections with people through the kind of music I play and through the people whom I play it with. All of the music that is going on is folk music; some of it is bad, some of it's lousy, and some of it's great, but it's all folk music. Everything from disco ducks to old ballad songs. It's all part of our heritage.

I think the thing that has concerned me the most is that, for almost two generations now, magazines who call themselves folk magazines and musicologist types have almost excluded the things that are current from our traditions. They have convinced a couple of generations of Americans that their music is not folk music and that their dance isn't folk dance; therefore, their thoughts are not folk thoughts and their hopes are not folk hopes. I've always been against that kind of thing. So, whether it's homegrown, or commercial, or whether it's this or that, I really couldn't care. It's all folk music to me.[7]

Pete Seeger quoting blues musician Big Bill Broonzy's definition of folk music: "It's *all* folk music; I never heard a horse sing it!"[8]

FOLK MUSIC'S DEFINITION ACROSS REVIVALS

Ever since the notion of "folk music" entered into popular culture, it has had as many shades of meaning as practitioners and aficionados. For some, a folksinger is a romantic figure out of a primitive past: a Paul Bunyan of song. For others, folksingers are a 1960s stereotype: "two beards and a blonde singing about a Negro with chains on his legs, and he is *very* far from home," as folklorist John Cohen writes.[9] Between these extremes, each folksinger or singer of folk music or folk fan will offer his or her own take on the genre's meaning and function. This breadth of opinion will lead to plenty of disagreement in this volume, as narrators revisit the genre at its peak and again today.

One of the original debates about folk music was whether new songs by the folk themselves constituted folk music. Early folk collectors believed that in order to be a true folk song, the work had to be age-old and anonymous. Collector Francis James Child at Harvard University had compiled a list of 305 English and Scottish popular ballads that came to be seen by critics as "a closed canon, like the Bible; no more could ever be added; the mould was broken, the ballad a lost art."[10] Newcomers to the field soon disputed this devolutionist, old school of folk collecting, arguing that traditional ballads were still being authentically reworked in remote areas. In John Lomax's forays into rural America in search of living, indigenous folk music, he went beyond this position to suggest that modern-day folk continued to generate songs:

> The work of [cowboys], their daily experiences, their thoughts, their interests, were all in common. Such a community had necessarily to turn to itself for entertainment. Songs sprang up naturally, some of them tender and familiar lays of childhood, others original compositions, all genuine, however crude and unpolished.[11]

Ultimately, as the parameters for what constituted folk music expanded, the realization grew that folk music was not as lost as its collectors had thought. Ironically, what the folk music collectors were "discovering" and protecting from extinction remained as living memory, even to those who did not consider themselves "folk" at all.

Ethnomusicologist Charles Seeger, on the folkness of the folk: Folkness of the folk theory: I call it "folkness of the people who think they aren't folk." . . . In the case of my family, my mother and father were full of things that the student now would say was folklore. But to them it was part of their own tradition.

When I had an argument with my father about it: "Oh," he said, "I hear you're interested in folk music in America. There isn't any, except the Negro spirituals."

"Well," I said, "didn't you know the old fiddle tunes?"

"Oh, yes, but they're not music."

He used to dance to them until he was sixteen.

By that time, the young people had discovered that in the big cities—Springfield was a small city then—they didn't dance to a fiddle anymore. They danced to music. Music, and that was Strauss waltzes from Vienna.

My mother was brought up to sing, to listen to the old bloody ballads, by her nurse. She probably knew a whole raft of them. But when she got to be a debutante, oh no, she sang the rah-rah-rah-boom sentimental things of the college glee clubs. And the other was not music. She put it behind her. Music was written music. Other music wasn't music. So the folkness of the folk and the nonfolkness of the nonfolk are really much closer together than we think we are.[12]

Singer-songwriter Si Kahn, on writing contemporary folk songs: Then we have the question of, am I, Si Kahn, writing folk songs? Do you have an answer to that? Because if I am writing folk songs and these folk songs are about what's happening here and now, if they were about what's happening yesterday, then it is not the music of another generation.

I write very consciously within the folk tradition. I had a discussion once with Utah Philips where he was talking about the difference between those singer-songwriters who are primarily influenced by pop and rock. It is those structures and those who are primarily trying to write within the folk tradition and use a different set of structures and musical references.

I'm not going to ask you to answer this because generations of folklorists and commentators haven't. But can one *write* a folk song?

My position is that you can write something that is like a folk song but might become a folk song. Whether it is a folk song depends on how people use it and treat it.[13]

OVER THE TWENTIETH CENTURY, MUSIC considered "age-old and anonymous" evolved into a vast and varied genre. Once folk music became popular, folk scholars and musicians and fans began debating the paradox inherent in "commercial folk music."

But this is not the end of the folk music debate. In this twenty-first century, the Internet furthers what first began with the advent of radio and affordable recordings: experiencing music from cultures and eras distinct from one's own. No longer does music come through the filter of a collector stomping through Appalachia, or the commercial filter of radio deejays and music industry talent scouts. Perhaps this new, borderless age of folk music is the most democratic yet.

FOLK MUSIC AND POLITICAL SONG

One aspect of folk music—so-called people's music—is its engagement with topical and protest song. Whereas the genre of folk music refers to the processes of composition and transmission, a song is protest and/or topical—the terms overlap more often than not[14]—by virtue of its intent and application. The term "protest song" covers a range of musical creation and views of society. Most literally, it is an utterance of opposition or resistance to an abstraction of society set for voice. A lament is not a protest song, unless it includes some form of opposition to the condition depicted. Nor is a work song a protest song, unless there is more resistance than bitterness to the worker's complaint. There is considerable variance in these standards. The folk song "Who Killed Cock Robin?" for example, may once have been a protest song, but its modern-day audience is largely unconscious of this past. Other protest songs, particularly those sung by African Americans during the nineteenth century, escaped attention as utterances of opposition. The topical song is one devoted to a particular subject, usually associated with the news of the day. In an era when the topics of the day are social protest, as was the case in the 1960s, the topical and protest song coincide. Of course, there are many other topics for song, from unrequited love to a baby's crying. Sometimes nostalgic, sometimes nationalistic, and oftentimes idealistic in application, folk music has attracted people inclined toward singing out.

Folksinger Pete Seeger, on protest music as a category: Even the words— "protest song"—you can laugh about the different definitions. I say somebody singing an unrequited love song is protesting unrequition. Many people have all their lives sung protest-ant hymns! So there's a very vague line between an ordinary song and a protest song. What would you call the song written by Walcott Gibbs's son singing in the bathtub ["Declaration of Independence"]?

> *He will just do nothing at all.*
> *He will just sit there in the noon-day sun.*[15]

THE HISTORIES OF FOLK MUSIC and political or protest song, however defined, are inextricable. The folk have always had plenty to protest about. Over the past century, topical folk music has taken on mine disasters, the Dust Bowl, Hitler, picket lines, nuclear bombs, segregation, Vietnam, gender inequality, apartheid, the environment, and the Iraq War.

Music organizer Leo Christensen, on music in the labor movement in the thirties and forties: [The Labor Chorus of the California Labor School] felt as a group that our basic approach was that we were trying to show the aims and aspirations of the working class and various parts of it, how music was represented and to what extent music was a viable weapon to be used in struggle.

[The Labor Movement] didn't seem to feel that music was really that important: "Let them sing their songs, but we know where the struggle is: It's out there getting hit over the head with a baseball bat or out there hitting the bricks!"

And we'd have arguments about this. I finally became very frustrated. I'd say, even Luther himself took songs out of the bars and made them into church music. Why did he do it? He said, "Because the Devil shouldn't have all the good tunes."[16]

Editor Irwin Silber, on folk music, politics, and activism: Well, the contradiction did not seem as stark at the time as it may seem to some now: it was the period in which most of us felt that the popularization of folk song was itself a political act.... We felt that we were, in reviving the authentic folk music; we were making a political statement and combating bourgeois ideology. That's what many of the political people felt. Other people may not have felt that way; they may have felt they just liked the folk music.[17]

John Cohen, on the New Lost City Ramblers' music and political impetus: We're more like someone who's performing a piece of music or, if not performing it, improvising or doing something with a piece of music. We're communicating that way. Also sometimes we're trying to transmit the circumstances in which the song would come from just to make people a little uncomfortable: that it's not just entertainment; it's a reference to another time and place and set of conditions. Those are things I would say we do.

The message that [some folksingers are] imparting sometimes is to get people to act responsibly or to take action. We do that in a much more obscure way. We sing "Battleship of Maine" and try to lay it out there to see the comparisons of contemporary America,

The charge was that folk songs being people's songs is a given, and that [the goal of] the Communist Party is to reach the masses; therefore it follows that we should be singing folk songs if we want to reach the masses.... In a strange way, what's involved there is how the folk song movement steered us to an American identity that led towards country music.[18]

FOLK MUSIC: A DEFINITION

It is hard to connect the near-infinite variety of folk and protest music accessible today to the surviving English ballads carried like treasure out of the hills of Appalachia by the early collectors. Historically, folk music shares core attributes as posited by a classic definition determined at the 1954 conference of the International Folk Music Council in São Paulo, Brazil: (1) continuity that links the present with the past; (2) variation that springs from the creative impulse of the individual or the group; and (3) selection by the community that determines the form or forms in which the music survives.[19] Rather than being art in and of themselves, static and perfectible, folk songs—however slippery to classify—have in common their engagement with the "folk process."

For the singer of folk songs Sam Hinton, the definition is more procedural than economic: "It must be admitted that there is no criterion of folk music that will enable us immediately to recognize it as such, and to separate it from other kinds of music. For folk music is not so much a body of art as it is a process, an attitude, and a way of life; its distinguishing features lie not within the songs themselves, but in the relations of those songs to a folk culture."[20] Thus, scholars prefer to focus on a dynamic folk process, situational and contextual, ever-changing.

Earl Robinson, on the folk process: The folk process...which all the great folk creators do, it's simply picking up an idea, and getting a tune, from wherever, to fit it, and saying what you need to say about something in the present time that bothers you. It can be a love song, or it can be a political one, or it can be anything in the world. One of the big reasons to this present day that I love folk music is they don't limit it. Well, this is just not true anymore; in the popular field, what they do is to push what makes money and sometimes the beautiful themes don't happen to make a lot of money.[21]

Pete Seeger, on authenticity and the folk process: The folklorist perhaps remembers an earlier version of a song, and he hears me singing it, and somehow it's gotten changed. And he says, well, that's not authentic. The funny thing is, from my own feeling about folk music as a process, I think one of the more authentic things I do is continually changing things. This is much more authentic and much more in the folk tradition of America; it's much more traditional to change things.[22]

Music producer Jim Musselman, on the folk process: It's the folk process. It's the same with Bruce Springsteen doing a song today. Pete [Seeger] once said to me, "The beauty of a song is to have it live on and be changed by people and be adapted." When we did "We Shall Overcome" with Bruce Springsteen, I got so much abuse over that. It was, "How can you take a civil rights anthem and have Bruce say 'baby' in it?"

I think the true folk process is constantly changing and moving. Somebody can listen to Bruce and say, that's not the way the song was sung a hundred years ago. The way the song was sung a hundred years ago is not the way it was sung three hundred years ago. The folk process is constantly moving. Whoever is keeping the songs alive is doing a good thing.[23]

Punk and traditional Navajo performer Jeneda Benally, on using the folk process: We recorded two unpublished Woody Guthrie songs. We wrote the music to these songs, and we even changed a couple of the words to these songs in true Woody Guthrie fashion, just to make it more personal. There's one song, "Indian Corn Song," we changed it because we're not singing about Indians; it's coming *from* us, so it's a different point of view.[24]

Si Kahn, on the variation inherent in folk music: Folks who doubt this should pick up the Library of Congress CD *Versions and Variants of "Barbara Allen,"* which has something like thirty-two different versions of "Barbara Allen."

Why are there so many versions of "Barbara Allen"? Because people didn't have wax cylinders, they didn't have phonographs. They learned it from somebody who learned it from somebody else, who learned it from somebody else, who learned it from somebody else. Once we have dominant media, a record that everybody can listen to, a radio station that everybody listens to, of course you get a more common version.

I'll tell you a story. My friend Jeff Keyser, who was a show preacher from eastern Kentucky, took a song of mine named "Go to Work on Monday." He recorded it for an album a lot of us were doing to raise money for textile workers who were suffering from brown lung disease, a breathing disease you get in the mills. And Jeff said to me, "You know I wanted to do to it exactly as you sang it because I didn't want to change a note and I didn't want to change a word and that is what I've done."

Well it is a wonderful sentiment, but the words are different, the notes are different. But Jeff really thought he had done the song exactly as I had done it. But because he is a traditional singer coming out of an old tradition of a singing family, what he hears and what he sings gets translated automatically. He really believes that he has done it faithfully. But no artist renders a song faithfully or faithful to the mechanics of it.

You can be faithful to the spirit; to the heart. He did a beautiful version, much better than my version. But it wasn't the way I sang it.[25]

Balkan folksinger Eva Salina Primack, on the transfer and translation of songs: I had an experience last weekend with a bluegrass musician, an autoharpist named Bryan Bowers. I was performing at a music camp. I did a little [Balkan] set by myself for an hour with my accordion, and he came up to me afterwards, visibly moved.

I had sung a single song, given a brief translation. It was about the second love of a woman, knowing full well that the first love is the sweetest. He went and got his autoharp, and he sang this song, "When You and I Were True," an Irish ballad he had listened to in his car until he could understand the lyrics....It was like, this is the same song. We're just passing it back and forth to each other.[26]

Pete Seeger, on folk music and change: All definitions change with the centuries.... The definitions of folk song and folksingers are liable to change also. Folk will insist on it.... Face it, folk traditions will change as the folks who inhabit this earth change... the person who beats his breast and says, "I will sing nothing but folk song" is either fooling himself or trying to fool someone else.[27]

OR, AS JOURNALIST GORDON FRIESEN WROTE: "If some folk-lorist a hundred years from now wants to call them folk songs let him go ahead—our dust will not object."[28]

One thing that is certain, folk music has entered the mainstream American vernacular—not as shared peasant roots, but as a shared cultural experience. For a group singing around a campfire—cowboys going "up the trail" in 1900, or Girl Scouts at summer camp in 2010—the semantic differences can seem trivial: there, around that fire, each is a part of the folk.

2

EARLY COLLECTORS

THE COLLECTING OF FOLK MUSIC in the United States largely began in the first decades of the twentieth century. Among the most important of the first collectors was Cecil Sharp, an English folklorist, who joined educator Olive Dame Campbell in her quest to uncover America's own folk ballad tradition. Of equal importance was a Texan named John Avery Lomax, who had insisted to his teachers at Harvard that the songs sung by cowboys were indeed literature and set off to collect them. Meanwhile, on the West Coast, the musicologist Charles Seeger was breaking new and contentious ground at Berkeley with his studies combining music and politics.

Kentucky songwriter "Aunt" Molly Jackson described folk music as originating when "our ancestors wrote songs about their own lives, their sweethearts, their husbands, their wives, their children, and their daily lives. Then they wrote a lot of funny little jigs about their pigs, their donkeys, their cows, and their good old hunting dog that treed coons, possums, and ground hogs."[1] These folk songs—as John Lomax's son, Alan, called them, "homemade hand-me-downs in words and music, songs accepted by whole communities, songs voted good by generations of singers and passed on by word of mouth to succeeding generations"—had long been overlooked by scholars and the musical elite and even dismissed as unimportant by the very people who sang them. This music existed in "a tradition quite distinct from popular song (made to sell and sell quickly) and cultivated art (made, so much of it, to conform to prestige patterns)," wrote John Avery Lomax, and for the most part it escaped notice.[2] In an introduction to Lomax's *Cowboy Songs and Other Frontier Ballads* (1910), President Theodore Roosevelt remarked on this oversight of folk music:

> There is something very curious in the reproduction here on this new continent of essentially the conditions of ballad-growth which obtained in "medieval" England; including, by the way, sympathy for the outlaw, Jesse James taking the place of Robin Hood. Under modern conditions however, the native ballad is speedily killed by competition with the music hall songs; the cowboys becoming ashamed to sing the crude homespun ballads in view of what Owen Winter

calls the "ill-smelling saloon cleverness" of the far less interesting compositions of the music hall singers.[3]

Historical precedents for the collection of Anglo-American folk music of the twentieth century include ballad collections such as Bishop Thomas Percy's *Reliques of Ancient English Poetry* (1765), Robert Burns and James Johnson's *Scots Musical Museum* (1787–1803), and Sir Walter Scott's *Minstrelsy of the Scottish Border* (1802–3). The most exhaustive early collection is *English and Scottish Popular Ballads* (1882), a twenty-seven-hundred-page collection of lyrics from 305 ballads in more than thirteen hundred variations, compiled by the Harvard scholar Francis James Child. Beyond being authoritative, Child's seminal work made folk song research respectable.

Ethnomusicologist Norman Cazden, on connecting musical trends and social trends in musicology: Historical musicology didn't pay any attention to social trends. Or to trends in the history of ideas. It didn't. It dealt with what would now be called historiography, the gathering of documentation for a history of music. And this did indeed begin not at that period, but earlier, and abroad. There was very little historical musicology in this country except for some prime innovators, among whom the leading light was Charles Seeger.[4]

Ethnomusicologist Charles Seeger, on folk music and its collectors: The folk revival movement, if you say it began in '40, well, I can say, oh, yeah, it began long before then. Goes back to John Lomax. Goes back to [Francis] Child. And then on back on to Herder, Scott, Burns, Bishop Percy. My gosh, to people working with folk music way back in the twelfth century. Only we don't know what folk music is.[5]

WHAT IS LARGELY UNIQUE to the twentieth century, however, is the extensive collection and publication of traditional materials from living, oral sources. Child, like Scott and Percy before him, researched ballads from manuscripts and printed matter. (These abounded: English ballads were printed in large numbers and widely distributed as early as the mid-1600s, and a significant number of them surfaced and were collected later from source singers of the oral tradition on both sides of the Atlantic.)

Child's protégé George Lyman Kittredge taught John Lomax, who in turn became one of the first field collectors of living folk music whose findings would later constitute a corpus of American song—starting with his *Cowboy Songs and Other Frontier Ballads* (1910). From Howard Odum's journal publications of African-American spirituals (1906 and 1911) to Cecil Sharp's and Olive Dame Campbell's *English Folk Songs from the Southern Appalachians* (1917) and on through Carl Sandburg's *An American Songbag* (1927), these were texts on which revivalists would later draw.

Folk songs were the oral equivalents of arrowheads: rare, elusive, and emblematic of an earlier and perhaps—for those who sought them—more idyllic time. Antiquarian collectors ferreted them out of the memories of rural people "dammed up" in remote or isolated places (from Appalachian mountain communities to segregated prisons in the South) and then, before they disappeared forever, wrote them down or recorded them on early phonographs.

In 1907, English folk song and dance collector Cecil Sharp wrote in the *Musical Times*:

> Up to the middle of last century the country-side must have been full of songs and singers, and a much brighter and happier place than it is now. Why the tradition came to an end at the period I have mentioned I cannot say. But that it did so is abundantly clear; for it is a very rare experience to come across a singer of the genuine traditional song under the age of sixty or seventy. This fact is a very important one, because it means that in ten years at the most there will be no more work for the collector to do.[6]

The folk songs were dying, went the thinking of the day. To maintain that link to the past, they had to be captured and preserved before they were forgotten or contaminated.

Folksinger Pete Seeger, on first encountering the Sharp ballads: My father mentioned "Barbara Allen" to me way back when I was ten or twelve years old. He was researching. He had a copy of Cecil Sharp's book [*English Folk Songs from the Southern Appalachians*], which came out in 1917. His own reaction was one of laughter, you know, not unfriendly, but you know, "hard-hearted Barbara Allen." He would quote to me that last line, or the verse:

> *But all she said as she passed his bed.*
> *Young man, I think you're dying.*

That kind of brevity appealed to my father. He thought that was a great line.

My father and I, as long as I can remember, always had long conversations where we would just ramble over every subject under the sun. I remember him mentioning "Barbara Allen," and another song, "Come All Ye Fair and Tender Ladies," [for] which he had the same type of twinkle in his eyes. He told me, "Here's a sad song but very beautiful and very moving," but he was smiling as he said:

> Take warning, come all ye fair and tender ladies.
> Take warning, how you court young men.[7]

Producer Moe Asch, on learning American folk music from John Lomax's *Cowboy Songs*: I was associated with American folk music since I was eight. Since Father sent me the *Cowboy Songs*. I still have the book. This is the original version. You know where I picked this up? I was a student in Germany—I'm an electronic engineer. On the Quay in Paris on a one-week vacation, I picked this book up. This opened me up to American folk music. Especially Theodore Roosevelt's introduction, that this is part of our heritage. And I still have it with me.[8]

SONGCATCHERS

Collectors' interests varied. Some included only songs still performed; others rummaged the libraries for printed (broadside) ballads. Whereas Francis Child had collected lyrics only, Cecil Sharp transcribed the musical notation and left his assistant to take down lyrics. Whereas Sharp was fascinated by the dying art of a preliterate, preindustrial peasantry, John and Alan Lomax were drawn to the living aspect of the music. Most collectors defined their searches by style or region or the demographic of the source: Sharp, Campbell, and others collected ballads of minimally corrupted British origin (read: cultural superiority); "Cowboy Jack" Tharp, like his rival John Lomax, collected cowboy tunes; Howard Odum and Lawrence Gellert collected African-American spirituals and protest songs; and Laura Boulton and Natalie Curtis (a cousin of the Seegers) collected Native American songs. The work of these early collectors developed a model for the folk revivalists who followed them: collecting texts firsthand; waging campaigns to introduce folk songs in school curricula and on radio; and trudging off to small colleges and folklore societies to inspire others with folk culture. Such words largely sum up the aims of the first folk revival.

The actual process of being a song collector was anthropological as well as musical. Cecil Sharp advised future collectors to "try to live the life and think the thoughts of people whose only literature is that which they carry in their heads, and in whom imagination takes the place of acquired knowledge."[9] Alan Lomax similarly explained that the collector "goes where book-learning is not. He lives with the underprivileged [and] has the duty to speak as the advocate of the common man."[10]

Few literary critics were convinced. One reviewer of Sharp insisted: "if there is one belief that should now be extinct, it is the belief that the unlettered had the power to create a striking or beautiful ballad that lingers in tradition. They can preserve and adapt and modify and transform, but they cannot, in any true sense, create narrative songs."[11] Yet collectors—educated elites—continued to cross class lines to collect songs from cowboys, chain gangs, and rural mountain people and carried examples (often purged of vulgarity or, in the case of Sharp's work, African-American influence)[12] back to other sophisticates.

Criticisms have long been directed at collectors, ranging from interference, filtering according to preference or bias, creating composite texts never actually sung, paternalistic condescension, or, more harshly, ventriloquism, appropriation, and full-scale exploitation of traditional materials. Other critics argue that the act of collecting and writing down or recording songs is like collecting butterflies or anything else ephemeral; it kills the living thing itself.

One anecdote from Sharp's work in Appalachia illustrates how recording music from oral tradition can irrevocably alter it: "I do not keep my mother's songs in mind as I used to," wrote the daughter of one of Sharp's key song sources. "But I know I have only to look them up in Mr. Cecil Sharp's book and they will come back to me just exactly right."[13]

Charles Seeger, on the danger of collecting: I don't think recording, in itself, necessarily changes the singer's attitude towards the material. Recording now, especially in newer techniques, without the bulky equipment, one can even keep the machine out of sight. That's the ideal way to do it. But don't take the people out of their context to sing. Never put them on the platform. The tradition just gets changed, more rapidly than it needs to be. If we want to keep it there, simply because we learn so much from it and we hope that more people would keep the old tradition of singing, the less we expose them towards city influences, the better.[14]

Pete Seeger, on folk music collection: Generally, [a popularizer] means someone from a city who has more contacts in the way of reaching out to broader audiences either through the printed page or recordings or concert halls taking some material which has been nurtured in a small area and bringing it to a broader area. And this can be good sometimes, although looking back over history, perhaps sometimes it's been bad. Maybe it's ended up by destroying the thing it's tried to broaden; bring something out of the closet and it's killed by the light of day.

Remember the Scottish woman who didn't want Mr. Sharp to write down a ballad:

"You've destroyed it now," she said. "Now that you've written it. It won't ever be the same again."

My guess is that any kind of mass reproduction of these things tends to throw the folk process out of kilter. One version of the song tends to become so much more important than the other. This is what happened, incidentally, with Nashville style fiddling almost wiping out a lot of local styles of fiddling.[15]

Editor Gordon Friesen, on how public performance affected traditional music: Folk songs [are] an intimate exchange of ideas and music between a group of people sitting around a table maybe over some beer. When the folksinger got on the stage or behind the microphone, it created a barrier, an artificial barrier which destroyed or at least seriously damaged what folk songs should really be.[16]

Charles Seeger, on differences of opinion regarding the performance of folk music: [The festivals] were wonderful affairs. But then they were discovered by the city, and the city would say, "now look, that string band got up on the stage and you couldn't tell when it began. They were fiddling around with the instruments, and well, it seemed that they weren't doing anything except just fooling around. And first thing you know they were all together."

Well, that's the way they were accustomed to do it. Well, the person from the city said, "that's no way to run a festival. They've got to go on the stage, bow to the audience, and then, begin. And instead of trailing off at the end, a ballad singer, half speaking the last few words, he's got to sing right up to the end, loud, so that he gets applause."

Well, you could see, the city influence began to come in. So I gave up going to the festivals, in my still-amateurish viewpoint.[17]

WHO OWNS A FOLK SONG?

More immediate conflicts arose because the sources of the collected artifacts did not, by sharing their song, give it up entirely. A song cannot be taken away and put in a museum like a pot or a photograph, an immutable object. For one thing, the pure, original keystone songs that Francis Child had sought in his day did not exist. For another, the singers of folk songs were necessarily connected to the music. These "folk" had their own opinions about the music and the "experts" who collected it, and they were not oblivious to condescension.

The question of copyrights further complicated tensions between source singers and the collectors. Initially, the fact that collectors copyrighted the songs they "discovered" held little significance, because they were not being issued on recordings. (Songs that were copyrighted earned 2 cents in royalties for each recording sold; this was split between the copyright holder and the publisher.[18]) Songs like "Home on the Range," which John Lomax had copyrighted, brought in revenue, but overall, holding the copyrights to folk songs had no apparent economic value. This would change quickly, however: when the Weavers made a hit of "Goodnight Irene," a song written by Lead Belly but copyrighted by John Lomax, the royalty earnings were substantial.

As copyrights on folk songs began to accrue value for collectors and, later, record companies and popularizers, the singers from whom the song originated (often belonging to communities that had been exploited before) cried foul. In response, the International Folk Music Council, a consortium of folk music experts from around the world, issued a statement declaring that folk songs should be copyrighted in the name of both the collector and the singer.[19] But some (the songs' sources in particular) continued to argue that authorship of a song more aptly belongs to those of whose history it is a part. Still others contended that folk songs inherently belong to the public domain. Leaving a song uncopyrighted, however, risks that somebody else even less connected to the song than a collector or arranger will claim it and reap the royalties. Copyrighting folk songs—music that is, by definition, communal and mutable—has endured as a point of dispute ever since folk music was "discovered" in America.

Charles Seeger, on the rights of a collector to copyright songs: Well, I had a big argument with Alan [Lomax] on [taking Emma Dusenbury's songs and copyrighting them]. But, he said, "but Charlie, how can I live?"

"Oh," I said, "but Alan, that's just what the bank robber says. How can he live if he doesn't shoot up the bank?"

He didn't see the point. (I was absolutely nefarious.) But, of course, it's different; it's complicated by this fact: the folksinger has got his song from someone else and that someone got it from someone else, or two or three other people. So there's a genealogy there of plagiarism in folk song. It's necessary. Sometimes people do invent a new stanza; or they put in a new twist in the tune. So there are contributions of each individual in the singing of each song. But they're slight, probably. The archaic tradition will last, if we just give it a little help and protection.[20]

John Cohen, on tensions between urban and rural folksingers: [In] 1951 I took my cousin and we hitched south for an adventure. I stopped in Washington at the Library of Congress. We looked up Virgil Sturgill and [Bascom Lamar] Lunsford. We worked our way south to Asheville. We stopped at the jail to sleep and they wouldn't let us. The guy there asked us what we were doing there. We told him we were looking for Bascom Lunsford. He said, "Well, let's see if we can find the number for him. Oh, he's out in Turkey Creek."

We called him. We told him we were from New York and he wanted to know who we knew there. Me, being very young, I'm trying to figure out who I would know that he had ever heard of.

I said, "Pete Seeger, Alan Lomax."

He said, "I'm busy!" ...

In 1959, when I first made my field recordings in the Appalachians, the first guy I met was a guy named "Banjo" Bill Cornett. He would sing for me, but he really didn't want to sing for me.

He had heard about other people copyrighting folk songs.

"Pete Seeger sat on my lap and learned everything he knows from me," he said.

I thought I was bashing around the hills of Kentucky, and here I am discussing copyright and Pete Seeger.[21]

THE LOMAXES AND LEAD BELLY

In the early 1930s, during the depression, John and Alan Lomax toured the United States in a car furnished with a state-of-the-art wire recorder provided by the Archive of American Folk Song at the Library of Congress. They were intent on compiling a comprehensive collection of American ballads and folk songs, which they saw not as relics but rather as living, shifting proof of America's everyman democracy. The folk songs they collected represented an impressive breadth of folk music genres and regionalism (including Cajun songs, blues, prison songs, country ballads, and Anglo-American folk songs); through this work, the Lomaxes would come to be seen as "canon makers" in the folk music field.

Charles Seeger, on Alan Lomax as a collector: He [was] probably the most brilliant collector of folk music living in his day. Nobody else can touch him. For quantity and for quality. People will sing for Alan but they won't sing for anybody else.

In Scotland, Alan said he wanted a milking song. So they went out to get the milking song. It was in about the middle of the morning. And the woman said, "Sure, I'll sing you a milking song."

"Well," says Alan, "I've got my machine right here."

"But I'm not milking now."

"Well, when do you milk?"

"Five o'clock."

"We'll be here."

So they go off. At 11 o'clock at night, Alan shows up. The woman is in agony and the cow is in agony. But the point is they waited for him. For the ordinary collector, they'd wait a little while and say forget about it. But Alan does that. He gets the informant bound to him somehow or other by that same kind of relationship that binds himself to an audience. And he gets stuff.[22]

NOT ONLY DID THE LOMAXES RETURN to the Northeast from their music-gathering sojourn with songs, they also brought the real item home with them. Lead Belly's role in folk music—as a chain gang captive, source singer, pet folk icon, teacher and model, and eventually, as a major figure in the first folk music revival—illustrates the complexity of the collected-collector dichotomy.

The Lomaxes had met Huddie Ledbetter (Lead Belly) at Angola Prison in Louisiana. Impressed by Lead Belly's extensive repertoire and musical ability, John Lomax arranged, upon his parole, for Lead Belly to come to Washington to record for the Library of Congress. John Lomax (who was accused of having a slaveholder mentality for doing so) hired the ex-convict to be his chauffeur and arranged performances for him, decking him out in chain-gang regalia.[23]

In 1936, the Lomaxes published *Negro Folk Songs as Sung by Lead Belly*. The same year, with some bitterness on both sides, Lead Belly and John Lomax parted company. Although widely acclaimed, Lead Belly was never commercially successful during his lifetime. Some of his widely covered songs, however (including the Weavers' chart-topping "Goodnight Irene"), became immensely so.

Pete Seeger, on Alan Lomax and Lead Belly: I think Alan was fifteen or seventeen when he said to his father, "I want to carry on your work." His father was sixty years old and feeling his age, and Alan was full of energy. He became real friends with Lead Belly even though [Lead Belly] didn't want to be friends with the elder Lomax because he had treated him like a child. When he told Mr. Lomax that he was leaving, Mr. Lomax said, "I did everything for that boy." That boy being fifty years old.

Alan went to Lead Belly and said, "You're absolutely right. Let me know if I can help you."

Lead Belly said, "You can get me some jobs. That's what I need."

Alan tried his best to get Lead Belly some jobs. He didn't succeed too well.[24]

Composer Earl Robinson, on Lead Belly: I was working in a summer camp called Camp Unity, a left-wing, progressive, Communist camp [in New York state].

And we heard about this man, Lead Belly. I had actually read his book, already, that the Lomax family put out. You know, [the Lomaxes] discovered him in a jail in the Deep South. And, he was happy to record all the songs that they wanted. He loved to sing, but he was also working for himself, as we all need to do, and didn't particularly like singing in that jail. So, he asked the Lomaxes if he would take a record of his to the governor. Which they were glad to do, and on the spur of the moment he composed a song to Governor Pat Neff.

A lot of left-wingers, especially black people, were upset with this man from the South—they called him Uncle Tom—because he would pass the hat after he sang, and do a little buck and wing, and they were trying to get out of that image, way back, as far as then, even, of Negro people being second class.

The first night he was [at Camp Unity] he sang songs about prostitutes and yeller-gals and gun-toting, razor-slashing, black "niggers" and stuff like that, and this was anathema, this was terrible for these people in this camp who were striving so hard for equality. And so, "what kind of person is this to bring here? What kind of good does he do for equality or anything else?"

I just didn't even notice; I was just enjoying this man so much. . . .

So, like I say, the Camp Unity was in an uproar the first night he sang. The second night we got him to sing "Bourgeois Blues" and "Scottsboro Boys" and a few others, and they were mollified, but there were somewhat wild arguments going on.

So Lead Belly was doing himself no good and the nation no good in a jail. His song to Governor Pat Neff had stuff like:

Mister Governor, you a good man.
And if I was in your place, I would free me.

Lead Belly never made very much. I would say about that man that he just came on just a very few short years too soon, because he would have been fantastic on TV. . . . whenever you could see him close up you understood the words. And if you didn't understand them totally, why he'd keep his twelve-string guitar pumping away, and he'd tell you, he'd explain, and create poetry at the same time he was doing it.[25]

Folksinger Don McLean, on revivalists performing Lead Belly's songs: It took four people to sing the music of people like Lead Belly [as in the Weavers]. The songs were too big for one person. . . . .

Lead Belly's version [of "Goodnight Irene"] is Lead Belly's version. The Weavers' version is the Weavers' version. Ry Cooder's version is Lead Belly's version. What's the difference? That kind of question is coming from an intellectual, purist place. What about verses Lead Belly left out? Some people have got to have a starting point with which they're going to get involved, if they're ever going to. If the Weavers hadn't got "Goodnight Irene" on the air, no one would have ever known about Lead Belly. Ry Cooder would never have been able to give a retrospective.[26]

Moe Asch, on Lead Belly's death (officially from Lou Gehrig's disease) in 1949: Lead Belly commits suicide. That's right. He died because he didn't wish to live. He couldn't foresee. He was torn: Hollywood promised him one thing, Bing Crosby and friends promised him another: he was going to be the number one folksinger and all that bit. He understood that afterwards; that everything was the kids. And he sang for Columbia University kids at the very end. Trying to tell them the truth.

It's a disease that comes to a person when he sees no hope. Same thing happened to Cisco [Houston]. Same thing happened to Woody [Guthrie]. You can call it whatever disease you want. But it is an unwillingness to live because you don't see in the future what you fought for as a youth. This is a terrible shock to a person who's positive and who sees the future as a positive thing, and you fight your way towards it.[27]

A SLUMP IN FARM PRICES during the 1920s, followed by the Great Depression of the 1930s, coincided with a particularly poignant time for the nation's "folk," or rural poor. Suddenly, romantic notions about the happy poor were difficult to maintain; and with mass migration under way, folk music enthusiasts no longer needed to tromp out into the wilderness to encounter old songs.

Folksinger Bess Lomax Hawes, on the economic climate: I was born in 1921; I was about eight. It was right after the crash, and the beginnings of the depression. And I remember my father coming in from the pit and sitting down at the table and saying to my mother, "I don't know what the country is coming to."

He had been on a car trip across Texas.

He said, "Every train I went by was black with men hanging on, to the top, to the sides, to anywhere they could get. And the railroad police aren't even trying to chase them off anymore. There's too many of them. I don't know where they are going, and I don't think they know where they are going either. They are just looking for some place where they can find a job. If it's this way all over the country, how are we going to handle it?"

It was an extremely impressive moment for me.[28]

RATHER THAN DYING OUT, folk songs—as the music of the people—
were about to take on lives of their own. Early collectors had drawn from
the elders of the country their living language and lore and, bundled
together with their own prejudices, presented this package to the nation
in books like *American Songbag* and *Our Singing Country*. In time, the country would again be singing these old songs. Yet before they would reach a
broad new audience in northern cities, they would have to overcome prej-
udice among conservatory-trained composers who initially regarded folk
songs as relics of a dying culture. It is ironic that a folk music revival would
arise from musicians trained at America's major classical music training
centers, who would, in time, turn away from an antiquarian attitude to a
preservationist one. (Perhaps no more ironic than the fact that in this first
revival, those collecting songs were generally not those performing them.)
For these collectors, reluctant revivalists, and popularizers, folk music was
the stuff out of which national character arose.[29] In their efforts to bridge
the distance linking the old and the new, the music of the backwoods
and the Next Big Thing on Broadway, they directed a stream of traditional
music into the river of popular music; which has never been the same for
its tributary.

3

MUSIC FOR THE MASSES

WHILE EARLY FOLK MUSIC COLLECTORS were searching out ballads and shanties on New England docks and in Appalachian enclaves, they largely ignored America's vibrant tradition of singing out and protesting in reaction to the news of the day.

The instinct to voice political sentiments through music is by no means new or uniquely American. Nor is political sentiment expressed in music unique to the twentieth century. During Europe's Middle Ages, anticlerical feelings found expression in the songs of wandering goliards. In seventeenth-century England, the egalitarian Diggers composed anthems of class consciousness, and the song "Lillibullero" (1689) helped topple James II from his throne. In 1703, the Scottish nationalist Andrew Fletcher wrote: "If a man were permitted to make all the ballads, he need not care who should make the laws of a nation."[1]

America's tradition of rebellion in song predates nationhood: many an antiroyalist ballad was sung in the age of the Boston Tea Party; during colonial days, New York governor William Cosby burned ballads critical of him. Abolitionists freely adopted hymns to their cause. Earlier, in 1829 (a full twenty years before the *Communist Manifesto*), the following lyrics were published in a union paper, the *Mechanics Free Press*, in Philadelphia, for a laboring audience:

> *The poor could live without the rich*
> *As every man may know*
> *But none that labor for their bread*
> *Could by the rich be spared....*
> *A truth it is both clear and plain*
> *Which every one may know*
> *That always in the richest earth*
> *The rankest weeds do grow.*[2]

Folklorists sometimes disdained such material, insisting that songs of discontent cannot be called folk songs because they are by nature ephemeral and limited by historical context, subject to quick forgetting (or updating). In the opinions of many of the early American folk music experts, because they did not fit the narrow literary definition set for folk music, topical and political songs were simply not legitimate folk songs.[3]

In the 1920s and 1930s, ethnomusicologist Charles Seeger (father of Pete, Mike, and Peggy Seeger) played a critical role in fitting protest music under the umbrella of the music of *des Volkes*, or people's music, which became a part of the folk music movements, or revivals, of the 1940s and 1960s. Charles Seeger was a radical thinker and composer searching for ways to meld his left-wing political convictions with music. He believed music could be revolutionary—that it could be used to empower the working classes to dismantle the political hierarchies in America—but it would take him and his family and friends many years to figure out a way to accomplish this.

Folksinger Pete Seeger, on Charles Seeger's early career: My father was convinced that great symphonic music would be the saving of the world. (He could look at a huge piece of paper with a thousand music notes on it and he could point out the first violin, the second violin.) After graduating from Harvard with high marks, he went to Germany and there found he was going deaf. He conducted the Cologne Opera there one summer. He had the discipline to say, "Well I won't be a conductor, but I'll compose." While he was over there he met the president of the University of California, who was impressed. He wasn't back in New York less than a year before he was appointed to build up the music department [at Berkeley].

His fellow professors radicalized him. One of them took him out to the lettuce fields and he saw little kids that could have been his own children working for pennies out there. . . . the migratory labor camps. He was horrified. After all, he had seen poverty in Mexico, but those were brown-skinned people. But here were fair-haired blue-eyed people, living in degradation. He was horrified. And he went back to San Francisco. Got up in a meeting, said, "Why, this is outrageous." And somebody stood up in the audience and said, "Sit down you lily-livered bastard. We've known this kind of stuff all our life; you're just discovering it." And he went back and shook his hand, "You know you're absolutely right, I shouldn't have shot off my mouth like this!" The guy, he was a Wobbly, and Father became good friends. . . . When World War I came, [Father] made speeches against imperialist war and got fired.

My mother said, "Can't you keep your mouth shut? You're not going to be drafted."

He came East and got the grand scheme to build a trailer. He built one of the first automobile trailers. My mother would stand on a platform and they would play. They had posters made. The trip was a disaster. People didn't come to hear their Bach and Beethoven. My mother had to wash my diapers in an iron pot over an open fire. Once they were nearly drowned in a flood; so my mother put her foot down. [They returned and] my father and mother taught at Juilliard in the twenties.

In 1929, the crash came and he was convinced that it was the end of the free enterprise system. Instead of just joining the Socialists, he joined the Communists who were among the bravest and most activist. The Socialists talked a good line, but to me, the Communists were doing more.[4]

THE COMPOSERS' COLLECTIVE

As the Lomaxes were traveling "50,000 miles by Cowboy song" (as they noted in their trip records) in search of America's indigenous music,[5] Charles Seeger became involved with an organization in New York City that was seeking a different sort of American music, a music that applied Communist analyses and might be used in the leftist movement that was emerging.

The Composers' Collective, a branch of New York's musical-intellectual Pierre Degeyter Club, consisted of rising musical talents fresh from Harvard and Juilliard—many of them members of the Communist Party—who collaborated to create what they hoped would become the revolutionary music of the escalating class struggle in America.

Ethnomusicologist Norman Cazden, on the origins of the Composers' Collective: This was a period when people in all walks of life were acquiring—by being hit on the head by economic circumstances—a radical outlook. Things weren't quite right with the present world. And the writers [in the Party] were firmly organized and had a headquarters [in the John Reed Club]. And they soon found attached to them people who weren't really writers or of literary interest directly; they were interested say, in theater, in playwriting, in journalism, which isn't quite the same as writing novels.

So musicians came around. Or people who wanted answers on how one finds a radical music to listen to. And so, finally, the Pierre Degeyter Club was organized as a home for the musicians and musically interested people who had the same general objectives as the John Reed Club but...were not writers. Where the Degeyter Club foundered was never determining whether to set musical standards for membership. A good many of the people who came into it were simply attracted to discussion of left-wing things in the arts but were not musicians. They didn't perform music. They didn't compose music. (Oh, they occasionally went to concerts.) But they would have a great deal to say about music.

Well, when you're dealing with an organization on that basis, pretty soon the organizational positions go to those who can speak well at a meeting—but they're not necessarily the best musicians in the place.[6]

"EVERY PARTICIPANT IN REVOLUTIONARY ACTIVITY knows from his own experience that a good mass song is a powerful weapon in the class struggle," wrote Aaron Copland in a 1934 review of the Composers' Collective's first *Workers' Song Book*. "It creates solidarity and inspires action. No other form of collective art activity exerts so far-reaching and all-pervading an influence. The song the mass itself sings is a cultural symbol which helps to give continuity to the day-to-day struggle of the proletariat."[7]

To this end, the Composers' Collective was inspired by the powerful and popular barricade song "L'Internationale," written in the aftermath of the Paris Commune by Eugène Pottier (originally set to the tune of "La Marseillaise," Pierre Degeyter composed music for the song in 1888). By the 1930s, it was the established anthem of the radical movement (and the unofficial anthem of the USSR). But the infectious, fist-raising bravado of "L'Internationale" was not the Collective's only aim. A frequent speaker at the Degeyter Club was the German composer Hanns Eisler, who maintained that true revolutionary music must not merely convey a political message; it had to musically progressive as well. Thus the composers in the Collective experimented with twelve-tone technique and dissonance, producing aesthetically complex music that aspired to serve on picket lines while simultaneously uplifting the supposedly poor musical taste of the proletariat. Examples include *Appalachian Spring* by Aaron Copland; film scores for Hollywood by Elie Siegmeister, Lan Adomian, and Alex North; and Marc Blitzstein's musical *The Cradle Will Rock*. Overall, the Collective's success at its mission was limited—the music it produced was largely unsingable, unless one brought a piano on the march—but its failure would ultimately pave the way within the music world and the radical Left for the acceptance and appreciation of folk music.

Pete Seeger, on marching songs: In the nineteenth century they thought that revolutionary songs that people could sing on the barricades marching down the streets was just what was needed. And that's how the "L'Internationale" got written. However, the invention of the phonograph changed things. People who tried to duplicate what the Wobblies did, you know, print a songbook, have usually been disappointed that the song book is not used much. It might have been used back in the Wobblies' day very successfully.... Needless to say, there are widely different opinions about what makes a good protest song.[8]

Composer Earl Robinson, on "L'Internationale": The Composers' Collective would really talk about the "Internationale" a lot and examine it—why is it so good, so wonderful, you know? They'd make attempts, piddling attempts, to try to write something like it, but just couldn't do it. And their heads weren't right for it either. That's too simple.[9]

Charles Seeger, on revolutionary music: *Workers' Song Book Number 1* has my song "Lenin, Who's That Guy?" That is a song that couldn't have been written before that time, of the development of music. It's a song typical of the good, creative thought of those days. But the harmony is very simple. It's the form of it that's irregular.

We went through the whole songbook with Eisler sitting there; and Eisler criticized everything, some of them devastatingly, and when at the end of it, he was sitting way down at the other end of the table, came to the last song in the book (which was the "Lenin, Who's That Guy?"): "Who wrote that?" That was the song he approved of in the whole book. And you look at it; the harmony is absolutely simple. It has a guitar accompaniment transposed for the piano. But the whole phraseology, the irregularity of the use of a stereotyped harmonic sequence of four chords over and over again, is absolutely new; it wouldn't have been thought of before those days.

One of the things we tried to do in the Collective: to use ordinary fragments of the technique in an unusual way, because we thought that was revolutionary and therefore was suitable for the workers to use, not giving them those same patterns in the usual way.[10]

Pete Seeger, on "Lenin, Who's That Guy?": [Lenin,] Who's That Guy? is a nice song to listen to [from the Collective] but I never sang it very often:

> *Lenin, who's that guy, he's not big, neither is he high,*
> *got two hands and a pair of eyes, just as human as you or I. . . .*

It has this very staccato rhythm that Eisler went in for. It was more of an intellectual tour de force than anything else. It didn't flow. It didn't have any warmth in it. The harmony was extraordinary. It went from G to A to D, G to A to D, G to A to D.[11]

Collector Herbert Haufrecht, on the members of the Composers' Collective: I think Earl [Robinson] was a breath of kind of freshness, his writing. That fresh breeze from the West, you know. I think many of us looked down our noses at his simple things like "Joe Hill." (I don't know "many of us"; I speak for myself.) . . . People like Blitzstein and others had many broader contacts and broader aspirations, beyond the movement. People like Copland, and others who were in the concert field, Henry Cowell, were never really in daily contact with the Collective, as many of us were. Their sympathy was there; they were affected by it, let's say.[12]

Earl Robinson, on the challenge of writing music for the masses: I remember a very leavening influence in that Composers' Collective was a man named Jacob Schaefer, who was head of the Jewish choruses—giant, left-wing groups. And Schaefer would listen to some of these tunes that came out of the these serious composers and he'd say, "I don't think it will work for my people." Jewish workers, you know: they had to have very simple stuff. They would probably sing Charlie [Seeger]'s thing, you know, but none of this other stuff. It was too highbrow, sophisticated, and not communicative on human levels.[13]

Norman Cazden, on Composers' Collective meetings: We met in a loft building, on what's now lower Sixth Avenue, really in the Village, around Eleventh or Twelfth Street, a second-story loft. And it may have been the week-round home of some other organization; and we would pay some very nominal rental and have it for the afternoon and evening. I seem to remember afternoon meetings, maybe evening. The attendance was fairly regular on the part of many of the members....

There was a great feeling of searching: what alternatives are we to look for in the world of music, and especially in creative music? For example, at the meetings, we would generally start out, not with any theoretical question, but with specific compositions that had been written by the members. You know, each one would speak up:

"I've just finished a song."

"Well, let's hear it."

And we'd gather around the piano.... There would be that kind of general discussion. And then some specific discussion of the musical techniques involved. Because people were trying to, let's say, gruff tone clusters at the bottom range of the piano in order to give a kind of percussive march beat to the music, rather than traditional harmony.[14]

Pete Seeger, on visiting the Pierre Degeyter Club: I remember Father giving lectures at the Pierre Degeyter Club on the history of music, relating Mozart's music to the culture of the eighteenth century. I attended one or two when I was home on vacation, but that's all. I remember hearing Aaron Copland speak there. Some stirring music in the German style: those Hanns Eisler songs sung by a chorus? They're very strong, very spare harmony, and strident as all hell.

They thought this was going to be *the* international style of *the* world's working class. And their theories sure went astray. Father had his doubts about it. I think he had more sense of humor than the others. His songs had some fine humor:

Oh joy upon this earth,
to live and see the day,
when Rockefeller Senior
shall up to me and say,
Comrade can you spare a dime,
Oh joy upon this earth…

And so on. It's a round. And a good round.

Well, I'd tried singing some of these songs. Matter of fact, my older brother and I and a friend went on a weeklong hiking trip through the Adirondacks in 1935, and we sang those rounds over and over again at the top of our lungs. We had a great time singing about:

Schwab, Schwab, Charlie Schwab,
life and happiness you rob,
from the workers in the mills,
from the miners in the hills.…[15]

Norman Cazden, on the technical side of composing revolutionary music: Twelve-tone and other such radical techniques of that period were billed as themselves revolutionary. Now they were revolutionary in a metaphorical sense, not in a political sense. They were artistic revolutions. But it was assumed an artistic revolution is part of a complete turning around of human consciousness. And music was to play its part in changing people's outlooks. It was a harbinger of a world still to come. That idea of course, is as old as Plato, if not older. The notion that music can actually change people's actions by changing their view of the world; and particularly, that this could be done by an art-like music.[16]

Earl Robinson, on Communism in America: The depression gave you something to look at. It really did. I mean, nobody was afraid—very few people were afraid—of the word "Communist." I mean, there were seventeen million unemployed.

I remember—the friend I drove to New York with was a real lefty, and I remember him saying, "Oh, the revolution is right around the corner; it's going to be any day now." I listened to him but I couldn't see it that clearly whatsoever. But the idea permeated.… It was clear that our system had to be overthrown here, and that the way to do it was the way they had done it in Russia and we totally supported the Soviet Union.…

My Communism is twentieth-century Americanism. I put an index card on my piano with this slogan. It just happened to suit where I was and my talent and the deep American roots were what really did this. The people element is something that came from reading Carl Sandburg's *The People, Yes*. It's a terribly important book to me. Yes, to this day I quote from the book... The Party line, in a sense was beside the point, as I look at it now. It stimulated my head. A good way of expressing it is a head trip, you know? It was a head trip.... I think where the Party was not able to allow themselves to be pushed off into a superleft position or weren't able to stand up and really claim their Americanism as Communists, that was probably part of the mistake....

When I think that if they had been clearer about where they were and what revolution in America meant and didn't mean, you know, I think they might have been able to handle that a lot better and not be isolated so easily.[17]

Pete Seeger, on Charles Seeger's radicalism: Father though had got in touch with the radical movement in World War I. They wanted Father to join them. But he said, "No, I'm not a worker. It's no sense in me joining the IWW [Industrial Workers of the World]." But that was when he started reading Marx. And so from an intellectual point of view, he was absorbing a lot. And in the early thirties, he tried to do more than just read about it.[18]

Charles Seeger, on coming into radicalism: I think the dissent that I got [growing up] was quite middle-of-the-road. In the University of California, before World War I, I ran across the real radicalism. And was much impressed with it. But in the twenties, I was in that trench, so to speak, where I pulled in my concerns with the society of my day. I had practically nothing to do with it at all. I was well enough off to have a nice place to live and have tailor-made clothes, and good meals, but not luxuries beyond that. I didn't have a car, except on and off. I experimented with a Stanley Steamer, for instance. But in those days of the twenties, I was definitely nonradical. So that when the depression hit me and the chance to make music for the people who were really suffering the depression, it was a great emotional experience....

By the time the depression came, I was full of it. [I had] an intense resentment of the situation that competitive capitalism had gotten us into. My revival of my old Marxism came out then.[19]

Earl Robinson, on arriving on the New York scene in 1933: So my idea in going to New York, what was in my head, was to go to Juilliard or Eastman and take advanced composition study.... I never went near Juilliard or Eastman. I went to Union Square instead, where all these radical speakers were. I was just getting ripe for it. I went to Union Square and they had all these various branches of radicalism. The Communist Party had a speaker. The Trotsky[ists] had a speaker. The anarchists had a speaker. The religious people had a speaker, you know? They were all competing with each other. So, I started immediately reading the *Daily Worker*.[20]

Charles Seeger, on protesting during the depression: It was a May Day parade, '33 or '34. Might have been '35. And we assembled up north of Greenwich Village somewhere. There were bands. And there were sound trucks as I remember. And some singing. The old union songs. Part socialist, part old labor union songs. We were in the Communist parade. The Socialist parade was, I remember, dignified by walking down Fifth Avenue at a different time. And so, there might have been clashes between the two. Just as in Germany, the damn fools fought each other instead of collecting together and fighting the real danger.[21]

REVOLUTIONARY MUSIC

The revolutionary impulse of the Composers' Collective was widespread in the early decades of the twentieth century, as agrarian socialist movements of the nineteenth century gave way to Progressivism, industrial unionism, then Communism. These political-economic movements vied with each other in advocating their solutions to the social dilemmas created by urbanization, mass immigration, and industrialization.

In 1905 the most radical union, the Industrial Workers of the World, was created to "confederate the workers of this country into a working-class movement that shall have for its purpose the emancipation of the working-class from the slave bondage of capitalism."[22] Instead of being craft- or industry-based, its motto was "One Big Union For All." As part of their mission, the "Wobblies" included women, blacks, and unskilled workers excluded from the American Federation of Labor (AFL). The Wobblies were among those who had been singing out against the exploitative working and living conditions that had come with industrialization; "there can be no democracy in a world ruled by industrial despots," argued the IWW's *Little Red Song Book: Songs to Fan the Flames of Discontent* (1909)—with songs such as "The Preacher and the Slave" by the labor activist Joe Hill:

> *Long-haired preachers come out every night,*
> *Try to tell you what's wrong and what's right;*
> *But when asked how 'bout something to eat*
> *They will answer with voices so sweet:*
> > *You will eat, by and by,*
> > *In that glorious land above the sky;*

Work and pray, live on hay,
You'll get pie in the sky when you die.[23]

In 1917, the Justice Department raided IWW halls across the country and arrested 165 union leaders, all of whom were eventually tried and found guilty under the Espionage Act. In music, the popular song "I Didn't Raise My Boy to Be a Soldier" was drowned out by "It's a Grand Old Flag" and "Johnny Get Your Gun." When the war ended the IWW leadership remained in jail, and the Socialist Party weakened. Strikes were staged across the country. Some were under the auspices of a breakaway new Party, the Communist Party USA, created in 1919 when Lenin invited the left wing of the Socialist Party to join the Comintern (Communist International). The Communist Party USA was soon forced underground by the arrests and deportations of Party members known as the Palmer Raids, America's first Red Scare (1919–21).

Meanwhile, American capitalism rode the wave of the "roaring" 1920s, until the stock market crashed, having lost three-quarters of its value, and the world's economies tumbled. In 1933—the year Franklin D. Roosevelt took office as president after a landslide election—the Great Depression reached perhaps its lowest point: a quarter of the population was unemployed.[24]

After 1935, radical musicians turned to many forms to comment on society: Trinidadian Calypso, popular in New York City; show tunes, blues, and race records circulating in African-American ghettos; and, of course, folk music (variously defined). Writing revolutionary music came with challenges beyond those inherent in writing original, creative work: concerns such as ideological purity and topicality weighed in the balance with aesthetics. There was also the quandary of how one might compose music that was technically and politically revolutionary yet appealing to the masses for whom it was intended.

Charles Seeger, on revolutionary music: No one had any idea what would be the nature of "revolutionary music," you see, and it took me a long time after this to realize that there's no such thing as revolutionary music. Music doesn't take any cognizance of the dichotomy between revolutionary and not revolutionary. To change the music technique is not revolutionary, outside music.

If I considered myself a musical revolutionist, it was simply by reversing the old technical device—you prepare a dissonance and you resolve a dissonance; but I turned it upside down and I prepared a consonance. My first species of counterpoint was all dissonance—well, that was revolutionary musically, but had no significance socially, it was not revolutionary at all. And it wasn't revolutionary musically; it was simply a change. A stunt that I could do. ...

My conclusion getting on towards '35 with the Collective [was] that the whole Socialist and Communist parties were city-oriented, slum-oriented and addressed to and springing from minorities of the population that didn't know America. The Communist Party, as I look back, didn't know the United States. They didn't talk the language of the country. They had a kind of confused jargon that they thought was the language of the country. "Workers." My God, no American wants to be called a worker![25]

Singer Bess Lomax Hawes, on the music of the Composers' Collective: Pete, I think, had The Workers' Song Book; or perhaps I saw them at Charlie's and Ruth's. [Composer Ruth Crawford Seeger was Charles Seeger's second wife.] Charlie, of course, had written some rather sophisticated songs, those rounds. He was also in touch with some of the European composers, Eisler and so on. I don't know whether he knew them personally, but he knew their work. He sang some of those and Ruth sang some of those, just around the house kind of singing with the piano.

I learned some of them. Never sang them very much, occasionally, but not often. They seemed to me too European, or too intellectual, or something. They never spoke to me very deeply. I didn't think that they were that interesting for American audiences.[26]

Norman Cazden, on contradictions in revolutionary music: There's some contradiction in the fact that the people involved in creating this new theoretical proletarian style were themselves not blue-collar workers. And that's no surprise, because blue-collar workers aren't trained in music; middle-class student-types are.[27]

Pete Seeger, on finding types of music for social change: Well, the Wobblies decided the pop song was the best form: "Everybody knows this tune; we'll put new words to it." One of the hit songs of 1912 was sung by a very popular singer: "Oh The Girls, They Go Wild Over Me." They made up this Wobblies version that was hilarious. I used to sing it myself. "The bull (the policeman) goes wild over me and the judge he went wild over me and the jailor he went wild over me."

Many people felt this was the best tradition. My father disapproved of it. He had a theory that a new society would require new music. Of course his theory didn't work out so well and I've often told people that the proletariat was not interested in the songs produced by the Composers' Collective in 1932 and '33 and '34. That's when he himself decided he should look into folk music.[28]

Charles Seeger, on becoming aware of folk music: I didn't know that there was any living folk music. I thought it was just a few old people, who were dying off. And popular music, well, popular music just tracks along; it does the best it can, imitating the concert music—that was my view of it. It's the last detritus, the last excrement, so to speak, of the concert stage. And it's not worth much bothering about. You can write about the beauty of cities and the importance of having beautiful architecture, without going into the plumbing. Well, popular music was the plumbing. . . .

These well-taught musicians trying to write music for ordinary people: they couldn't, because they couldn't imagine what an ordinary person *was* musically. So I went to Aunt Molly [Jackson], and I told Aunt Molly, "We're all on the wrong track. You are on the right track."

She could write music that the people would sing. And some of them are damn fine songs too. Why that "Harry Simms," it makes gooseflesh come in your backbone.[29]

AUNT MOLLY JACKSON AND MUSICAL LEFTISM IN NEW YORK

Aunt Molly Jackson (called "Aunt" in reference to her profession as a midwife) arrived in New York in 1931 fresh from the strikes of Harlan County, Kentucky. She had been "discovered" that year by a committee of leftist writers (including Theodore Dreiser, John Dos Passos, and Sherwood Anderson) who visited the Kentucky coal mining region. Aunt Molly Jackson had a rough, rasping voice: undoubtedly authentic, ripe with class rage. She'd lost most of her family to the mines. The alienation and straitened circumstances of mine workers—the isolation of working underground and the near-feudal system under which many miners worked and lived—ultimately produced the most extensive collection of labor protest songs of any American industry, and Aunt Molly Jackson knew (and wrote) her share of them.

When Charles Seeger first encountered Aunt Molly Jackson in New York—a living, breathing (singing and cursing) sample of Appalachian local color, touted (much like Lead Belly) for her authenticity—he saw in her the merging of old folk songs—homegrown American music of the sort he'd begun to read about in books by Lomax and others—and left-wing politics.

Seeger did not know it yet, but it was Aunt Molly Jackson's music—not twelve-tone, not dissonance, not the complicated compositions the Collective was generating—that would prove most revolutionary to him (and others) and would stimulate their interest in traditional music.

Bess Lomax Hawes, on Aunt Molly Jackson: [I heard of her] through my brother Alan and through Mary Elizabeth Barnicle, who was a folklorist at New York City. She had been pretty well collected. Alan, I think, recorded her in Kentucky. They went back to see her when she got up to New York and recorded in her apartment quite a number of times: her life history, her reminiscences, plus her songs. She was still composing at that time. I went and sat in on a number of those sessions.

Her half-brother Jim Garland was also there. Jim Garland had developed the eye disease that comes from malnutrition in part and was never cared for; he was pretty well blind then. He had composed quite a number of songs by that period. "I Don't Want Your Millions Mister," Aunt Molly sang that and Pete [Seeger] learned it from her and so on. I wouldn't be at all surprised if Pete's later development of interest in topical political song didn't develop out of that Kentucky model. Because there were a lot of good songs coming out of the South at that period; Aunt Molly and Jim were in the forefront of that whole idea.[30]

Pete Seeger, on Jackson's visit to the Composers' Collective: In 1933, [Father] brought Aunt Molly Jackson around to the Pierre Degeyter Club. There was Aunt Molly:

> I am a union woman, just brave as I can be,
> I do not like the bosses, and the bosses don't like me.

Well, his fellow musicians just listened to her in amazement. Says, "Well, isn't this a freak. Just a freak."

I've often told the story about him bringing Aunt Molly Jackson to the Collective and they listened to her for half an hour and they said, "But Charlie, this is music of the past! We're supposed to be creating the music of the future."

And they didn't see any point in trying to carry on the kind of music, I mean, she's a relic of past centuries. Something that Charlie Seeger dug up out of the hills. It's something to be listened to with amusement. But it doesn't have any relation to the music of the working class of the world.

But Father played these records to me. I didn't actually meet Aunt Molly 'til 1937, I believe. But he [then] felt that the music of a nation would arise out of the peoples' music of that nation.... And so, Father gradually moved away from Eisler as a model; though he still really loved Mr. Eisler as a person, Father felt that the music in *this* country, while it might learn something from Eisler, was still going to have to come out of American experience....

He takes Molly back to her little, one-room apartment and said, "Molly, I'm sorry, they didn't understand you, but I know some young people who are going to want to learn your songs." And I'm sure he meant me.[31]

Bess Lomax Hawes, on Molly Jackson and the folk process: Almost all of her songs were based on [traditional tunes], I don't know whether they recognized it or not. Aunt Molly thought about the text, that's what she was interested in. When she wrote a song, it was in effect writing a poem. She would never say it as a poem; she would always sing it. But the part that she was writing were the words, and she sort of put them to the rhythm structure that she had in the back of her head to some sort of an old tune that was knocking around in there. She could sometimes identify it, but sometimes not. But I think that's a very common process of folk composition.....

I think Alan [Lomax] saw Aunt Molly and Jim [Garland] and that movement in terms of the folks, in terms of traditional singers, as exactly in step with what had always happened in folk song. That they were doing exactly what the earlier bards had done. What the unknown cowboy singers had done who wrote "The Range of the Buffalo," which was a political song of its period (based on an earlier tune knocking around). He saw the contemporary movement to create new songs, particularly by people like Aunt Molly and Jim, as exactly parallel to Elizabethan bards singing scandalous songs about queens and their goings-on. That, in terms of the folk song academic movement, was a very radical position in that day. A folk song had to be old in order for it to be a folk song. You couldn't, by definition during that period, have a "contemporary" folk song.

Aunt Molly's stuff was more organic to her own experience [and the product of] a process that had been going on for a very long time within traditional communities.... It was always sort of, "This terrible thing happened, so I wrote this song." That's the kind of thing I remember her saying, rather than, "I wrote a song for a particular situation." Now, she may have done that. It always seemed to me that Aunt Molly's songs were more reflections of her personal experiences at first hand. Even though she might start out with "I hate the capitalist system," she always got down to particulars.[32]

FOLK MUSIC, LEFTISTS, AND THE NEW DEAL

If Aunt Molly Jackson's 1933 encounter with the Composers' Collective had not gone well, history was on her side. In 1935, the Communist Party sought to reground itself in populism and radical patriotism, a movement known as the Popular Front. Folklore and folk music came to be associated with this search for native radicalism. Over the course of the 1930s, streams of interest in folk music converged: the older collector-lecturer-author types who had been active for some time met the new pro-American culture, Popular Front Left forming after mid-1935.[33] These groups turned to folk music as nationalistic and patriotic. With such diverse perspectives, the conception of folk music had to shift. According to Library of Congress folklorist Ben Botkin, those interested in folklore turned away from "the realm of antiquarianism and chauvinism" in favor of modernity and living sources and concerns.[34] In practical terms, this meant unearthing American radicals, and American radicalism, from within American musical history.

Musical radicals looked for antiestablishment songs in working-class and popular music—in folk music. Prior to the arrival of Aunt Molly Jackson in New York (or the union balladeer Ella Mae Wiggins from Gastonia, North Carolina, earlier) discussions of using folk music by thinkers on the musical Left had been limited to foreign models, particularly Russian compositions steeped in folk song. Composers such as Shostakovich, who incorporated Russian folk songs into his concert music, were admired (at least until his denunciation by the Soviet Union).[35] But the musical intelligentsia still saw European and Russian folk songs as something altogether different from—and superior to—the "low" music Aunt Molly Jackson was singing. As Carl Sandburg, editor of *American Songbag* (1927), wrote at the time, "There are persons born and reared in this country who culturally have not yet come over from Europe."[36]

Over the course of the 1930s, the Lomaxes' notion of folk music as the voice of American populist democracy would join with the Composers' Collective's quest for progressive music to radicalize and move masses. And as mass song and American folk song began to merge, the conception of folk music was evolving (to the disapproval of many early collectors): folk music was no longer merely vestigial; it was also germinal. The seeds of revival had been planted.

Norman Cazden, on the contemporary meaning of folk music: In the first place, by folk music, in New York at the time, we would not have meant American folk music, certainly of the hinterland of America. New York City was very largely a city of immigrants, of first-generation or second-generation immigrants, to whom, let's say, Cecil Sharp's research on English folk songs of the southern Appalachians was quite unknown. The banjo and guitar were not familiar instruments. The balalaika was and the mandolin was. . . .

Anyhow, there was a lot of Jewish folk song, a lot of what passed for Russian folk song, which was really nineteenth-century Russian cafe music. There were Greek folk songs, any nationality you'll name.[37]

Pete Seeger, on Russian folk music: Maybe people will say it's inevitable in the Soviet Union that folk music was costumed and put on a stage and killed that way. See, the socialist countries killed it in a different way, and they really did. These beautiful, fluid Russian folk songs they wrote down note for note. They formalized them. I'm only sorry that I've never been able to find a way to say this to Russian audiences: "You're killing your own folk music by the way you're formalizing it."[38]

Norman Cazden, on the radical movement and the folk: There was a feeling that, if the radical movement was ever to command the support of the majority of people in this country, the radical movement had to learn the language of the people, the manner, the substance. It had to steep itself in local history, in things that really mattered to people. And not look with disdain upon this as simply being a heritage of old culture.

Some of this was greatly influenced by the improved study of folklore in general. It was no longer the simplistic view that scratch a worker, and he is immediately a disgruntled revolutionary who's been unemployed and is ready to turn the political situation upside down.[39]

Earl Robinson, on music in action: I remember down on the waterfront once, being part of a strike situation, but everyone was having a helluva time and a lot of young people and this one guy, who with a gang of young people were singing "Casey Jones," the [Wobblies'] version, "Workers on The SP Line." It was so vital, so alive, so incredibly there, compared to what the Composers' Collective was doing that this had to influence me deeply.[40]

Guitarist Ry Cooder, on the depression songs of unemployed railroad workers: Up 'til the decade of the thirties, railroading began to fall off in its scope and number of miles, amount of equipment used. They didn't have much of a highway system in this country until 1933 or so.

It was mud and dirt, and it was hard to get from out there to out here, so the trains were the main thing, and the boomers were the guys, the train workers who were put off [the job]. They were union men, and apparently the unions were broken up by the train companies. Organized labor was under attack because it had gotten big and powerful. And so these train men would be put off the trains; but what they did do, they continued to ride the trains as hobos, and they were called "boomers."

So then, hobos became, during the depression, greater in number and more of a problem. They were considered bums and no account and bad people, but the boomers had a certain honor, and a certain status. Boomers were simply guys who had a job, had a calling and a profession, and then they didn't have it anymore. It was not their fault. As the song "Boomer's Story" says, "I hear another train a-comin', I guess I'll be on my way" is about the size of it. They never stayed very long in one place.

Who writes songs like that? I mean, you can't imagine somebody sitting down [to write it]. It's obviously not by a professional songwriter, it's not a Tin Pan Alley song; it's far from being a rustic song too. It's not a hymn-tune structure tune like many of the nineteenth-century cowboy tunes. (They were actually taken from hymns or some other source.)[41]

Charles Seeger, on people's appreciation for their own music: I could see from the history of folk music that people, regardless of what stratum they live on, have a desire to make music in the tradition of that stratum. And the music from other strata, well, they'll listen to it sometimes but they don't want much of it. They like their own music and what can be made out of it.[42]

SUCH WAS THE IDEALISM of the thirties-era folk revivalists, and this sort of radical patriotism led Roosevelt to include in the Farm Security Administration a federal agency dedicated to creating communities across the country to house (and employ) struggling families. The Resettlement Administration itself was short-lived (1935–37), but its Special Skills Division sponsored both a photography project (participants included Dorothea Lange), community-building through music, and the recording of American folk music. The federal government also began supporting the Archive of American Folk Song. Former Collective members Charles Seeger, Earl Robinson, Norman Cazden, and Herbert Haufrecht joined other New Deal folklore activists on the government payroll.

Herbert Haufrecht, on folk music in the Resettlement Administration: I was supposed to organize musical activities in the community. That was my function. And among the things I had to do was, I organized a choir for the church.... And among the choir members was an ex-boxer with his nose flattened out. But he loved to sing. In the southern style, they sang the solfège, you know, note reading, but shape notes. And you'd see this husky pug and he would love nothing better than to sing. People from all over. There was a miner there from Georgia, his name was Sexton and he brought the blues, played guitar. They came from all around. There were young fellows who played what we called hillbilly somewhat influenced by the more commercial music. There was a carpenter who was a psalms singer.

And they're suspicious of foreigners who come in there. See, this was a new community—a mixture of people from the area and from distant lands, and I had many problems. They had secret societies. They met at night. They had passwords. There was almost lynching parties and all that sort of thing. And I was supposed to soothe all this with music!

But anyways, it came to a head at one of the square dances. Some days I traveled as far as forty miles away to get a certain caller I heard about.

That was rough going though: down onto a ferry, crossing up on the other side—I had just learned how to drive at the time. The road disappeared in the streams, real hill country. This guy was going to get his uncle. He had to go by foot over the hill. I had to stop at the car. So I was waiting a half hour. His uncle finally came with his fiddle, his wife, his daughter, her kids, about eight people in a little Chevy, just loaded to the gills. So we all came back for the square dance, flat tires and all. And I got there about nine o'clock, a little late, and everybody was worried. So we had these square dances. But on occasion, the opposition [the Republicans at that time] would booze up. And break in and try and break it up. I had to send in a report to Washington what happened. That was in '36, my first [direct] association with folk music: a wonderful experience, I must say.[43]

Pete Seeger, on the end of the Resettlement Administration: In 1936, '37, '38, Father tried to bring out some of the progressive songs that they ran across in their collecting:

> *The farmer is the man,*
> *Lives on credit 'til the fall.*

And "The Candidate's a Dodger." Henry Wallace went up to Capitol Hill to see if he couldn't get the Resettlement Administration reapproved by Congress. And there was a conservative southern Senator, said, "Mr. Wallace, you want me to vote for that Resettlement Administration of yours, look what it produces." (Slap! Down on the table went a copy of "The Candidate's a Dodger.") "Did you expect me to vote for that?" And that song was one of the reasons that the Resettlement Administration folded. The Farm Security Administration picked up some of the program. And my father's work got shifted over to that.[44]

Charles Seeger, on the Resettlement Administration: Well, if you look at my instructions to my field-workers, you'll see that they were to go into the resettlement as somebody from Washington—they couldn't help that, they couldn't help it being known that they were musicians, but I said, for God's sake, there let it stop. From there on, you're a human being.

You've got to make these people like you, you've got to have them trust you, or else you'll never get anywhere with them. The first thing for you to do is to find out what music the people can make. Then put that to the uses that you're sent to the community to use to make the people in the community get along with each other instead of fighting with each other. Because you see the community was ordinarily a place where several bigoted religious groups would start fighting with each other, and then you'd have trouble.

Mrs. Roosevelt and [Rex] Tugwell and the other people there in Washington had that idea, that music might be able to harmonize some of these difficulties. And I had that from my work in the Collective that that was what music *should* do....

Well, I'll tell you one story, of Margaret Valiant and Cherry Lake. There's the advantage of it. Her success was absolutely phenomenal because she went to the women and found that they had poor clothes, and she knew how to make the clothes better and had them put on a fashion show so that they could sing their favorite song. And then play along with the local hillbilly band.

Musically, I knew what I was doing. I was absolutely sure, and I had enough chance to test it out: that music must serve. That you must use the music that the people got in them already. There's no use pumping foreign music into something that's a perfectly going concern and you can make use of....

Socialism in music was what we tried to practice there. But, of course, Congress gradually found out what was happening.[45]

Activist author Stetson Kennedy, on the WPA: I was employed as a WPA [Works Progress Administration] writer there in Jacksonville, and it must have been '37 or '38 when Charles Seeger came to town. Charles did a talk to the WPA Music Project in Jacksonville and somehow a transcript of his talk came into my possession—I still have it, a report on the recording of folk music in the Soviet Union. For Charles Seeger to make such a talk in a city like Jacksonville in 1937 was really remarkable.[46]

Norman Cazden, on folk music collecting and the WPA: The WPA projects of the 1930s also meant a rediscovery of roots. I have recently been going again over the research in folk music of WPA days: no political content. It's the hoedown, the local songs, the narrative about a girl in the nineteenth century who got murdered by her sweetheart, the story about Old Joe Clark and his love for chicken pie. This is not political content; self-consciousness in the sense of recognizing that there was indeed a repertoire of song and story and tradition and music of their own; that, yes. This was bringing new awareness that there is such a thing as roots, and that there is a depth to people.[47]

FEAR OF COMMUNISM in America ultimately ended the Resettlement Administration (and much of Charles Seeger's career as well). Applied folklorists (those working in the public sector) who had become radicalized during the depression—such as Ben Botkin, Alan Lomax, and later Charles Seeger—were attacked professionally and forced out of their jobs.

Members of the Composers' Collective had connected to folk music. Elie Siegmeister was now describing folk song as "one of the richest, most exciting types of music on earth.... Folk song, the natural expression of our people who 'don't know anything about music,' is the deepest, most democratic layer of our American musical culture."[48] The rest of America was already there—listening to radio barn dances and tuning in to the first National Folk Festival in 1934.

By the late thirties, convincing people that folk music was alive and well in America was no longer a struggle. Out of the depression would come folk music groups such as the Almanac Singers and People's Songs; and folk music, protest, and the American Left would remain connected for decades. And the place where they would connect was in a small, oddly shaped district of lower Manhattan where bohemians had roamed since World War I: Greenwich Village.

Lightnin' Washington and his work group at Darrington State Prison Farm, Texas, sing for John and Alan Lomax, 1934. *Photo by Alan Lomax, courtesy of the American Folklife Center, Library of Congress*

Banjo-picker Pete Steele, with his family in Hamilton, Ohio, 1938, was an early influence on Pete and Mike Seeger. *Photo by Alan Lomax, courtesy of the American Folklife Center, Library of Congress*

John Avery Lomax, an early collector of living folk music from across the United States, stands beside his mobile recording unit. *American Folklife Center, Library of Congress*

Members of one of folk music's first families often sang together: ethnomusicologist Charles Seeger with composer Ruth Crawford Seeger and their children, future musicians Mike and Peggy, about 1937. *Courtesy of the Seeger Family Collection*

The songbook *Songs of Labor and the American People* (February–March 1947), with union hero Joe Hill on its red cover, was published to mark the first anniversary of the pro-labor singing organization People's Songs. *Courtesy of the Labor Arts Archive's Henry Foner Collection*

The Almanac Singers performed pro-union, anti-war, and anti-Nazi music; from left, Woody Guthrie, Millard Lampell, Bess Lomax Hawes, Pete Seeger, Arthur Stern, Sis Cunningham, New York City, 1941. *Used with permission of the Woody Guthrie Archive*

Folklorist Alan Lomax (center, at microphone), bluesmen Muddy Waters and Memphis Slim, and Pete Seeger backstage at Carnegie Hall in 1959. *Photo by John Cohen*

The Weavers—Lee Hays, Fred Hellerman, Pete Seeger, and Ronnie Gilbert—brought folk music to mass audiences in the 1950s; here, they appear at the Old Town School of Folk Music, Chicago, 1958. *Photo by Robert C. Malone, courtesy Ralph Rinzler Folklife Archives, Smithsonian Institution*

The New Lost City Ramblers (Mike Seeger, Tracy Schwarz, and John Cohen), a classic, "old-timey" string band, perform at the Newport Folk Festival, 1965. *Photo by Diana Davies, courtesy Ralph Rinzler Folklife Archives, Smithsonian Institution*

Anonymous musicians pick for Sunday crowds in Greenwich Village's Washington Square Park around 1965. *Photo by Diana Davies, courtesy Ralph Rinzler Folklife Archives, Smithsonian Institution*

Guy Carawan, Fannie Lou Hamer, Bernice Johnson Reagon, and Len Chandler bring freedom songs to the Newport Folk Festival, 1965. *Photo by Diana Davies, courtesy Ralph Rinzler Folklife Archives, Smithsonian Institution*

Civil rights activist Jimmy Collier inspires protesters with song during the Poor People's March in Marks, Mississippi, 1968. *Photo by Diana Davies, courtesy Ralph Rinzler Folklife Archives, Smithsonian Institution*

Navajo protest singer Klee Benally, a member of the socially conscious punk band Blackfire, which has recorded Woody Guthrie songs, at the Grassroots Festival in Trumansburg, New York, 2008. *Photo by Jeff Folkins, Rochester, NY*

Holly Near sings out against the Iraq war in New York City, 2003. *Photo by Diane Greene Lent*

Pete Seeger sings at a civil rights rally in Searsville, California, in 1963. For decades, such audiences have come to folk music for its power to forge community and motivate social action. *Photo by Robert Krones*

4

GREENWICH VILLAGE

1940s

IN JANUARY 1917, as the salons buzzed with talk of "Wobblies and Freud, cubism and free love, anarchism and birth control" and playwright Eugene O'Neill and the Provincetown Players were revolutionizing American theater on MacDougal Street, six conspirators (including artist Marcel Duchamp) climbed the Washington Square Arch and declared Greenwich Village a "free and independent republic."[1] In its way, Greenwich Village has always been so.

The burghers who settled lower Manhattan Island skipped over this district—as erratic in its geography as in its inhabitants—whose narrow alleys prevented deliveries by wagon. Radiating out in a street pattern all its own from Washington Square Park, New York's bohemian capital welcomed the iconoclasts. Among these were many of America's major artists who deviated from the mainstream and needed a haunt for freethinkers. In the early years of the twentieth century, Greenwich Village was home to the writers E. E. Cummings, Willa Cather, John Reed, Dylan Thomas, and Edna St. Vincent Millay; the painters Tom Benton and Jackson Pollock; and a large slice of the avant-garde that was shaping the intellectual and artistic ambitions of the times and the nation—including the Composers' Collective.

Though subjected to criticism as elitist, abstract, and even naïve, the left-leaning politics of Greenwich Village were always mixed in with the painting and music.[2] Here the Marxist New Masses, following in the tradition of Max Eastman's work The Masses, published "what [was] too naked or true for a money-making press."[3] Even Leon Trotsky himself had lived briefly in the neighborhood. As Eastman recalled:

> The whole scene and situation lent itself to my effort and my then very great need to romanticize...the revolution. The talk was radical; it was free-thought talk and not just socialism. There was a sense of universal revolt and regeneration, of the just-before-dawn of a new day in American art.[4]

Folksinger Oscar Brand, on hanging out in the Village: I gravitated to the Village [from upstate New York]; I thought it was marvelous that here were these people singing the songs, some of which I knew by heart. And they were singing them the way I ought to sing them: freely and happily and enjoying the syllables and the music. That was something that I hadn't had too much contact with.

The Village is where the wind carried me. I enjoyed it there very, very much. I enjoyed the people. I got to know them. The playwrights and the writers and the sculptors and the painters. It was a very exciting thing for me. But I couldn't stay there. Had no place to live, to sleep. I didn't know many people there. So I had to go home almost every other night. I was out of school. And then I went to work on the farms in upstate New York. I would come in when I had a day off; "Day off" meant part of Sunday; that was the day off.[5]

Journalist A. B. Magil, on leftists in New York: There's no doubt that the greatest strength of the movement was in New York: politically, organizationally, culturally. After all, as far as culture is concerned, New York has been the cultural capital apart from anything the Left contributed. The movement, the radical political movement [of the 1930s], was national. It had activities in many parts of the country. (That doesn't mean that it was numerically strong, except in a highly relative sense. It doesn't mean that it had activity and influence in every part of the country.) There were large parts of the country where there was no Left activity whatsoever.[6]

AMID WAR AND RUMORS OF WAR, amid the political and cultural unity forged by the Popular Front and the New Deal, the 1940s began. A better world seemed within reach, and a new crop of artists picked up their instruments to sing for it. As if by some gravitational pull, they came together to talk politics and play music in New York City: Alan Lomax was promoting and collecting folk songs; Pete Seeger and Woody Guthrie were returning from traveling America, jumping off freight trains, and swapping songs with strangers; Aunt Molly Jackson from Harlan County was singing for union events; Lead Belly was serenading kids; and bluesman Brownie McGhee was teaming up with blind harmonica player Sonny Terry. Their coming together supercharged an unusual fusion of music and cultural insurgency, as the first folk music revival reached critical mass in New York City.

What had begun as a revivalist instinct among urban, college-educated musicians and researchers now took a new turn. The Archive of Folk Song was in full swing; at universities, folk music was no longer dismissed as vulgar and archaic; and Alan Lomax was bringing folk music to millions via radio. Now this folk music revival movement, whose hub had been in Washington at the Library of Congress, moved uptown. Or, rather, downtown, to the Village, where the apartments were cheap and the food ethnic and inexpensive.

Early folk music enthusiasts—including the painters Benton and Pollock—made their living rooms ring with old songs as the depression ended in Greenwich Village. Among the leaders of this budding folk music movement were the Almanac Singers, an "agitprop" group who performed old-time southern and western tunes with new lyrics, based on the topics of the day. At first, there were rehearsals in a basement, and soon after, in a house famous for its salad bowl the size of a washtub; it was hootenanny time at the musical co-op known as the Almanac House.

New York City may have been exciting to the hootenanny crowd, but it wasn't easy living. In the process of changing from a coterie pursuit into an underground subculture, folk music was beginning to find some commercial viability, egged on by radio. "Tossed into the commercial boiling pot, [folk music] is now being processed for radio and every conceivable outlet,"[7] composer Roy Harris remarked at the time. But the remuneration was negligible. People who would one day be credited with launching a second folk music revival were struggling to scrape by. Of course, the lives of young musicians in Greenwich Village differed from the poverty they sang about—not like coal mining in West Virginia, or fleeing the Dust Bowl—but it was poverty all the same.

Almanac Singer Bess Lomax Hawes, on poverty and the Almanacs: Everybody was poor, but we weren't poor in the sense of the people we were talking to. They were poor and didn't want to be poor. We were poor and didn't notice it. It wasn't that we were trying to look poor—we were!—but we hadn't thought of ourselves as dressing up or dressing down, as dressing any way in particular. We had the same kind of naïveté when we started to make it in that few months there. We didn't have any presentation, we just straggled up to the microphone and started to sing.[8]

Almanac Singer Lee Hays, on surviving in New York City: [In the beginning] there was just a booking Pete Seeger and I did together [at the Jade Restaurant in December 1939]. Someplace that somebody got him to sing at. He gave me the five dollars. He said he didn't need it and I did. I remember he used to take me into a saloon; he taught me how to put hot pepper sauce into cold beer to pep it up, make you less hungry.

We didn't have a hell of a lot of money. In this first apartment with [Millard] Lampell, this little place, that is where we met [folksingers] Cisco [Houston] and Josh [White] and Burl [Ives] and that is where we had the famous soup pot going all the time, where everybody brought in a potato or a piece of meat. I don't know how I was living in those days but anyway we had a famous stewpot, that a lot of people ate out of, perpetually cooking on the back of the stove.[9]

Almanac Singer Millard Lampell, on getting by in New York City: No one ever cared about money, or where the money was coming from, or whether you were going to have enough to live. We got scraps of things; Mother Bloor [the radical labor organizer], or someone like that, would come over and bring us a basket of apples or carrots from her farm. Lee would cook big loaves of bread—you know, he'd been used to cooking for seventy or eighty at Commonwealth [College] anyhow—and we'd have a pot of stew going. It's amazing how little you could live on. We paid virtually no rent. We got very little for the singing, and no one really cared.[10]

Almanac Singer Gordon Friesen, on the Almanacs' inspiration: The Almanacs had no use for the establishment. They studied Joe Hill, Aunt Molly Jackson, and—you know the songs of the struggles in the mines—Jim Garland, and Sarah Ogan. They appreciated those kinds of people, Sonny Terry and Brownie McGhee. They were drawn to Josh White because White's first album was religious songs under an assumed name, but his second album was about the chain gangs, *Southern Exposure*. They were drawn to him because he was telling it like it was amongst the black people down South; as it really was.

I think it was all popular consciousness. It just so happened that they had this house in Greenwich Village because before they had the house, they were making these national tours. Once they started out for the West Coast. They made several trips to the West Coast. And they sang a lot in Detroit to the United Automobile Workers organizing drive. There was a long period there in which they really had no base, such as Almanac House became later on.[11]

Millard Lampell, on New York's folk music community in 1940: I'll tell you what the whole scene consisted of....There was Lead Belly singing his Southern chain gang stuff; there was Josh White who was very slick but had done a chain gang album; there was Richard Dyer-Bennet doing the sharp versions of folk songs in concert in a very stylized way—sort of English style; there was Burl Ives doing rather hokey stuff, and there was us.

You have to remember, in those days if you walked along a street carrying guitars and banjos, it was like you were leading a giraffe. No one had ever seen anybody carrying a guitar or a banjo in New York, much less playing on the subway, which we often would do on our way to a booking. Oh, people really got excited, fascinated. Well, you know New Yorkers, some of them would look up and then look back to their newspapers—they can't be taken with anything. But certainly at the places we played, people were very romantic about, particularly in the left-wing movement, "America." It was a kind of Carl Sandburg, Archibald MacLeish, Steven Vincent Benét feeling about America. We all had that.

Then, suddenly, it was as though the music of "America" had come to New York. Kids loved it. We were asked to play a lot of schools, like the Little Red School House [in the Village], and so on. But mostly it was the Left, in general. I can speak for myself—I think Lee [Hays] was much more hip to what was going on—but I just was swept up in the kind of romantic atmosphere; I think Pete [Seeger] was the same way. It was political in a very emotional way; that is, not in a particularly organized way. It was much more a populist feeling, because all of our songs came from working people.[12]

Ethnomusicologist Charles Seeger, on the gradually shifting definition of folk music: In the early days, oh you must sing traditional songs. If a group didn't sing traditional songs, they weren't folksingers. Then Peter was one of the first to introduce, for the city audience, some songs that weren't folk songs. They were like folk songs, in this respect: that the average person, after hearing it a few times, could and would sing it, so that the definition of what was a folk song began to include that.

The person could be a folksinger even though they sang songs that would have been thrown out a few years before; because they had not gone through oral transmission and change over several generations, people began to let down on that several-generation currency definition of folk song. And if it were something like "Kisses Sweeter Than Wine" that could be sung by anybody and would be sung by anybody, after hearing it enough, if they liked it, then, well, people regarded it as a folk song.[13]

THE ALMANAC SINGERS FORMED in early 1940, initially as a trio that included Pete Bowers (a pseudonym for Pete Seeger), Lee Hays, and Millard Lampell. When Dust Bowler Woody Guthrie showed up in New York later that spring, he joined up. Other members included Pete and Butch Hawes, Bess Lomax (Alan Lomax's sister), and later Sis Cunningham and Gordon Friesen (two radicals newly arrived from Oklahoma), along with fringe members such as Burl Ives, Earl Robinson, Arthur Stern, Tom Glazer, and even Alan Lomax. The group sang for peace, for unions. After Hitler invaded the USSR, they abandoned the antiwar position of their first album, *Songs for John Doe* (1941), and began singing out against fascism.

The Almanacs lived in Greenwich Village and held rent parties and cause parties in a tuneful commotion: Woody Guthrie wrote his book *Bound for Glory*, tossing the pages on the floor next to his gallon jug; Pete

Seeger played his banjo until his roommates made him practice outside; and everyone wrote songs, talked politics, and sang some more.

Bess Lomax Hawes, on Greenwich Village life with the Almanacs: Yes, it was a bizarre household in the extreme, Lee [Hays] being passed out upstairs and Woody working his own particular way, totally individualistically. Pete Hawes, who lived in the back bedroom, was a rather elegant figure, Bostonian elegance, upper-class elegance—he relatively lived to himself. He had two Siamese cats at the time and Siamese, as you know, scream. Woody referred to both of them as "Sexy"; that was his name for them.

He said that Pete [Hawes] should release them, in fact, threatened to throw them out of the house. Pete, of course, had bred them very carefully—this was one of his hobbies at the time—he was constantly getting into battles with Woody over that. Woody would threaten to open the window and let the cats out.

Meanwhile, Pete [Seeger] and I shared the front bedroom [with a sheet hung down the middle] in perfect sobriety and isolation and being very careful to not impinge on each other and be private from each other.

Woody was writing absolutely constantly during that period and we were all working with Woody. He was doing the *Bound for Glory* material, which as you know was edited down. About a tenth of what he actually wrote came out in *Bound For Glory*. He was absolutely unstoppable. He never even crossed anything out. Pete [Seeger] made up a song about him at the period [sings]:

> My name is Woody Guthrie,
> I'm the great hysterical bum,
> highly saturated
> in whiskey, rye, and rum.
> I've wrote a million pages
> and I've never read a one
> I think that's about the biggest thing
> that man has ever done!

And it was absolutely true. I picked up the pieces of paper off the floor and put them in order and read them. Woody never did.[14]

Oscar Brand, describing some of the Almanac Singers: The Almanacs? They had better lyrics than most groups ever have. They weren't just street writers with chalk on the pavement, as I've seen many. They were with Pete, who was educated—he may have left college early but he didn't lose the stamp of Harvard—and Millard who could write very, very well, and could change and fix when they made a mistake; and the prosody was tough.

And Woody Guthrie never cared about prosody. He used to accompany me. My god! I used to go crazy because he would play wrong chords. He did it on purpose. They all made fun of me. First of all because I was Canadian. And I was obviously Canadian in my speech and everything else. So they made fun of me. Also, I didn't drink or smoke. And that wasn't the easiest thing to do so I used to buy the liquor for them so they would accept me. And I didn't have a banjo. I've never been a musician really....I thought maybe one day if they kept going maybe I would join them, which was foolish.[15]

Millard Lampell, on the musical influences of the Almanacs: [Pete Seeger] had picked up a lot from Uncle Dave Macon, who was his idol— the guy who was the first banjo player in the *Grand Old Opry*. Pete had a lot of old 78 Uncle Dave records. We were in the course of time to put together quite a library collection of records of all that stuff that was made during the thirties. A lot of it was folk music; some of it was country music. (There was a lot of that recorded. It was sort of the white equivalent of the race records for the blacks.) It was white music meant to play in the South. You know, the early guys who were later to become the granddaddies of what became country music, hillbilly: the Carter Family, the *Grand Old Opry*, some of them folk and some western. Some of them were novelty numbers. The early versions of country music coming from the twenties and thirties. The Coon Creek Girls, I remember, absolutely, we'd play. Woody loved them too. "I'm going to marry them all," he'd say.

The favorites that we played over and over again were Jimmie Rodgers, a number of the black blues singers, Blind Lemon and T-Bone Slim, and a bunch of those guys. So, we'd listen to that stuff all the time. Of course Pete had been collecting songs and had worked in the Library of Congress with John Lomax—you know, Alan's father; I'm sure he'd gotten a lot of the stuff from Ruth and Charles Seeger.[16]

Composer Earl Robinson, on his role in the Almanac House: I see folk music as a living thing, which lives by changing all the time. And I contributed to the change. And the Almanac Singers really did that. We who were in on it [the first folk music revival] thought of ourselves as kind of special people because we were honest, truly honest, about folk music and about its living qualities, bringing it alive and on the other hand resisting the ossification process which would be expressed in 365 versions of the famous song....

Every Sunday afternoon they'd have this performance open to the public; you could just drop in. Kids on the floor and a marvelously relaxed country feeling right in the middle of New York. It was a beautiful, beautiful place. The Almanacs grew and developed there. I felt kind of like a father-confessor in a sense to the Almanac Singers. I was just the elder statesman. I'd sing with them occasionally and just glory in my children. Really, it's funny; I never quite put it that way before this, but, I was just two years older than most of them, you know, three, four, whatever, and famous, you know, but this Almanac group was by far more important to me than anything that was happening on Broadway.[17]

Almanac Singer Pete Seeger, on hosting Greenwich Village hootenannies: By and large, it was music every day and jokes. I remember when I was playing the banjo sitting on the toilet and Woody saying, "I've seen everything now."

In the *Daily Worker* we'd have a little ad, three lines, "Almanac Hootenanny" and give the address. We didn't have a mimeograph machine, but there were some hand-drawn posters we could put up in some meeting place. Yeah, that's what we would do, when we would go and sing somewhere, we'd leave posters: "Hootenanny at Almanac House Tomorrow Afternoon. 35¢." We'd get twenty-five or fifty people, sometimes sixty.

I wouldn't say a pint of whiskey would make the rounds, maybe Lead Belly would drink some on his own, he was trying very hard not to get in trouble. I think he was trying to quit alcohol. Lee drank too much beer, and he would want to have a keg of beer; but I think we persuaded him that that wasn't that necessary.[18]

Oscar Brand, on singing with the Almanacs: I sang in the chorus—though there was no real chorus—of some of those early recordings the Almanac Singers made....I don't know how it was done. I only knew that I'd follow somebody. We'd go over. Maybe it was Moe Asch's cellar or something. And we'd just hang around the outside and then there were the group who were going to do the recording. They were at the microphones. But if you listen to any of those, you'll find there are people singing "loyal." All these people singing "loyal"—I was one of them.

When the recordings were being made, like most of the folk music that recorded all these years, it was not written down. You want to do a recording—I've done a hundred of them—you need a certain drumbeat, you go to the drummer if you're doing drums: "Bap-a-da-da-da," and then the guy picks it up and then he does a better job. Similarly, with all the instruments, if you were in charge, then you tell him what to do. If you're in charge, well then, you just make sure they know what they're singing, if they know what they're recording or playing or anything.

This scene was different, more like the scenes that I met when I was traveling. You had a couple of people on the porch singing, playing, just because they liked the sound. They liked to be part of that sound. And so they'd be playing and singing and you could join in if you wanted. If you didn't know the song you were screwing them up; they didn't care for that.[19]

Earl Robinson, on Lead Belly at the Almanac House: What was very lovely were the times that Lead Belly would be there. Lead Belly would be totally relaxed and my son Perry, who was only four years old at the time, would play on the floor and Huddie would throw a verse at him and then back again to the whole group. He was marvelous with kids, and so he fitted right in, that was the sense of the Almanac hootenannies. What Lead Belly had, Pete and Woody and the others learned a little bit, or took something from him. For a room like this and twenty people sitting here, he would take "Goodnight Irene," and he would make a verse with everybody's name in it, sing a verse to everybody in the room. And this ability to improvise was something that Woody had terrifically; Pete gradually developed it if he didn't have it. Mill Lampell was great at it. Mill could always throw out a line. Lee had the ability. Everybody there had this kind of spontaneous quality. That was what was probably so marvelously characteristic of it, besides the music, the sense of fun.[20]

ALTHOUGH THE FBI WAS CONVINCED OTHERWISE, not all the Almanacs were members of the Communist Party USA; their political stances did mirror that of the Party, however, including their decision to abandon peace songs after the Soviet Union was attacked by Germany. But unions were the Almanacs' foremost audience. In the spring of 1941, they sang for twenty thousand Transport Workers' Union members in Madison Square Garden. That summer, the Almanacs crossed the country, singing for the National Maritime Union in Cleveland and Harry Bridges's Longshoremen's Union in San Francisco, among others.[21]

Singer Leo Christensen, on the early Almanacs: The Almanacs first came out as a group in connection with a rally that was held by the ILWU [International Longshore Workers' Union]. Pete, Woody Guthrie, and Huddie Ledbetter came, and I sang along with them on the same program. It was kind of a hootenanny situation. Longshoremen strikes were going on all the time. There was a big strike in '36. This was 1940.

'38 was the sellout in Munich. '39 was the invasion of Poland. While that was going on, there was a movement among the progressives opposed to getting involved in what we thought was really a phony situation. Matter of fact, I wrote a song, "The Yanks Will Never Come." Because the real intentions of the Western Allies was to promote Hitler and to try and get him to go to war against the Soviet Union so the two of them would fight to the death. Then they'd walk in and take over. They particularly wanted to see the Soviet Union destroyed. Pearl Harbor got us involved.

At the point where we felt we shouldn't intervene was where I heard about the Almanacs. I still have the records.[22]

People's Songs bulletin editor Waldemar Hille, on ethnicity and the Almanacs' music: [The Almanacs] always stressed the idea that progressive songs or songs of America don't just come from the minority groups. I know that this sometimes got Pete into some rather hot arguments because people felt that he was arrogant and sectarian even. He [and the others] were interested in the cowboy songs and the songs of the West. And the songs which Alan Lomax was collecting which were "Casey Jones" and all of that.[23]

Bess Lomax Hawes, on her brother Alan's take on the Almanacs as folksingers: I don't know whether Alan felt that the Almanacs were exactly the same thing as Aunt Molly's and Jim Garland's compositions. There you had a slightly different situation of people who were not singing directly from their own experiences, not using a given grown-up-in set of artistic variables. They were picking things from here and picking things from there and learning songs from the West, and songs from the South. And deliberately also making a conscious statement of, "I'm going to use this song to present this point of view." Whereas Aunt Molly's stuff was more organic to her own experience.

I don't know how Alan saw that. That was a sort of new development. That was a conscious use of what was basically—not an unconscious, that really isn't the right term for it—a very conscious use of a process that had been going on for a very long time within traditional communities.[24]

THE ALMANACS BROUGHT TOGETHER music from all parts: shanties from the Northeast; cowboy songs from the West; blues from the Midwest; old-time Methodist hymns from the South—a musical cross-section of America. To them, folk music was people's music; it was familiar, audience-friendly, and patriotic in the sense of the Popular Front's "twentieth-century Americanism." And it was fun.

Earl Robinson, on the musical role of the Almanacs: The emergence of the Almanacs was one of the most exciting things of the time, for a lot of reasons. The musical reason was that they were really using folk songs. They based themselves totally on American folk songs and composing that went on was in that style. Take a piece like "Wasn't That a Time," Lee Hays is responsible for this flat seventh, da, da.... That's a folk thing that crosses all borders; a flat seventh is a part of every folk music of every country on earth.

They were so superb in contrast to what the Pierre Degeyter Club and the Composers' Alliance [i.e., Collective] did; you couldn't even speak of them in the same league, in the same breath. The folk song, new words to the old folk songs, making them come alive, making them so living for now: this was a breath of fresh air to the whole popular music of the thirties, you know?[25]

Ethnomusicologist Norman Cazden, on the musical roots of the Almanacs: Had the Composers' Collective and its members not existed at all, I think there would still have been the Almanacs. I think their antecedents would be found in the late thirties, not in the Composers' Collective, but in the renewed interest in Burl Ives's songs, in Woody Guthrie's songs, in Lead Belly's songs. But someone needed to prepare the ground for that. Someone needed to be an articulation of the notion that music is a means of agitprop. Since that's the social function that music served. The agitprop idea was there, but this was agitprop, through the medium of the traditional folk song adapted to this purpose. But that's not the Composers' Collective's contribution....And so far as agitprop activity, well, Jacob Schaeffer was doing that in the late twenties, but in Yiddish. And the notion that one could find comparable material in the American folk tradition rather than in the Russian Jewish folk tradition, that was the new ingredient. Earl Robinson, in particular, held out for it. And Charles was right along with him. The rest of us didn't disagree, but it was always not necessarily the thing we were into.[26]

***Sing Out!* editor Irwin Silber, on the influence of the Almanac Singers on the young Left:** We were all influenced by the Almanacs. I had been to the mass rallies before the war where the Almanacs sang. The Almanacs had a very liberating effect on the Left, for both good and bad reasons. The dominant music of the Left, until the time of the Almanacs, was twofold; it was the European revolutionary tradition, and it was American popular music. In fact, a lot of myths have been created about how folk music was the cultural expression of the Left.

Well, maybe by the 1950s that came to be the case, but not—what's the name of the creepy guy who wrote a book [*Great Day Coming*]?—[R. Serge] Denisoff. He makes out like the Communist Party sat down one day and plotted it out. The fact is that in that period, the dominant musical things you found on the Left were really just political words to popular songs. I mean [the musical] *Pins and Needles* was typical; the composer Harold Rome took the normal course. In general that was the kind of music that the Left associated itself with. That is what the "Americanism" thing was in the thirties.

Those of us interested in square dancing and folk songs, we were looked at as sectarians. When the YCL [Young Communist League] held its dances, they were with big swing bands; they weren't holding square dances, I assure you.

[The Almanacs' music] was very liberating because—at least for people of my generation who were rejecting the values inherent in commercial music and didn't have that sense of identification with the European tradition, and didn't want to—we wanted something that was American. But the thing that was American that was given to us, we had to reject in value terms.

It wasn't just the Almanacs, it was Woody, and Lead Belly and Pete [Seeger] and so on, pulling it together that made a connection between the musical and the political values that made a lot of sense to us.[27]

Through oral tradition, songs of political dissent have entered and changed American culture. The most populist of art forms, song has given voice to sentiments that have no other outlet, from slave songs sung under the whip of plantation foremen to the Wobblies' objection to inhumane labor conditions. Songs provide musical enfranchisement and reveal community dynamics and history. In an ethnological context, music's primary effect, as Alan Lomax commented, "is to give the listener a feeling of security for it symbolizes the place where he was born, his religious experience, his pleasure in community doings, his courtship, and his work—any or all of these personality-shaping experiences."[28]

Pete Seeger, on compiling political folk songs: Alan Lomax was at that time [1939] putting together the collection of songs which later became *Hard Hitting Songs for Hard Hit People* [1967]. He saw these songs as a very important development in American folk music and they were being systematically excluded from all the respectable folk song publications. Really systematically excluded. In other words, folklorists would come so along and say, "now that's a political song, so that's not a folk song." So Alan made a special collection of these, and two years later, he gives them to Woody and me.[29]

Bess Lomax Hawes, on the temporality of topical songs: Woody's response to the whole problem of the topical song—he felt we really ought to make songs that would last beyond ten minutes [laughing]. He was continually frustrated by the curves of history that were wiping out our repertoire and making it nonsuitable for singing. He really wanted to write songs that would last for a while. So, in one of his attempts to explain his point of view on this, he did a parody on a humorous song that he remembered from his youth. About a young man who had a bad reputation (that was the tag line). He wrote a song "On Account of That New Situation" that expressed his point of view on it. The only verse I recall, went:

> I started out to write a song to the entire population,
> and soon as I got the words wrote down,
> here come a brand new situation.

There were about four other verses, all more or less to the same rhyme. This was another kind of case in point where he thought he had written a constructive song about the air raid situation and it went out.[30]

Pete Seeger, on singing for the unions: In New York, 1941, it was Mike Quill and the Transport Workers Union that showed me what an organization could do. We were singing for fifteen people here and twenty-five people there, but one of the heads of the union said, "We have a strike on and we have twenty-thousand transport workers; let's get them in Madison Square Garden. Don't just give them a speech, let that gang of people that call themselves the Almanac Singers in." We made a song for them about the train that never returned. Lee Hayes mostly did it. (Later Bess Lomax Hawes rewrote it as the "MTA Song" in Boston.)[31]

Gordon Friesen, on the Almanacs' relationship to the unions: I think the only person among them who was really fighting for socialism, who really wanted and needed socialism, was Woody. Pete's from a well-to-do middle-class family. He didn't need any money. Mill was wheeling and dealing to make his own. Hays, I don't think cared about whether we ever got socialism or not, never mind Communism. The Almanac Singers were in the union-organizing drive, to organize the unorganized.

They especially sang for the UAW [United Auto Workers], who were in the throes of finally reaching organization after a long bloody battle, the sit-down strikes, the Ford attack on the workers. They also sang for the National Maritime Union. It was organized here by Joe Curran, who became a fat-assed reactionary. They sang for the transport workers, who were then in the process of being organized. In fact, Mike Quill, Red Mike, was known to be (or seemed to be) a Communist, as was Curran. One of Red Mike's dying wishes was that Pete would come and sing at his funeral, which Pete did, although their ways had separated some years before.[32]

Bess Lomax Hawes, on the Almanacs' use of topical song: After you come out with a song [you find the source]—I frequently did this with Lee [Hays], told him the name of the tune that he had used. He was never conscious of having used it. He was always surprised. He had simply started from a tune, but not a tune with words that he was playing on. That process I think is far more common on the folk level. Pete [Seeger], on quite the other hand, very deliberately selected tunes and was aware of the tunes that he was working from because he is much more of a musician. . . .

We thought about developing songs that people could learn. We thought about songs within particular areas of usage. That is, we occasionally tried to write songs that could be sung at demonstrations or at picket lines, a song that people could learn very quickly and that didn't have very much in the line of text. "We Shall Not Be Moved" was the kind of song we had in mind, that people learned and sang in on immediately. We thought about songs for passing information along. There were a lot of structures of songs that we thought about. We thought about "zipper songs" as we called them: where you could take the same song and zip one word out and zip in another, so that they were infinitely flexible.

You could take a song in support of a candidate, and sing it for another candidate in another borough during an election. We thought about songs for improvisation where we could put in topical verses or take them out or make them up to suit the particular occasion. We had several songs of that kind that we used deliberately in that way to try to personalize these songs so that they spoke to particular local issues. We did a lot of composing songs about towns for that reason: Pittsburgh, New York City, Chicago, and various other city songs. There was always an attempt to leave songs behind in that sense, to make up things that spoke to people's particular interests in the hopes that they would remember them, in whole or in part.

Our programs were talked about ahead of time, with not too many solo performances. Always something that the audience knew already, that they could sing with us on. We'd do "Solidarity" or "We Shall Not Be Moved" or a spiritual. Always a song with a good chorus that people could learn or be taught very quickly, usually some song that had to do with specific problem of that particular group. If we didn't have one, we'd make it up, or we'd adapt another song for it.

The programs were very carefully thought about in that sense. We tried to analyze the function of song within a group and to an audience and structured our programs that way. We didn't have the star problem because most of the songs, one or another of us could take the lead enough, if there was going to be a good chorus with everybody in on it. And, we were very good at involving audiences. One of the places that we fell down was in not analyzing audiences properly. We were really bringing in only one part of the cultural spectrum.[33]

People's Songster Mario "Boots" Casetta, on discovering politicized folk music: Who knows why anyone is attracted to the age-long struggle for the liberation for mankind? What strings are touched in your background. . . . When I was a young man in my early twenties and in the service, and stationed in San Francisco, I walked into a music store. I picked up an old Asch-Stinson album, whatever it was, of Burl Ives. And I listened to "Black Is the Color of My True Love's Hair." That was the beginning for me of music for political action. When I heard that, I said to myself, "You've tumbled onto something. There is a whole world. This obviously is some well-stream. You've got to find somewhere where it is and get in on it."

That's when I started buying records and listening closely. And asking the guy in the record store. And then when I first put on the album of the Almanac Singers, and I heard the same flavor, the same. In some cases, modal structures, it went one step further. Not only was that stuff good, but *here* is the way to do it. Here: be something for the good guys. And from that moment I became involved. And whatever it was, and my background was not the usual one, because my parents came out of vaudeville and show business. I was partially sophisticated, partially college educated, partially ruffian, a wild-ass little character, whatever. Somehow, that hit my gong, and the reverberations have never stopped.[34]

Bess Lomax Hawes on the influence of New York on the writing and performing of folk music: I have wondered myself, what would have happened if we had really moved outside of New York City? We did take a couple of tours, but the base of the organization was always New York.

As I say, culturally speaking, I think we were in the wrong part of the country—we were not living the life we sang about except in a sort of an extension. We were mixing cultural styles, we were way out in Left field, operating in a peculiar time, responding in a very naïve way to a lot of things that were going on. At the same time, I don't think we would have, probably, produced the same songs outside of New York City.[35]

SINGERS AND SONGWRITERS were not the only people forging new audiences for folk music before World War II—if they had been, "revived" folk music might never have traveled beyond Washington Square. The folk collector and friend of the Almanacs Alan Lomax ceaselessly proselytized. He broadcast and recorded Lead Belly and Woody Guthrie for the Library of Congress, and the owner of Disc Records (later Folkways), Moe Asch, recorded folk music and kept some of its producers afloat.

Bess Lomax Hawes, on Moe Asch: [Moe Asch] had Disc [Records] at that time. He went bankrupt about seven times and always started back in again. Always the same way, always the same old reliable, sweet Moe. He never paid you a cent of royalties, but if you were really flat—and most of us were—you could always drop by to see Moe and he would invite you to lunch! He never would let you pay a cent; he would take you and feed you up and would slip you a few bucks. He did that for every single member of the Almanacs and for many, many, many other people, consistently. He really supported most of the singers. It was quite a routine in a funny kind of way. You didn't ever touch Moe for a real loan, but you used Moe as your last resort, and he understood that this was what was happening.

He always handled it like a perfect gentlemen, always made you feel good, gave you a couple of dollars just so you could take a taxi home. He also supported Woody almost one hundred percent when Woody was really down. He hired him at twenty-five dollars a day to sit up there and record every single song he knew. And Woody, you know, had them all written down in those notebooks. I remember going up there frequently and there was Woody on the stool with notebook over here, and he'd turn the page and start the next song, get through that and turn the page and sing the next one. And he literally recorded his entire repertoire, and Moe had no use for it at all. But, it was a way to pay Woody and keep him alive.[36]

Folkways Records founder Moe Asch, on recording folk music: I had a very interesting situation of recording. I had a room like this, with a little window and in back of the window was my equipment. The door was open. At any time you'd see Pete Seeger, Woody Guthrie, Sonny Terry, Lead Belly, you name it, come in and just walk off the street and get together there and record: "Hey, Moe, put the damned thing on," and I would. They let out all their guts in it, see?

"Solidarity Forever"—those were part of the union songs that we did for the CIO-UAW for Alan [Lomax]. Burl Ives, then, went for bigger, greener pastures. The reason I recorded Burl Ives's one album—he was with Columbia or Okay Records—he was given this letter, and the next day he had to be in camp. He was a friend of my brother who was with the Agriculture Department in Washington.

My brother made the motion pictures and wrote materials—Nathan Asch—and see, they were all a clique: very well-known authors got together and Burl was always part of that. So Burl came to me and said, "Hey, I'm going tomorrow in the army, I've got to make an album."

Okay, so I don't want to do it. So, I called Alan and I said, "Burl wants to do an album. I don't trust the guy, you be down there and you supervise the album."

In ten hours we made an album of six sides [*Songs for Victory*, 1944].[37]

IN THE EARLY 1940S, the Almanac Singers were trying to find a niche for themselves. As pacifists, they found resisting the momentum of the escalating war a challenge; it forced the group to return to the prounion roots of their music. There was also the inconvenient issue of making a living, which often interfered with the idealism they were trying to hone and maintain.

Bess Lomax Hawes, on the politics of appearances: We really were awfully young and awfully green. We didn't really know how to present ourselves in any kind of sense. We just did what we did and made it on the basis, I think, of the sincerity that was, I'm sure, very apparent. But we didn't know what we were, really; we didn't fit anywhere. We didn't have any persona that we really understood.

I remember being on one union booking one time up and having an older union man come up and ask me afterwards whether I belonged to a union and I said, "No, I didn't."

He said, "Does your folks?"

I said, "No."

He said, "Well did any of you kids ever have any union experience?"

I said, "No, I don't think so."

He said, "That's very interesting because I don't understand why you feel the way you feel."

I tried to explain it to him and he said, "Well, I think there's one thing I ought to tell you. When we go to a union meeting, we always dress up."

We talked about that for a long time afterwards. I think it was a very revealing moment to us because we hadn't thought about ourselves in any sense except that we were going to go and sing. And that we were making any kind of statement beyond that, what we had to say, I think was something that we really hadn't thought about at all. We always wore whatever we happened to have on at the moment.[38]

Gordon Friesen, on group dynamics: Woody would get mad. One time he wanted to shoot Mill Lampell. Mill was a wheeler and dealer. He'd taken Woody along somewhere, to midtown somewhere, to some plush executive office where he was going to try and make some kind of musical deal with Woody involved. And Woody was sitting off in a corner playing on his harmonica, quite faintly. Mill finally turned around and told him, "Put that away. Don't you know we're talking big money here?"

So Woody'd put it away but, pretty soon he'd have it out again. And Mill walked over and snatched it out of his mouth and Woody got up and stalked out and he was so furious that when he got back to Almanac House—at that time we were living on Hudson Street (I think Pete had already gone into the army)—to borrow $7.50 from me or Sis. (Woody was living with us.) He said he'd go to New Jersey and buy a gun there, and he was gonna kill Mill Lampell.

Fortunately or unfortunately, we didn't have the money either. But he was so furious, he had bought a mandolin at a hockshop a few days before, he took it and smashed it against the wall and jumped up and down on the pieces.[39]

Bess Lomax Hawes, on philosophical differences within the Almanacs: Mill [Lampell] was, I think, attracted to the group because of its political position, because he saw this as a very viable way of getting a political message across and he thought the tunes were good. He enjoyed making up songs. He was a good man with a lyric. But, his style was—to use the term from the period, which sounds very old-fashioned now—agitprop. His contributions were very much in the line of political slogans. He was a good sloganeer. Woody disliked that very much. He regarded these songs as eminently forgettable, which I think he was right about, ultimately. Although Mill added a lot to the group at that period.[40]

Millard Lampell on the Almanacs playing at Rockefeller Center's Rainbow Room: We were all on the booking at the Rainbow Room, the famous Rainbow Room. I forget who had brought that agent around [to the Almanac House], I have a feeling it was either Norman Corwin or Alan Lomax.

By that time it was almost like the Almanac House was almost like a salon, it became very chic for people to come down to the place and hang out there and listen to the music. It was very new and exciting for people. All kinds of people dropped in. People from radio: Norman Corwin loved the stuff, so he brought down his musical director Mark Warnow because he was thinking of doing *A Note of Triumph*, and in fact we did sing on it: "Round and Round Hitler's Grave."

The minute we came in the Rainbow Room, we hated it. We were thinking the big thing was we could get enough money to publish *Hard Hitting Songs for Hard Hit People*. But the minute we walked in, we realized—it's incredible how naïve we were—what kind of costuming and staging there would have to be![41]

Bess Lomax Hawes, on playing at the Rainbow Room: We were in this enormous nightclub, deserted, with the tablecloths on the tables, looking out over this enormous view of Manhattan. I'd never been in any place like that. I had never been to a major nightclub. We had sung in the Village Vanguard and places like that; but this was an upper-crust society place. The people in it were sharp businessmen running a big nightclub. They thought of us as an act, and treated us as an act; and we didn't know how to respond because we never had been treated as an act except occasionally in concerts where we would come on as part of an evening and we would be backstage and then we would go on stage and sing five songs or they would tell us how many.

We were used to that, but we weren't used to putting on a show. It was so clearly the wrong place. As soon as we walked in, everybody knew immediately that this was nothing we could ever do. It was nowhere we could ever be.

William Morris, the agency, of course, didn't know what to do with us either. We clearly had something, but what it was, they didn't quite know and neither did we. We had no way of telling them what to do with us because we had only done what we had done. There was absolutely no possibility with that group of developing any kind of act or any kind of presentation that would be acceptable. All the people there could think of was that we should wear blue jeans and bandanas. They thought of us as a country hillbilly act. The reaction to that! Anything concerning costume was completely out of anybody's realm of thought. It was the wrong time, the wrong place, the wrong moment for us.[42]

Gordon Friesen, on the Almanacs and the Rainbow Room: All that business about the gunny-sack rags and the men wearing Little Abner overalls, that was all a side issue. The real thing was that they were red-baited out of existence at that point. I had gone with them. They had signed a contract with Decca Records, which was very big at that time. They signed up with William Morris. William Morris laid out the money for their union dues. They had been, although singing for unions, they had been nonunion up to that stage. They had to join 802 to become professionals. And Morris was lining them up a nationwide tour when this red-baiting article, as I remembered it, appeared on the front page of the *New York Post*, of all places ["Peace Choir Changes Tune"]. But within the next day or the next two days, despite all these signed contracts, they were told not to come back to the Rainbow Room; Decca said contracts are canceled; William Morris said "this is the end of it."

I don't know why it should have happened so fast. It seemed awfully fast to me but we were older and we had gone through red-baiting periods in which one thing was one thing one day and the next day it was the opposite. The FBI could have been in back of it.[43]

Pete Seeger, on the end of the Almanacs: I wouldn't say we hit bottom with an icy thud. We were struggling, like always. We just didn't get any place, we hoped that we'd be singing for unions; instead, just a few left-wing unions would have us and masses of right-wing unions thought we were dirty Communists and a whole batch of middle-of-the-road unions didn't know anything about us. And a whole lot of Social Democrat unions didn't like us either. So it wasn't like we hit bottom. We never went up—we were still struggling at the bottom![44]

BY DECEMBER 1941, the union songs, too, were obsolete. During World War II, the Communist Party dissolved into the Communist Political Association, which began asking unions for a no-strike pledge. Class-conscious songs like "Talking Union" were put to pasture for the duration; the Almanacs had dug themselves into an ideological hole. Gradually, the folk music scene in Greenwich Village dispersed, and with it the Almanac Singers. The Almanacs' network remained: those who could be there sang at Pete Seeger's wedding in Greenwich Village. But it was a time of action, and the Village lost its young performers, temporarily, to other theaters.

Pete Seeger, on marrying Toshi Ohta in Greenwich Village, 1943: I don't remember if Lee [Hays] was there or not. As I remember, Bess [Lomax] and Butch [Hawes] were there. Lead Belly came. And Alan Lomax. And we just sang and sang and sang the whole evening. Out in the backyard, we used to do a lot of singing. There was a little backyard with buildings all around so you got a lot of good echoes. Some of those New York backyards are great for singing. I don't know if you've ever been in one, two or three high brick walls around you and the sky's directly above you, so you're out-doors, technically, but you get a resonance, a reverberation that you don't normally get if you're outdoors.

It was quite a party. Then, back to the army.[45]

Bess Lomax Hawes, on the effects of the war: The Almanac world, as you say, was somewhat sheltered. We all grew up during the war; it was a sobering experience. I think it's difficult for people who are not of the [World War II] generation to realize that it had an enormous emotional effect on Americans.

It was a unifying experience that was tremendously important. You began to feel that there were possibly ways in which people with varying points of view could get together.... That was a very, very important thing for us to go through. It's too damn bad you have to have a war to do it, but...

We thought of ourselves as educators and really as [political] artists, not in the refined sense. I don't think that was our effect, though.

I think we all learned a lot. I think [being a part of the Almanacs] had a profound effect on Woody, possibly more than anyone else. It kind of socialized him; it gave him a place to be. So that his later production, I think, was even better than the Almanac period. I think his Maritime Union songs and particularly his Washington and Oregon and Cooley Dam songs were simply superb.

He couldn't have done that without the Almanac experience, I don't think. He would have been too damned individualistic and too ornery and too horrible![46]

Singer-songwriter Arlo Guthrie, on his father's political leanings: I read an article in some magazine recently with a great quote that said: "In an atheist country, rebels go to church." I think that's basically where Woody's coming from. He's your basic rebel. That means that if he was in a group of people where there were sixteen Hindus and three Jews, then he's a Jew. If he's in a world with sixteen Jews and three Hindus, he's a Hindu. He's always on the wrong side. He's always on the side of the little thing, the littlest guy. He's there because that's where he likes to be. To a certain extent this country likes that, we like that as a people: we're for the little guy.[47]

Mario "Boots" Casetta, on discussing politics and music with Pete Seeger during World War II: [In Saipan] I asked Pete Seeger about the Almanacs. I was terribly curious.... He talked about New York. He told me there were people around, names I was just getting onto, through records.

He envisioned some kind of a loosely knit organization, but nonetheless, some structured group where people could get together and exchange songs and ideas and maybe print them and this and that. I was terribly gung-ho and I got all excited. And he said, "You know what, you could do the same thing in LA. I'll do it in New York and you try and get it started in LA."

Which is what happened.

I was on Saipan, I guess six months before the war ended, and when I got back to LA, I was contacted by Earl Robinson. And he said, "Pete gave me your address and all that. We're getting together a few people who are interested in this."

I went to Earl's house in LA and met several of these people. I saw what was going on and I was terribly interested and fascinated and dedicated and everything else. I've never been a real singer myself. I have a kind of master of ceremonies cheerleader complex; I was very good in getting people to sing.[48]

PEOPLE'S SONGS

On December 31, 1945, in a basement in the Village, a group of folksingers, chorus directors, union officials, and others met to discuss the next step: forming an organization to "spread these songs around, to bring as many people as possible, the true democratic message that came out of [people's] music."[49] They decided to call the new organization People's Songs. Early participants—among them Lee Hays, Woody Guthrie, Bess Lomax Hawes, Irwin Silber, and Earl Robinson—joined in hopes of reaching out more. People's Songs moved its headquarters north from Greenwich Village to an office near Times Square, where participants organized hootenannies, maintained a library, and produced a bulletin called *People's Songs*. They were making performers available for rallies and picket lines, and laying the groundwork for a later folk song revival by printing songs of traditional singers, particularly those with antiestablishment themes. People's Songs spread even further when Mario "Boots" Casetta, whom Seeger had met in Saipan during the war, started People's Songs West, based in Los Angeles. Within the first year, chapters had formed in several American cities and in Canada.[50] According to Irwin Silber, "We thought that the world was worth saving and that we could do it with songs."[51]

Community educator Norman Studer, on the first People's Songs meeting: Just [after] the Second World War, a group of people who had been involved in a folk song movement before the war were interested in starting a folksinging group at that time. Woody Guthrie was there, and a number of the people who were involved in the Almanac Singers. This was a sort of informal, community meeting—it was in Greenwich Village—a meeting where they were organizing People's Songs. I was there at the beginnings of it.[52]

Mario "Boots" Casetta, on People's Songs West: The reason People's Songs was successful at that time in that space is because we were dealing in an oral tradition with people who had traditionally expressed themselves that way. And the poor people of the world have never owned presses, they've never owned radio stations, but they've had a voice. They've been able to sing and pass their songs on. And we were able to tap that vast reservoir of people who not only could sing but who were receptive to singing songs they could remember their granddaddy used to sing.

What is People's Songs? It was to use songs for political action, in a broad sense, whatever that might mean. Whether it was a supermarket where maybe somebody was being discriminated against, in hiring practice, or maybe local plumbers were out on strike and had a good cause and needed a helping hand, or to do something for the UN, whatever it might be. I became a paid employee. I was the only one. And in order to keep the little office going (we had two or three different locations in town) and to pay my salary, which was minimal, and the telephone, we had to find a source of income. Now what was that source of income? Pete said to me that they used to get together and have concert-type things which people would sing and they found a name that they liked called hootenanny....

We had our first hootenanny in Hollywood, and it was great. And we used to have those hootenannies with some frequency. Sometimes once a month or every couple of months, in different parts of town. Sometimes big halls, sometimes small halls, cheap, fifty cents or a dollar to get in. And we had such talent. Woody Guthrie would come into town and sing. Pete Seeger, when he came in town, would sing. And I usually acted as master of ceremonies and did some song leading. And New York was following, similar but different.

One of my fortes was we'd start singing, not necessarily something heavy political but maybe a folk song like "It Takes a Worried Man," and we'd start out with two or three people, banjo, guitar and I'd be leading. And I'd jump off the stage and go out in the audience. People used to love this. And I would swing my arms around. And I would exhort them to sing, sing. And this drove Pete wild when he saw this. He'd see one or two of us hopping off the stage and going out into the audience and saying, "Sing! Sing, damn you! Sing!"[53]

MEANWHILE, FEAR OF COMMUNISM was escalating in postwar America. Although the House Committee on Un-American Activities (HUAC) and the FBI investigated individuals, their ostensible interest was in the organizations to which these individuals belonged. In the folk music world, this meant People's Songs (1946–49). Though People's Songs was founded to promote union choruses, by 1948 there was little harmony left in the unions. Could the isolated movement planned on Saipan by Pete Seeger, Boots Casetta, and others succeed against the currents of its time?

Oscar Brand, on how People's Songs got started: [After the war] Pete came over to me. I sang a song I'd written in the army and one that I'd written afterwards, and Pete said, "You know, we've got to start something." (He was very quiet because someone was singing. He was very careful not to interfere.) He said, "I'd like to start a magazine or something like that where we can put the songs we're writing today." He said "they got lots of books now of songs that were very popular for the last six hundred, five hundred years," he said, "but I'd like to put in some of the songs of today."

I thought that was a great idea. I said, "I'll tell you what, you can have a magazine."

He said, "Well we'll probably do something, mimeograph or hectograph"—that's what you had in those days.

They asked me to join the group. So I was a member of the board of *People's Songs* on the first issue. And the second.[54]

Mario "Boots" Casetta, on People's Songs picket lines: When the Technicolor strike was at its height [in the late forties], the organization itself got an injunction against mass picketing, so that they were only allowed a token picket of three to five people. And there were cameras. And for this I will always be engraved in the files of the FBI and everything else. Because the union, whichever one was involved, really used their head.

"All right, we got a token line," they said. "Do we have four or five guys walking around with signs or are we going to have some people with guitars, since we're under the constant scrutiny of radio and film?" So they asked us if we would help. And I went down there. Hundreds, if not thousands of people on both sides, the scabs on the inside, the strikers on the outside, the public at large and more goddamned cops than I've ever seen in my life surrounding that place. And cameras on the roof and everything. And I would go out on the sidewalk, with two or three singers, and one or two union members. And we would revolve. We would keep going down the street, singing. You could hear a pin drop. Everything was concentrated on us, amongst these thousands of people. We'd make two or three circles. Then these one or two union guys would drop off, and the next two would come on. And we would keep this thing going.[55]

Irwin Silber, on the politics of People's Songs: Mao says there's contradiction in all things, of course. There was contradiction in People's Songs. But, in the center, most of the people shared an interest in both political song and folk song. Their emphases might have been slightly different, but there was enough overlapping. However, there would be people over at the extremes.

I mean, Bob Claiborne got pissed as hell at People's Songs after a while. He thought that anything that moved away from politics was bad. It's hard to imagine dear old Bob Claiborne being ultraleft, but he had that urge, you know, for a few moments. There were others who felt that way, but, more from the Right. But their association with the organization was short-lived. You see it in letters to the editor that appeared in *People's Songs* bulletin from people who said, "I thought it was a folk song group and you're shoving all these politics down my throat," and so on. But, if you want to judge where it really stood....Well, look at what finally turned out, what kind of an organization did it turn out to be? Did it turn out to be an organization where the main emphasis was on folk music or the main emphasis was on politics?[56]

Mario "Boots" Casetta, on the political underpinnings of People's Songs: It wasn't a political organization in that sense of the word. We were not there gathered to formulate programs based on issues and take appropriate action. We were there because each of us somehow were freaks about folk music and its application to whatever struggle we might think was worthwhile....

As for California, in People's Songs, there were some members in the CP just as there were some Democrats. We probably had some Socialists. And then we also had some Independent-type people who didn't want to be affiliated with any group in a narrow political sense. I say this to you with the utmost sincerity, there was never any undemocratic railroading in a People's Songs meeting. If there were members of the Communist Party, they never by the slightest gesture made it known. Whatever they felt it was valid for People's Songs to be part of, they then raised it as individuals and it was hammered out and discussed.[57]

IN 1947, WHEN PEOPLE'S SONGS held its first national convention at Hull House in Chicago, FBI director J. Edgar Hoover received an urgent telegram reporting that the members of People's Songs "play folksongs…where the hoity-toity red intellectuals gather."[58] Two months later, in the U.S. Army's *Weekly Domestic Intelligence Summary*, the FBI cited People's Songs as a Communist front.[59]

People's Songs went on to support the Progressive Party's presidential candidate, Henry Wallace, in the 1948 election. Pete Seeger and Paul Robeson toured with the campaign and sang for its rallies.

Mario "Boots" Casetta, on performing for the Wallace campaign: This was the final big Wallace rally in which Robeson appeared and, of course, Wallace himself. Everybody you could possibly think of who was involved in the Progressive Party was there. At an early part of the program, Pete [Seeger] and I led songs, the songs of the campaign, the political songs, "The Same Old Merry-Go-Round" and others. Someone had taken a movie, I suppose eight-milllimeter, which I once saw. That picture is of Pete playing the banjo and me waving my arms in huge, broad gestures so people could see clear across Yankee Stadium.[60]

IT WAS WALLACE'S DEFEAT, not FBI infiltration, that ultimately put an end to People's Songs. But before long, People's Songs' Communist Party–oriented successor, the booking agency People's Artists, was formed, as was the folk-protest song magazine *Sing Out!*

Earl Robinson, on *Sing Out!* during the Red Scare: People's Songs really went all-out in the period of the Wallace campaign, and there was a marvelous singing movement, some great songs, and after the loss, they disbanded and created *Sing Out!*—I mean, soon after. They saw the need for a folk music magazine but on a different basis, not so political, although Irwin Silber was still in there and it would still retain its political character, but I think it did become broader, related better to the needs of the new period.…

[The readership of *People's Songs* bulletin and *Sing Out!*] was a combination of Progressive Party people, cultural-minded leftists, and a lot of ordinary people who just liked folk music. They had quite an audience I would guess, especially *Sing Out!*—more than *People's Songs* maybe. *Sing Out!* [founded in 1950] had an audience of quite a few people who didn't necessarily go along with some of the politics. There would be letters occasionally in *Sing Out!* opposing this or that political line. And it didn't influence Irwin Silber or anybody else hardly at all but that kind of letter would happen. And there was, every once in a while, a person would drop their subscription.…

The House Un-American Activities Committee didn't do anything like they did with *People's World* or the *Daily Worker*. That was clearly Communist Party. *Sing Out!* maybe they would have an occasional quote from them. They would have had to try and prove that *Sing Out!* was Communist-dominated or inspired and they would have had a hard time. They really would have. They could imply it, but you wouldn't get that too often.[61]

Sing Out! editor Irwin Silber, on People's Artists: People's Artists was, first of all, a booking agency not just for political singers but for blacklisted performers. We found work for actors either driven out of Hollywood or blocked from getting there.… The People's Artists hootenannies—we put on three or four every year—maintained a Left public presence during those years when, aside from trials and witch hunts, much of the Left had been made invisible.[62]

Norma Starobin of People's Artists, on their hootenannies: Irwin Silber and I used to give out *Sing Out!* We were producing People's Artists records (we did the packaging and mailing); we did bookings and ran hootenannies. One of the things about the hootenannies that I was critical of (having done some theater work and technical lighting) was that they were run very informally. I was critical of it because only Pete Seeger and maybe Leon Bib had a natural stage presence and technical knowledge of how to use the microphone and a sense of grouping. Other members who would perform were too natural, too informal. They didn't want to become slick and professional. I felt they should have rehearsed more.

When the name "hootenanny" got taken over by college groups, they did very well with it and were making money. We were always going broke. I think part of it was this insistence in keeping everything very folksy and emphasizing the content rather than making it slick and professional.[63]

People's Songster Leo Christensen, on Cold War mindsets: I became aware that the Cold War was emerging before the war was even over, when

I was working in the shipyards [in San Francisco]. I would talk to these guys; most of them were automobile salesmen, insurance salesmen who had avoided the draft by getting into war production. They were scared to death and particularly scared to death of the Russians. They would say, "We're going to have to take those Russians on."

The atmosphere had been created somehow. I think it represented a real fear on the part of leadership of a certain powerful section of the country. And I can't identify that. But realizing that the Russians, when they fought, they fought for keeps. Stalingrad. I think they foresaw that as a result of this, there was going to be a sweep of Communism throughout all Europe. And they had to begin to take steps to plant in the minds of the American people that we're going to have to stop this.[64]

BY THE END OF THE 1940S, the leftward movement had cooled in America. The Communist Party had moved away from its Popular Front stance (leaving behind the broad, populist approach of People's Songs) and toward a more defensive and sectarian approach. President Harry Truman's administration was attacking the unions and Communists who had helped elect Roosevelt. The prewar heyday of the Almanac Singers seemed long ago and irretrievable.

By the 1960s, Greenwich Village would again be the nexus of folk music when a new batch of young musicians would sing for Moe Asch's Folkways Records, or pick their guitars in the back room of Izzy Young's Folklore Center, or perform at Gerdes Folk City or the Gaslight, among them the folk greats Peter, Paul and Mary, Ramblin' Jack Elliott, Tom Paxton, Judy Collins, Phil Ochs, and Bob Dylan.

Before moving uptown to Tin Pan Alley from the Village's subterranean haunts, however, folk music's community would have to survive its greatest challenge: the blacklist, and with it the odd notion that singing folk songs was a Communist plot. Before the second folk music revival could sweep America, many musicians would run a gauntlet of attacks, FBI investigations, and congressional hearings—and then still find themselves blocked from singing on TV and radio.

5

"AM I IN AMERICA?"
THE RED SCARE

THE ALLIED VICTORY in World War II reduced the threat of fascism; but by the late forties, dreams of wartime prosperity had given way to national shortages of jobs, houses, and schools. Visions of united nations had disintegrated into an escalating fear of annihilation.

For the folk-musical Left, a turning point was reached during People's Songs' support for Henry Wallace, whose anti–Cold War stance gave rise to virulent opposition. In Burlington, North Carolina, an angry crowd refused to let the farmer-statesman speak, until Wallace became so riled that he grabbed a bystander and shouted at him, "Are you an American? Am I in America?"

The mood in the United States was bleak. President Truman's administration responded to rising anti-Communist hysteria by requiring loyalty oaths to purge the federal government of New Deal liberals, activists, and Communists. The hotly contested Taft-Hartley Act—called the "slave labor act" by its opposition—curtailed the power of labor unions and limited their capacity to strike.[1] Even unions took a conservative turn; some began expelling the Communist organizers who had been instrumental in their formation in the first place.

THE PEEKSKILL ANTI-COMMUNIST RIOTS

Out of this fear and frustration, violence boiled up. In the fall of 1949, signs and bumper stickers around Peekskill, New York, read "Wake up America, Peekskill did!" The town was proud of having prevented the openly Communist black opera singer Paul Robeson from performing in their community. Anti-Communist protestors had accomplished this by mobbing the stage of Robeson's scheduled concert and leaving behind a burning cross. Music had provoked the United States' first anti-Communist riot, which was eerily similar to the incidents of anti-Semitic in Germany in the early thirties. But now Robeson and his sponsor, People's Artists, were back; and his fans were determined that the show would go on, whatever it took.

Peekskill locals believed their town was being invaded by Communists; the concertgoers believed they were being persecuted by fascists and a right-wing coup was in the making. People's Artists recruited twenty-five hundred union members who linked arms and formed a human chain around the grounds so that the crowd had their chance to belt out the anti–Cold War mantra "If I Had a Hammer." But when the right-wing demonstrators outside were not dispersed at the appointed time (despite record numbers of police bussed in from around Westchester County), apprehensive concert organizers wrapped up the concert early so that everyone could leave before dark. Daylight, however, was not enough to hold back the anger welling beyond the gates.

Folksinger Pete Seeger, on Peekskill, 1949: It happened so quickly that you didn't have time to get scared very much. I remember driving out the gate and there were policemen there. I wanted to turn left because it was the quickest way home. He said, "No. Everybody this way." There were three ways you could have gone; straight, left, or right. Everybody had to go right. There were still maybe fifty or a hundred people there hollering epithets: "kikes," "nigger lovers," "go back to Russia." It just went on continually.

The cars moved very slowly down the road. This is a local road, ironically named Division Street. Think of the divisions of the people. Instead of Unity Street, it was Division Street. We'd only gone about a hundred yards when I saw glass on the road, and I said, in my innocence, "Uh-oh. Watch out; maybe somebody's going to try and throw a stone."

I turned the next corner and there was a pile of stones, thousands of stones, each the size of a baseball, piled waist high, and a strong, young man just heaving them into every car that went by. It was a six-foot range. Around the corner was another pile of stones. Finally after the third or fourth pile, there's a policeman standing there, just a hundred feet away from them. I say, "Officer, aren't you going to do something?" He says, "Move on, move on."

I look around and the car in back of me is getting it. Because I'm stopped, he has to stop. Because he's stopped, he's a sitting duck, getting stone after stone after stone. I start up my car so he can get out. I keep my head up high, above the glass flying all around lower, and everybody else down low.[2]

People's Songster Mario "Boots" Casetta, on the Peekskill violence: When we left the grounds, they told us to roll up our windows as we came up; our own people told us. They said roll up your windows and go as fast as you can; there's nothing we can do about it. When you came out of the grounds, this huge meadow, there were ropes in various directions. The police purposely blocked off all the exits except one road that they shunted us down, to the right. And that is where we were massacred because there were people up on an embankment. Some of the stones were big and went right through the windows of Greyhound buses.

To heave a boulder from a fairly high embankment and then have it hit the windshield of a car or bus going sixty miles per hour was like a cannon ball. We were in the Jeep, and it was rocking, rocketing. Also the highway was strewn with large boulders, like going through a battlefield. We could feel the buffeting and the rocking and the terrible noise of these huge stones hitting the car....

Well, I was frightened like that. I expected that any moment that damned car would roll over. Then I heard this terrible noise, a crack. And then somebody said, "my God, Greta's been hit." A big, big rock had come through the window and hit her just above the eye. It opened up her eyebrow, a bad gash. We got to the end of the run and there was an opening in the clearing and we stopped. There were some people sitting on a bank, a grassy bank away from the trees. And we said, "Do you know the way to the nearest hospital?" And they all started laughing and cackling. I remember one woman rocking back and forth, slapping her knees, like she'd heard a good joke. It was unbelievable. It was like I would imagine Nazis would have been in those early days in street gangs in Berlin.[3]

Pete Seeger, on the message of the Peekskill riots: We thought of Peekskill as a terrible attack of fascists upon American civil liberties and Robeson in particular. It had gotten worse, as some people thought it would, on the Right as well as on the Left. I told you about the signs in Peekskill saying "Wake up America, Peekskill did!"

They were calling upon the rest of America to do the same thing. In other words, "Whenever you find there's a Commie around, you do something about it. You don't wait for the long process of the law. You do it right away because our country is in danger."[4]

Sing Out! **editor Irwin Silber, on the aftermath of the Peekskill riots:** I never will forget a letter [People's Artists] received back in 1949 from the Ku Klux Klan of Westchester County. It thanked us for our activities, the Peekskill concert in particular, saying that this had enabled them to recruit hundreds of new members. The reason, they said, was that "people in Westchester County really don't like Negroes and especially they've got no use for red niggers like the kind that you're promoting. And so we thank you for all of your efforts on our behalf."[5]

WHAT THE CONCERTGOERS could not have known was how this not-so-Cold-War rift would spread across the United States over the next decade, with folk music close to the core of the controversy. In the eyes of some, folk songs and their singers formed an insidious conspiracy.

THE GREAT FOLK MUSIC PLOT

Folk music, which in 1950 had just begun climbing the pop charts, was not exempt from red-baiting and impassioned condemnation by anti-Communists. "Along with the handclapping, the guitar strumming, the banjo picking, the shouting and the howling, comes a very subtle, but highly effective, presentation of standard Communist Party propaganda," howled one article in the John Birch Society's bulletin *American Opinion*. A musical menace was apparently loose in America; fiddles and banjos started to look subversive, and folksingers, songwriters, folklorists, and union organizers experienced FBI scrutiny, or worse.

Folkways Records' Moe Asch, on avoiding political association either way: I didn't want Folkways to be associated officially with any political area, whether it was Communism or socialism or Marxism. I only issued material that I felt was contemporary and needed to be exposed. I never issued Communist propaganda. I've issued both sides, including the Un-American Committee [HUAC] with Brecht. Would they [radicals] record for me? Fine. But to be associated, I wasn't interested.[6]

Broadside **editor Gordon Friesen, on the privacy of politics:** A person's politics are his own business. It's none of your business to ask me if I'm a Communist or not. That's why we have a secret ballot. We're a democracy. They're still arguing whether Woody Guthrie was a Communist or not. They're still questioning it. You know they're making a film about him. They asked Harold Leventhal, "Was Woody ever a Communist?" And Leventhal says, "No, he was a Communist in the sense that he had a lot in common with other people. With other down-and-outers."[7]

Guitarist Happy Traum, looking back at the role of Communism and folk music: It can be said that the left wing brought the music to the masses and developed the whole folk movement as we know it. It could also be said that because people are biased that the Communists moved it into an area and used it for their own purposes and twisted it so they rewrote history in a way. Both points of view are valid.

My own point of view: I was becoming involved with a lot of radical people when coming into the folk music world. My political thinking was certainly formulated by those people. I wasn't raised from infancy in that kind of environment. I look at things maybe with a little more detachment. I could see where there were biases. Reading *Sing Out!* history from the earliest days, it's very obvious. Looking at it now it's embarrassing, some of the early issues. They certainly are serving their own interests in that magazine and not the interests of the music itself.[8]

Guitarist Danny Kalb, on the anti-Communist perspective: In a way I don't know that it *was* a sad era: because this Stalinist Communism wouldn't have changed by itself, because of the world situation, the American situation. Perhaps it's for the better that lives were lost, or careers ruined. I wouldn't want to have Stalinist Communism being dominant in America, like it was in so many countries. If they ever came to power, we'd all be dead. This is what happened in Stalinist situations; they were crazy to the point that they shot Bukharin and all the Central Committee people.

That's what they did. Tens of millions of people lost their lives under the Stalin purges in the thirties, forties, fifties. So you can understand the feeling of people like anti-Communist Congressman [Francis] Walter or [Joe] McCarthy or people like that....This [Communist] guy comes up here and says that these labor camps were only for fascists and Trotskyites. They can say that. Everyone knows that that isn't true; and this Communism you're talking about is so good that you think it counted for this-and-that happening in other countries. You can see how they [left-wingers] can justify it to themselves—being the fascists they were.[9]

ALONG WITH SENATORS Joe McCarthy, Pat McCarran, and other opportunistic anti-Communist legislators, FBI director J. Edgar Hoover was determined to unravel the perceived Communist insurgency in America, and this meant identifying Communist fronts and tracing them back to their leadership. Anti-Communists such as the editors of *Counterattack* identified the leader of folk music's subversion as none other than Pete Seeger.[10]

Manager Harold Leventhal, on the blacklisting of Pete Seeger: Why was Pete so singled out? Pete was the constant target for all of the *Red Channels* people and for the John Birch people. So in any quote that one might casually say that Pete Seeger being on such-and-such a program was considered, there would be a barrage of things. There wouldn't be a barrage equal to that if they'd said Joan Baez or Judy Collins or any other person.

It came through various right-wing books, loads of material on Pete, that he was singled out, not only in terms of ever attempting to get on radio or television, but—at concerts that you'd see—we faced constant picketing. For years, there was hardly a concert which was not picketed, whether by the Legion, or the Birch, or whatever, local so-called anti-Communist groups. He was the guy, he was the leader they were after. He "poisoned the minds of young people." . . .

Well, Pete always took the position that he did when he was on trial in the House Un-American Activities Committee, that his political philosophy was purely his own business. So even, and I don't recall that particular letter, how it was released or when . . . but it would be almost correct to say that it perhaps reflected the thinking at that time; it was so broad, whatever was our thinking back then, it was our business. It was nothing to do with the fact we were singing songs on radio and television. "Regard us as performers and entertainers." And, in fact that was the stance, I think, of a lot of the Hollywood people as well.[11]

Ethnomusicologist Charles Seeger, on his son's risks during the McCarthy era: Peter was on the outside and I was underground. McCarthy came on, what was it, '49 to '51? That was a long time from the Composers' Collective; all that had been forgotten. I was tremendously appreciative of Peter's whole stand. His willingness and his ability to run a risk. I was willing enough; I just didn't have the ability. Nothing I could do, except in a small way. I could write, I could give a lecture and that sort of thing. But that wasn't carrying thousands of people along with me in a public concert.

Naturally I expected [Peter to be targeted]. That was in the cards. In these days, the reactionary and ultraconservative groups had been very militant in this country and were, always, from ancient times. And they weren't going to lie down and take that sort of thing without their same tactics, to the extent they could. They couldn't take him out and lynch him in Washington. I had no fear of that. But I think he sometimes ran a risk down South.[12]

Political songwriter Malvina Reynolds, on the establishment's resistance to folk music: It just seems ridiculous. What kind of an enemy is this, you know? It's a pretty common feeling amongst reactionary people that folk songs are radical. I have a theory that these songs came out of poor people's experience and it was making something socially interesting, exciting, dramatic about the lives of ordinary people. And that would be a radical thing to establishment-type people. This is kind of a proletarianization of popular music and so they objected. And also, people who were interested in folk music would tend to be writing songs for progressive types of things. Though it's almost a world fact that the reactionaries have very few good songs; they don't have the feeling or something.[13]

(WHAT'S LEFT OF) THE COMMUNIST PARTY USA

World War II had temporarily unified the nation, but in the uncertainty of the postwar era, a fear of imminent Russian invasion was sparked and stoked—though the Communist movement in the United States had now declined dramatically in numbers and influence. Nonetheless, a nostalgic idealism toward the music of social reform had drawn in musicians in the thirties and forties and now still kept some musicians in the orbit of the Party as fellow travelers, influenced by its stances.

Folk-blues singer Barbara Dane, on singing for the Party: Well, I had a good experience in the beginning in Detroit, being a young person just attracted to the Party, and having no idea what role I could play. I was given very good direction from a particular person who had actually come from New York but was assigned there as a Party organizer, and who was setting me off on the path that I wound up being on the rest of my life! I didn't realize that at the time. I was a singer already, but I had no idea of the value of one kind of song over another. I sang whatever music I was attracted to at the moment....

When I got around to the movement, I got from this particular person very good support and very careful pointing in the right direction of, "Why don't you learn some of these kind of songs?" or "Why don't you go down and sing on this picket line here?" And then making sure that people started asking me to come and do them, and then, after I got pretty good at it, he organized a concert there.[14]

Earl Robinson, on the Communist Party in the 1950s: The political movement of the Communist Party was becoming so decimated and so unimportant, so put-down, so sad in relation to where it was before in the thirties and some of the forties too. I, along with some others, tried very had to stay with it and help in our small way. I suggested teaching them how to write better, offering in a small way, trying to improve the propaganda message, to see that it got out all right. And we were pretty unsuccessful; it really was a losing struggle and for a lot of people it was the coup de grâce when Khrushchev came out with the Twentieth Congress Report [in 1956]. He admitted that Stalin had been bad in a lot of ways, had been responsible for killing quite a few Russians, apparently not just out of being anti-Jewish or several aspects like that, but out of paranoia, you know, fear of being overthrown....

The Khrushchev report, that was the turning point. Because if we're supporting the Soviet Union all this time and Stalin, the king, is a murderer—it was a little bit hard to continue with the same unthinking support, which they had got from us until then, you know. And so a lot of people dropped out. I stayed; I stayed a little while longer.

But it was tied to the blacklist too. There was a time there when, our union, the musicians' union, conducted a little bit of a red purge. We were urged by our lawyers to go in front of the union and say, "I'm not a member." That's all. "I'm just not a member." You couldn't take the Fifth with the union, you know. And I did this, and I remember at the Party meeting in front of it, they asked me to do this, and I wanted to say—and I'm not sure that I said it, "What am I doing this for? What is the Cause?"[15]

Pete Seeger, on "Commies": What's so dangerous about Communism? The fears that humans have are really hard to explain. . . .

The words "freedom" and "justice": only Commies talked about things like that. The word "peace" was also something only Commies talked about. I guess our great thing was simply in our Christmas song where we said, "Peace, Frieden, pace, pakòj, shalom: the words mean the same, whatever your home."

That was our big progressive stand in 1951.[16]

PARANOIA RENT AMERICA during the McCarthy era. Though it has been estimated that the Communist Party in the United States had fewer than one hundred thousand members when this Red Scare began, a total of 6.6 million people were investigated between 1947 and 1952; even President Truman would ultimately refer to the period as the "great wave of hysteria."[17]

By the late 1940s, many had come to believe that the United States was under Soviet attack from within. There was a "force of traitorous Communists, constantly gnawing away, like termites at the foundations of American society," J. Edgar Hoover explained to the nation; now, as the Cold War heated up, it was time to root the "termites" out. Among those on Hoover's extermination list were singers of folk songs.[18]

For the next twenty years, the FBI assigned agents to investigate folk musicians. Many of their investigations ended up in the files of police "red squads" and before congressional hearings.

From 1940 through 1968 (at least), the FBI, the CIA, and a half-dozen other intelligence agencies—including those of the Departments of Justice, the army, and the navy, among others—illegally collected information on America's folk musicians.[19] These documents, amounting to some five thousand pages, reveal a trail of phone taps, trash carriers, and informers planted by the FBI in the folk music community.

Author Bob Reiser, on the FBI in the 1950s: My parents moved to avoid being harassed by the FBI, moved away from all their old associations. They wouldn't have done it for themselves, but my grandfather worked for the government, and he had gotten threats that he would be fired if my parents continued. For his sake they broke all their ties. I had learned that any kind of political feelings were things to be kept to yourself. That was the fifties—keep it to yourself. I was lecturing some kid in the street on Marxism, and my mother started screaming at me. I learned to keep my thoughts to myself.[20]

Pete Seeger, on the mindset of the Red Scare: A lot of people on the Left, as well as on the Right, were convinced that there was going to be full-scale war between the Soviet Union and the United States of America very shortly. And that in order to prosecute this war, the American ruling class would have to call for a dictator, whether it was a McCarthy or somebody else, under the plea that our country was endangered by traitors, that they'd have to clamp down on civil liberties. We'd be in jail or running for our lives.[21]

Charles Seeger, on responding to the FBI: [Earl Robinson] was staying with me in Washington, and there was a big reception at the Soviet Embassy and he went and the next day the FBI called on me. I think I told them when [they asked why] I drove him, that anybody can go the Soviet Embassy if they want. It's the embassy of another country, duly recognized in Washington; and what was the matter there? I would have gone myself if I had had an invitation. Then they went away and didn't bother me. But it may have been partly that and a couple of other things that gradually got them to crack up on me.[22]

Earl Robinson, on being "graylisted": What happened to me is my agent stopped being able to find jobs. That's all. I was on the "graylist." My name didn't get in any papers.[23]

Folksinger Oscar Brand, on being scrutinized by the FBI: The FBI was at me all the time. They thought I was lying. That I knew these people. That I knew things about them. They kept asking me questions. I said, "I don't know." One day they asked me "Do you know 'Boots' Casetta?" I said, "No," because I didn't. I didn't know the name. He says "Oh, you don't know. Well, okay." They went off for a little while. They didn't trust me at all even to call.

Then one day my mother gave me a book of cutouts from the newspaper and one of them's a picture—headlines, "Oscar Brand with 'Boots' Casetta, so-and-so, so-and-so, and so-and-so." If I was them, I wouldn't have trusted me at all. Because, obviously I'd lied to them as far as they knew.

They came right to me because I didn't hang up the phone or do anything like that. To me the FBI was a good organization. I didn't know anything about them. I only knew that in the South they had gone against the Ku Klux Klan, and to me that was very, very good. And as far as I knew they were like the Canadian Mounties. They were honest people. I did discover later what kind of people they were. But they would come and ask me questions.[24]

Charles Seeger, on being pursued by the FBI: I had many sessions with the FBI during my life in Washington, coming in to ask me about people. And I had managed to acquit myself pretty well. To save the FBI from knowing what I knew and yet not giving the impression that I was holding back anything. I had been successful. But in the McCarthy period, they got hold of me. I was then making a yearly trip to Europe as one of the founders of the International [Folk] Music Council. I had a diplomatic passport from '49. I didn't have to go through customs. I had all kinds of emoluments.

The next year I quickly got my passport, but it was an ordinary passport. I said, well, I wonder if they're beginning to find out something. The next year I had a limited passport. In '53, I was still a member of the newly fledged UNESCO group. There were only three personal members and I was one because I was recognized as the founder of it. I used to read papers and then I presented the Constitution for an international organization of music education [the International Folk Music Council], which has since been a tremendous success.

They wouldn't let me have a passport. I saw the head of the passport division. He was an elderly man. And he said, "Well of course, I know I'm not against you personally. I know you'll just simply realize that your job wouldn't be worth two cents before Congress in its present state of mind."

I'll go around to the Pan American Union and I'll retire. "Oh," he says, "why did you do that?" I said, "Well, I'm of no further use to my organization. I don't sit anymore." Well, he tried to persuade me not to but I went around the next day and asked to be retired. I had a right to, although I had still two more years. To keep things down!

I didn't want to have them think I was going to go battling them. I wanted to show as much subservience as I could. Now, they undoubtedly reported that back to the FBI and said, well, he's so cast down about this, that he's retiring two years before he has to. And I bet they called up the chief of the Pan American Union and "is it true that Professor Seeger has"—oh no, in Washington, everybody's Doctor—"is it true that

Dr. Seeger has retired two years before he had to?" "Yes, he didn't give any reason." I had a feeling that perhaps that might make them a little bit more delicate in handling it.[25]

Oscar Brand, on being questioned by the FBI: The first time the FBI came to talk to me—I think this was the first time, I don't know—the guy came to my door. Black suit, black tie. I think I remember that part. And he said, "Mr. Brand, we have some questions to ask you. Would you answer them?"

I said, "Well, sure."

He said, "Well, I can't ask them here." It was my little apartment in the Village. He said, "But we have a limo parked down there and a couple of my friends would like to hear this too."

And I said, "Okay," and I went down. I think I must have put on a coat—it must have been cool. Went down and about a block and a half away was this car with two other guys there, all with black suits. Hard-eyed. I've met them before. Many times before and many times afterwards. They're guys who believe they know what's right, and they don't care if they step on you with boots. They really don't care.

The first thing they did—before "Boots" Casetta—they were asking me if I knew this guy, and this guy, and was he a Communist?

I said, "I really don't know." I kept telling them in order to know, you have to be a member. You couldn't guess. I have friends who are socialist friends. I didn't want to say it, but by then I was so angry, I said, "Look, I have very close friends who would not vote for Franklin Roosevelt because the Communist Party was for him. That's how bad they feel." I said, "If I even said a nice word to you guys, they would cut me off their list. My best and good friends. Why? Because they feel that anyone who even talks to you is a menace, a horror. So I hope you'll excuse me."

He says, "Well, we may call you. Keep around."

And they were asking me questions like "Do you remember so-and-so. Did you do this with so-and-so?" and I was like some rabbit that they'd caught in a trap. I couldn't answer them false things; I just couldn't. My memory isn't that good. So I kept telling them, "No, I don't know him. I don't know him." And, "oh, yes, I know him."

"Well is he a Communist?"

"I don't know."

But they knew that I spent much time with these people—he says to me, "Stay away from Peter Seeger"; that was why I was in *Red Channels*.

This was the substance of a long conversation and finally he says, "You want me to drive you back?"

I said, "No, I think I can walk."[26]

Charles Seeger, on FBI questioning: They came around later, about the day they discovered that [my wife] Ruth [Crawford Seeger] had incurable cancer, and really grilled me. And then I confessed to the Composers' Collective. And some other things: too much of a leftist stand from the time I was a conscientious objector in the First World War and refused to buy war bonds. . . .

I'd be perfectly public about Carl Sands, [my] Composers' Collective identity. Of course, when the FBI wanted the names of people, not *a* name. Although some of them went by their own names and may nowadays admit it. But I won't say it. If somebody comes along and I tell the story of the May Day song and Aaron Copland winning the prize, I make a point that he was not a member of the Collective, but he was sympathetic. And Aaron's quite frank too. He doesn't deny that he wrote a May Day song, quite militant words. . . .

There were not too many possibilities for additional earnings at sixty-seven. We had a growing family, and Ruth had just reached the point where she had been in her teaching before she left Chicago, where she had all the pupils she could take and could charge what she wanted. I felt that I wouldn't live forever, that I must keep Ruth's ability to support the family and herself from being harmed by my activities there.

So, I told them, "Sure, I was a member of the Collective."

Peter said, "Why did you do that?" Peter wouldn't.

I said, "I know it's not any of their damned business, but my business is to not interfere with Ruth's professional life because it looked as if she would be the person who would be able to send Penelope [Penny Seeger] to college, if Penelope wanted. But I couldn't. I didn't look forward to much of an income. Three or four thousand dollars a year. Pensions and things. There were very few chances then.

Universities weren't asking me. Oh, Yale had asked, given me a visiting professorship in 1950, but it was a freak. There was not much of a chance of people after sixty-seven being given university positions that paid anything anyway. But it wasn't until that blessed Institute of Ethnomusicology got started at UCLA that I was taken back into the university. I had been out of it since 1918, 1919. Thank heavens![27]

Folksinger Peggy Seeger, on being harassed for traveling to China: I was very surprised at the size of the dossier they had on me, though. Oh yes, they brought it through. They said, "In 1957, you said this," and "Would you say this is a likeness of you?" and they hold up a picture of you in a Moscow crowd and I hadn't done anything.

They turned me back; they wouldn't let me in. April 1958. What happened was, I went to China when I wasn't supposed to. It was written in our passports then that you're not allowed to go to the People's Republic of

China. There were about eight or nine countries that you weren't allowed to go to. I was at the Moscow festival and they invited us to go to China. I thought, "This is the chance of a lifetime, I'll go." And the minute we announced that we were going, two hundred of us were invited and about 150 decided to go: Moscow was barraged with phone calls from anxious parents, "Don't go darling, they'll eat you alive," that kind of thing.

Then Christian Herter, who was then the State Department fellow, made personal calls to all of us. He said, "If you go, you'll lose your passport and you're liable for up to a two-thousand-dollar fine," et cetera, et cetera. So, in the end only forty of us went, and for that they wanted back at us. They traced us wherever we went, and you got so that you went across the border holding onto your passport with two hands. You don't let it go or let anybody take it. And if anybody said, "I'll take your passport in the back room," I said, "Right, you take it while I'm holding onto it," and you'd follow them in. So they did try to get us back. I think I was one of the last ones.

But the dossier was amazing! They had conversations with people in China, people in Moscow, France. And that's why I don't worry about what I speak about now, because I would never have thought then that I was talking to anybody dangerous, so I mean why bother?[28]

THROUGHOUT THE FIFTIES, the FBI actively recruited informants (ex-Communist witness-informers were rewarded with celebrity and often career opportunities), including some who went on to small and large careers in folk music. The Bureau would approach a singer known to be on the outs with People's Songs' circles, someone who would not do benefits, for instance. The agents would appeal to the individual's patriotism, to his or her "good reputation," and occasionally to private information at their disposal. Even more common was placing "volunteers" in People's Songs or People's Artists as informants. Customarily, the infiltrators' function was nonmusical—to report on meetings and steal documents. If they played the guitar, so much the better.

Of course, Woody Guthrie and others were aware of this surveillance. As he once sang (improvised to the tune of the folk song "Acres of Clams"):

> He asked, "Will you point a gun for your country?"
> I answered the eff-bee-eye, "Yay!
> I will point a gun for my country
> But I won't guarantee you which way!"[29]

Organizer Toshi Ohta Seeger, on spies: I think you have to go back to way after the war. We always lived with the knowledge that there were FBI and CIA around us anyway because of my father being in Intelligence during the war. I don't think we really gave it much thought. It was a normal thing. It happened.[30]

Peggy Seeger, on being under surveillance: Only at one or two American concerts, that was noticeably in Houston and Austin in '60, when they were sitting in the front rows. You could tell them. They sat too straight. They had cold eyes and they're very, or at least they used to be, very identifiable.[31]

People's Artists' Norma Starobin, on attacks on hootenannies: I think I only worked [for People's Artists] about two years. Then the hootenannies were severely attacked by young hoodlums. I remember we had a terrible evening. It was square and folk dancing on West Fifteenth [Street], at the Teachers' Union Hall.

Well, these neighborhood kids heard the music, and our policy was to invite them in rather than turn them into enemies. They got in there and just started to break our furniture. They must have been planted by either their church or the FBI. If you have two or three teenagers coming in off the street, that's one thing, but this was a gang. The children were really endangered by hoodlums that came in.[32]

People's Songs organizer Leo Christiansen, on being aware of spies: I participated in meetings where I was aware that we were being observed by FBI agents. I think it was pretty hard not to be aware of that. You'd see the same people pop up at meetings and you saw them there but you never saw them anywhere else. A "flatfoot" is pretty hard to conceal. If you look at people who are listening in a group, sometimes, and there's a kind of spark of enthusiasm which you would detect and then all of a sudden you were looking down a row of faces and get one guy who is kind of dead faced. Something's going on.

We always recognized the fact. Of course, we subsequently found out that very often informers were informing on informers. So we thought it was kind of a joke. Everything was so open, what in the hell was going on, but also we knew that it was vicious, because we knew that somewhere along, someone was going to be confronted with accusations and not be able to face their accuser. But what could we do? That's life.[33]

Pete Seeger, on surveillance: You assume there's a possibility of it. In other words, every time you're on the phone, you assume there's a possibility that the phone is tapped. This is probably part of the plan, too; the whole intimidation of the country.[34]

AN UNKNOWN FBI INFORMANT filed this report on People's Artists:

June 12, 1954

    On Friday night, June 12, 1954, I attended the official opening for the office of People's Artists it was a closed affair where people were admitted by invitation only. The purpose was to show the office to people with money and to get them to contribute, funds are badly needed the organization is almost broke. Leon Bibb acted as the master of ceremonies and introduced Pete Seeger who sang three songs. Edith Segal was then introduced she recited a poem she wrote for Paul Robeson which introduced him. Paul sang one song and spoke for 15 minutes on the importance of the organization and the job it was doing for the progressive movement. He then showed the audience a Soviet magazine which was published in Russia and had a picture of the cover of the new songbook "Lift Every Voice" and had quite a lengthy article on P. Irwin Silber then asked the people for money starting with $50 contributions._____
_____[redacted]

    Those present who I could get to know were:

_____   _____

_____   _____[redacted]

Pete Seeger, on the spy "Harvey Matt": Well, Harvey. How would we describe him? Pudgy, medium-short. He was one of these active little people. You know often there's a new convert who's busy and helping out, volunteering for this and volunteering for that. He liked to sell literature and he was pretty good at it. He came into People's Songs and said, "I've got a great idea."

    [My wife] Toshi was suspicious of him. She'd say, "He doesn't have much income; look at him driving a new car."

    After about three or four months, he said, "Gee, this isn't really working out." He was going to sell records and books. The profits would go to help pay the rent of this poverty-stricken little organization. After a few months he says, "I'm sorry, I just can't afford to do it anymore. I can't afford to contribute my services."

    And I said, "Thanks for trying, Harvey."

    He'd been sitting there all the time just keeping track of who came in the door; and not paying the bills. He'd ordered one hundred dollars' worth of records. After he left, the bills kept coming in. We had hundreds of dollars of bills to pay. One of the main reasons that People's Songs owed three thousand dollars was that there was maybe one thousand dollars' worth of records, which he had ordered and never paid for. We were stuck with it. He had taken the money and used it for his own salary. Then we were accused of being dishonest businessmen before the [House Un-American Activities] Committee. What a sly trick.

I guess I found out he was an informer when he went to the Committee. It burst like a bombshell. We were all saying, "Hey, did you hear about Harvey?"

Almost every year there was a new spy making a bombshell.[35]

Irwin Silber, on People's Songs mole Harvey Matusow: [At People's Songs] Harvey was at the front desk, sort of a receptionist. But at that time we also, as a means of income, operated what amounted to a little book and record store right within our office, and he managed that for us as well. So, he'd greet you, he'd answer the phone, he'd sell you a record, sell you a book, and do whatever chores around the organization needed doing. Afterwards I kept trying to recall how he came around and I don't remember.[36]

IN SPITE OF THE OBSTACLES, a new movement was starting in Greenwich Village. First, folk music had come in from the hills with artists like Aunt Molly Jackson, Lead Belly, and Woody Guthrie; it was debated, disdained, and ultimately welcomed after the Composers' Collective's failure; recorded, collected, and broadcast by Alan Lomax and Moe Asch; adapted and applied politically by the Almanac Singers; and then catapulted into popular consciousness by the Weavers. Neither the FBI nor HUAC could stop it, and neither would the New York City Red Squad.

In 1949, following the Henry Wallace's campaign for president, Lee Hays and Pete Seeger returned to Greenwich Village in a new quartet called the Weavers, with Fred Hellerman and Ronnie Gilbert. As the Cold War heated up, they lost the few bookings they had. Their only choice was to sing commercially. Their intent was to reach out beyond what the Almanac Singers had done before the war; and their experience and rehearsal served them well. They had a repertoire of songs no one had heard, and their four-part harmony stunned crowds. By the summer of 1950, "Tzena, Tzena" and "Goodnight Irene" were on the pop music charts. Greenwich Village folk music was suddenly coming out of living-room radios across America.

The Weavers signed with Decca Records and, backed by the big band sound of arranger Gordon Jenkins, soared up the ranks of the *Hit Parade* with polished versions of folk songs like "Kisses Sweeter Than Wine," "So Long (It's Been Good to Know Yuh)," and later "On Top of Old Smoky" and

"Wimoweh." Ironically, the mainstream music industry welcomed them. With four platinum albums in just two years, the group was promptly accused by left-wing colleagues like *Sing Out!* editor Irwin Silber of compromising "both their political and artistic integrity."[37]

This comment reflected an age-old debate on the value of popularizing folk music—shouldn't it be performed as traditionally as possible? Or, should every song be a weapon in the class struggle?—as it would recur in the second folk music revival, also centered in Greenwich Village. While a few hundred folklorists and activists debated, the Weavers were the toast of the town.

The Weavers' Lee Hays, on that band's first gig: We were wearing corduroy jackets and blue washable pants, as I remember. This was when we went to work at the Village Vanguard, our first job.

I think Toshi [Ohta Seeger] went out to the army-and-navy store and found something to fit me. It was a presentable corduroy jacket, the only jacket I owned. And one pair of pants. I think my only other pair of pants was a pair of blue jeans.

I remember being a little baffled by the nightclub life, which was new to me. I don't know that I'd ever been in one. But I don't remember any debate about it, except the fact that this was a way to Earn a Living. As a matter of fact, we were getting fifty dollars apiece a week at that point and that was considerably more than we were getting anywhere else.

The Greenwich Village audience was pretty great in the Village Vanguard. It was the most consistently faithful audience we ever found, which surprised me, since it was a nightclub audience. Don't forget that years before a group called the Reviewers had appeared at the Village Vanguard, including Judy Holliday and her friends, doing satirical political comedy. The club was known for innovative stuff. In fact, all the clubs [in the Village] were known for material that was a little bit outside the mainstream.[38]

Mario "Boots" Casetta, on the Weavers' rise in popularity: I went to the Village Vanguard when the Weavers sang.

The [songs] didn't have narrow, narrow political action that you might make up for a rally. But other general things: "The Hammer Song," "Wasn't That a Time?" and other folk songs. It was like a hootenanny performance.

I remember that I was happy for the Weavers and absolutely flabbergasted. I wanted to stop people on the streets and say, "Listen to that, those are friends of mine. They're really radical as all hell, or Reds, or whatever, and you're clapping for them you asshole, and why didn't you recognize them a long time ago?"[39]

ON JUNE 25, 1950, just as the Weavers' records were arriving in shops, the Korean War made Communists the official enemies of the United States. Greenwich Village folk musicians were being actively blacklisted, investigated by the FBI, and subpoenaed to appear before HUAC. The Red Scare of the 1950s would deal a death blow to many artists' careers; even the chart-climbing Weavers would soon be untouchable.

The Cold War persecution of "Reds" had plenty of precedents in this nation's history. As early as 1798, laws were enacted that defined "enemy aliens," and the 1918 Sedition Act made disloyal references to the American flag, government, or Constitution subject to twenty years in prison.[40] When efforts to rout out subversives were unsatisfying, however, the overzealous turned on all things German.

Eventually, "liberty cabbage" became sauerkraut once more, but the censors soon turned their sights on Russian Communism. In 1930, the House of Representatives approved the creation of what came to be called the Fish Committee to seek out "all entities, groups, or individuals who are alleged to advise, teach or advocate the overthrow by force or violence of the Government of the United States."[41] In 1945, HUAC was made a permanent standing committee of congress, with subpoena powers. Then, in 1950, a relatively unknown senator from Wisconsin made a speech in West Virginia in which he announced, "I have here in my hand a list of 205, a list of names made known to the Secretary of State, as being members of the Communist Party and who nevertheless are still working and shaping policy in the State Department."[42] Joe McCarthy never shared this list, but McCarthyism was born—"contributing, along with [President] Truman's loyalty oath for federal employees and the attorney general's list of subversive organizations, to an atmosphere of social and political paranoia."[43] A second Red Scare was sweeping America.

However apolitical the Weavers' hits, popular success did not shield the group from the groundswell of Senator McCarthy's blacklist. In June 1950, the Weavers became, according to *Variety*, "the first group canceled out of a New York café because of alleged left-wing affiliations."[44]

Folksinger Don McLean, on the Weavers: The Weavers were superstars. In my opinion, that group is one of the most important quartets in musical history, the musical history of this country. It's only because of the blacklist that people aren't told that. Their work is present all the time, everywhere. I'm talking now from a very unique position because I've been through this. There is a thing that happens—it's very heavy—when your style is so powerful that it turns on the public, as opposed to a cult of people who might appreciate what you do.

The Weavers exploded out of that; what that does is very heavy. Who knows what would go down in terms of conflict, because you are faced with a very explosive situation that is out of control. It's like a shot in a rocket ship....The Weavers found out what it was like to be valuable property. The individuals in the group and their reaction to being a valuable property may have ultimately sealed the fate of the group.[45]

The Weavers' Ronnie Gilbert, on dodging HUAC: They never called me [to testify before HUAC]. What happened was when I finally was going to be called, there was a message for me. I was having dinner at Harold and Natalie Leventhal's and Natalie said, "Somebody called earlier and left a message to please call."

And I did, I called this woman named Mrs. Scottie. I later found out she was the finger woman for all of the New York stuff.

"Mrs. Scottie, you wanted to talk to me? This is Ronnie Gilbert."

"Oh yes, Ms. Gilbert. You can't hide from us. We know exactly where you are."

"Oh, who's we?"

"Well, the Committee. The Committee would like to interview you. Everything will be very private. We understand you are married now, and girls don't like to tell their husbands everything." (I'm using this in my book.)

Anyway, so they were going to call me and she said, very politely, "When?"

I said, "Well, can I call you back?"

She said, "Yes, but don't wait too long. The Committee is eager to talk to you."

I called a lawyer and he said, "Get out of town fast if you don't want to get subpoenaed."

But we had a concert. So he said, "Well, here's what you do. Do the concert and when you get to the airport don't call her until you are practically on the plane. You don't have to call her if you don't want to."

But I did. I said, "Tell Counselor I'm really sorry but I can't do that right now. I have to get back to my two-year-old child. If you need me I'm in the phone book in Los Angeles."

(I didn't tell her which book in Los Angeles.) I didn't hear from them after that....

We had one year, literally, of "stardom" and then it began to fall apart. All we had was two years and the last year of that was very hard, very rough.

Well, we flew to Ohio to be sure that we did what the contract said we were supposed to do, which be be there. When we got off the plane, I remember stepping down the stairs and being accosted by a reporter.

There were reporters, press people standing around. Most of them went to Pete first, the one that came to me asked me questions. I treated it like "I'm just a girl, what do I know? Just a girl. All I want is my husband; I have a baby." I did the whole woman thing, disgusting.[46]

AT THE ONSET, persons suspected of links to Communist organizations were named in hearings before state and federal anti-Communist investigating committees. Those testifying were given a choice of incriminating themselves or being blacklisted, which cost many their jobs, families, houses, and reputations.

The arts and entertainment industry was particularly targeted. In November 1947, the Hollywood blacklist kindled as the "Hollywood Ten," a group of screenwriters and directors, were cited for contempt of Congress, for invoking their First Amendment right of free speech before HUAC, and then fired under the auspices of the Motion Picture Association of America. In 1950, *Red Channels* published the names of 151 people (including musicians such as Leonard Bernstein and Pete Seeger) linked in some way with the Communist Party USA, and the blacklist swelled.

The Weavers' manager Harold Leventhal, on *Red Channels*: Let's say you had sixty names. It is possible that fifty-five never continued participation in any of these things at the point in which they were named in *Red Channels*. Or gave up whatever political backgrounds they had.

Every week there was another entry for Pete [Seeger] and this infuriated them. Pete was continually active in the area they resented. The fifty-five others may not have been. They didn't have anything new on the guy. But after they had attacked him, he'd keep on going.

Pete didn't say, "Well, I'm going to cool it." He didn't cool it. He continued, proceeding as he always wanted to proceed. I remember the first tour of the Soviet Union. It was picked up by the papers. This is [fourteen] years after the original *Red Channels*.

No other American performer had appeared in the Soviet Union. Then you have Pete going to the Soviet Union. This added more material and made him the prime target.[47]

Lee Hays, on the Weavers and politics: If you're talking about associations with Communists, we had plenty of them. One of my best friends was Bob Reed, that's what got us blacklisted. He had something to do with the cultural part of the Party; I never knew quite what he did, but I finally decided after a great deal of thought that one of the basic thrusts of our stage work—I'm not so sure about the Almanacs, but certainly of the People's Songs and the Weavers—had a very highly religious bent.

A traditional Weavers concert—couldn't get more religious than that. In a very broad folk sense, and I think this appealed to something in the left wing, some kind of sense of good old Americanism or some sort. I would tell preacher stories, even antipreacher stories; had a lot of fun with country-type stories involving preachers and churches, and we'd illustrate lining out hymn techniques, and sing shape-note hymns, and tell stories of how it was done in the days of Billings. Basically a lot of this was, I believe, more religious than political.[48]

Don McLean, on the Weavers and the danger of song: This is the notion of dangerous songs—danger has to do with the environment that it's in; sing "Tzena, Tzena" to the Arabs and watch what happens. Pete has always managed to find songs that are dangerous for their time and place. Because the kind of danger, the point of view that sees these songs as dangerous is an establishmentarian point of view, not from the point of view of letting people live decent lives. It's only dangerous to those people who would want to stop that. From the point of view of the individual, it's nothing but beneficial. A dangerous song is the most dangerous form of art there is; you can never kill a song.

This is what all the Weavers understand so fundamentally. In terms of understanding what might have happened, the chances are that everybody was rather naïve. This would explain the feeling, "sure we'll get a group together, and we'll sing songs of everybody, from every land, we'll get people to see each other and shake hands." And suddenly, *whack!* down comes the axe: the reality of just how dangerous this music was, how threatening it was to someone.[49]

Harold Leventhal, on the Weavers being blacklisted: I don't think any of us were unconscious of the *Red Channels*, and the whole temper that was going on there. None of us believed that we could beat it; everyone knew it was just a matter of time until it beat us. There was never the feeling that we could really compromise on that issue. We could play around it for a while...to gain a little time, we were going to get it. It was just a matter of waiting to get it and how. So I don't recall any incident, or any meetings we had or discussions, none whatsoever that they could make the statement "Let's deny this whole incident—let's denounce that background."

None of that ever happened. It was our country and it was a feeling that we got away with it. Takes years, months...this was it.[50]

ON AUGUST 9, 1951, the governor of Ohio, Frank Lausche, wrote the FBI for information on the Weavers, who were scheduled to appear at the Ohio State Fair. His request put Hoover on the spot. The files requested were clearly confidential; no private individual, not even a governor, could legally examine them. Hoover's zeal got the best of him, however, and he passed along the information.[51] The Weavers' engagement was canceled so quickly that there was not enough time to take their names out of the programs.

Ronnie Gilbert, on the Weavers being blacklisted: Well, this happened just preceding the Ohio State Fair, which you know all about. When the press began to pick up . . . it was a great surprise to us that we weren't blacklisted long before that. We were on borrowed time and we knew that perfectly well. The decision to try to keep going, try to outrun the blacklist by taking advantage as much as we could of our stardom, of the thrust towards starhood and all of that, that was a very hard decision to make because it meant cutting ourselves off from the Left.

We couldn't have it both ways. If we were going to pursue that path, then we were going to pursue that path. Pete [Seeger] did try to have it both ways. He would sneak off and try to do some singing over there. That was going on all the time. We pretty much knew that at some point something was going to happen. It was a great surprise when it didn't. We did this show, we did that show, you know? We did appearances on television shows.[52]

Pete Seeger, on being blacklisted from television: The Weavers were on network TV in early 1950. We had a flurry of programs. *The Tonight Show*, when Fred Allen was on it. He got off a wonderful crack. He asked, "When did you Weavers get together?" And we all started talking at once. So I said, "Mr. Allen, you better ask us one at a time." So he said, "Well, Mr. Seeger, when did *you* get together?"

We were on the *Milton Berle Show*, a whole batch of real big shows.

Later on in 1950, the blast came out and we stopped getting network shows.

You know, the first time I can say I was blacklisted was in the early sixties when David Susskind interviewed me. This was a syndicated show. It was taped and then syndicated around. He was willing. I said, "You know you're going to get letters."

He said, "Well, I'll face that. I like to challenge those people, they're stupid." He said, "Would you mind taking questions and answers?"

I said, "No, fine."

After he was interviewing me, someone stands up and said, "Mr. Seeger, are you blacklisted from TV?"

I said, "Well, frankly, I don't know. I don't get jobs. A show like this is the exception that proves the rule."

Susskind interrupted and looked me right in the eyes and said, "Mr. Seeger, you are blacklisted."

I figured, he must know.[53]

Harold Leventhal, on audiences during the blacklist period: The unions were literally closed through the whole McCarthy period. Where we did have unions, the doors were shut. The left-wing groups that one would sing to were being shattered bit by bit. So whatever door was open, you'd go. And at least in New York these independent community-type schools, or progressive schools, opened their doors to [performers like the Weavers]. They were self-dependent. They didn't depend upon any city funds, or they weren't open to this kind of criticism. It didn't matter to them. So you'd go where the door was open.[54]

Earl Robinson, on Pete Seeger performing during the blacklist period: Well, Pete did one very beautiful blacklist thing: the guerilla method of singing. I mean, certain places if they found out about him in advance, they would picket and maybe manage to cancel him out. So he really got into this habit of getting in and out fast.[55]

Pete Seeger, on "guerilla singing" on TV: I'd drop in on local TV shows. I'd call them up myself. Or else get a local publicity person. I'd say, "Is there some local TV show I can come on?"

They'd say, "Who are you? Pete Seeger? What do you do?"

I'd say, "I sing folk songs."

They'd say, "Oh, that Burl Ives stuff." Or, later on they'd say, "That Kingston Trio stuff." Or, "Oh, you're with the Weavers. Sure, I remember 'Goodnight Irene.' Come on up. We'll chat a moment. I'll play your record. Singing at the college tonight, good."

So, I'd be up there and I'd talk with him for five or ten minutes and he'd play some song and I'd be away before the American Legion could mobilize itself to protest this Communist fellow on the air.[56]

Former congressman Hugh DeLacy, on the Weavers: Of course when you've got some real musicians such as the Weavers were, they had the capacity to extend themselves beyond the sociopolitical origins. Their origins. They did. What happened, of course, is that when you bring the songs of the people to a vast audience which does not recognize itself as being "of the people," if I can put quotations marks around that—then the music itself isn't compromised, but its original purpose is sort of dissipated....

And so someone could say about this music that it may very well have been primarily used to give a little spirit to the people who were engaged in struggle, and why shouldn't it be? People who engage in struggle have to have spirit. . . . We do have something of a people's culture in this country. Which, culturally, is revolutionary, really, when you start to think about it. Because we talk about the media and they're always telling us what to think, and what to sing, and the rest of it. And here suddenly there's a strain [in this folk music], which goes in the back, which may go into the future.[57]

Pete Seeger recalls a blacklist anecdote: Well, there we were at Daffy's Bar and Grill and some drunks hollered, "Bet you can't sing "The Star-Spangled Banner."

Ronnie said, sweetly, "Suppose we do it when you're all sober." Because they were all very drunk. Hugh DeLacy, the former left-wing congressman, came out to hear us.

He pointed out to me, he said, "You know, the Red Squad is placed all around here. They got their eye on me, frankly, more than you, because they want to see who I speak to. Now watch what I do." He went around to every table in the room, shaking hands. "Hello, I'm Hugh DeLacy. I live over here. I'm glad to meet you."

People wouldn't refuse. "Who's this guy? Okay." Shake his hand. He shook hands with everybody in the room.[58]

Ronnie Gilbert, on the blacklist: The truth is I would have been happy to sing those [Weavers] songs anywhere and I think that's true to some extent for everybody in the group. I could be wrong, but I don't think there was a lot of thought given to "Oh God, we were so good, we had these great things and now we have nothing."

I remember [later], being interviewed by a young woman and that's what she wanted. She was very young; it was for some publication. She said, "How do you feel that the worst possible thing that could happen to you happened? You lost your work."

I said, "What? That is not the worst possible thing that can happen." And at the time people were being tortured in Guatemala, you know? So I said, "What's the matter with you?"

She didn't realize. To her, that was the worst thing that could possibly happen. The worst thing was that America was giving in to this terrible thing of blacklisting.

Our own field was the smallest part of it. Academia was being destroyed by it. Unions were being destroyed.[59]

Pete Seeger, on gradual improvements: Every year since the end of the Korean War, I could measure the increase in civil liberties in America. The Korean War ended in '53. McCarthy was censured in late '53 or '54. In '55, things got better. Even though I was called up in front of the House Un-American Activities Committee, things were still getting better.[60]

HUAC AND FOLKSINGERS

HUAC did not get around to folksingers until 1955, after the list of perform-ers who garnered more headlines was exhausted. In 1955, Pete Seeger and Lee Hays of the Weavers were called to testify. Hays took the Fifth as his defense against self-incrimination; and Seeger took the First Amendment, freedom of song:

> Mr. Seeger: I feel that in my whole life I have never done anything of any conspiratorial nature and I resent very much and very deeply the implication of being called before this Committee that in some way because my opinions may be different from yours, or yours, Mr. Willis, or yours, Mr. Scherer, that I am any less of an American than anybody else. I love my country very deeply, sir. . . .
>
> Mr. Scherer: Let me understand. You are not relying on the Fifth Amendment, are you?
>
> Mr. Seeger: No, sir, although I do not want to in any way discredit or deprecate the witnesses that have used the Fifth Amendment.[61]

On March 27, 1961, six days after Pete Seeger's conviction in a jury trial, New York's parks commissioner, Newbold Morris, banned singing in Greenwich Village's Washington Square. Eventually, most activists in the folk music community were subpoenaed, as HUAC explored the folk music plot. Even those who were never subpoenaed suffered blacklisting for their associations, including Mike Seeger, Pete's half-brother.

Oscar Brand, on being called before HUAC: I got a call. They wanted me to come down. I think it was near WNYC, a big FBI building there. And I think that HUAC was there. Well, I drove up to Pete's as I had done many times. I helped him build that place. (I didn't do too much, because I was working.) I said, "Pete, they just called me for the HUAC. They want to talk to me. Shall I go?"

He said, "You have to go."

I said, "Well, I have nothing to tell them."

He said, "You do what you have to do. I did what I had to do. You do what you have to do. And the only person who could tell you what you have to do is yourself."[62]

Earl Robinson, on HUAC's intent: They wanted to scare any organi-zations that might do good things. Stand up against the war in Korea, say, and influence a lot of people. This is how I would put it. The war in Korea had to be supported by the American people and anybody who was against it had to be labeled a Red or dangerous. They were moving toward arming against the Soviet Union also. The atomic bomb contest was going on, who could produce the bigger one.[63]

Musician Mike Seeger, on the McCarthy era: It was horrible. I remember a very good friend of my father's, who was given as my reference, was intimidated by the government and asked to testify at a hearing on my behalf when I had applied for a job working at the Social Security office. I ended up quitting because I was trying to do too much—going to school and working full time and playing music. I quit before they completed their investigation.

The government later sent me a dossier on my father, brother, and sister, asking me to comment on it. I told them that I preferred to answer questions only about myself. They asked me if I was a Communist and I told them that it was unconstitutional for them to question me on that subject, unless I was involved in advocacy of a violent overthrow of the government. I said, "I'm a pacifist. I just spent two years working in a state hospital because I don't believe in that." From there on I refused to answer because I had already answered by doing my time.

They told me that if I didn't tell them yes or no (as to whether or not I was a Communist) I would never have a government job again. Unfortunately, I capitulated—I was very young at the time.

That was ridiculous: me, a member of the Communist Party. At that time, this happened in '58, I was living with country people who really had a dislike for black people.

[In the sixties] I had a run-in with a man named Tom Paley, who was a member of a square dance troupe that was on the attorney general's list. Paley [a member of the Ramblers] wouldn't say that he was sorry for belonging to it, so we were blacklisted from television. The Ramblers were never seen on network television after that. We had been on the *Today Show* on Independence Day where we purposely did "Battleship of Maine" because it was the time of the Cuban missile crisis. They asked us back on the condition that we sign loyalty oaths, saying they were sorry. We didn't want to do that.

The last thing to happen was the funniest: the Social Security had a radio program using traditional music in the midsixties. They wanted to use the Ramblers, asked us to do a show, and then called back saying it would be too embarrassing—they'd have to answer too many questions. They told me that I was too controversial because of the name Seeger. We were a little bit upset at that. When the opportunity came to back up Maybelle Carter on one of these shows, my friend Ralph Rinzler arranged for me to be one of the musicians without the Social Security people knowing. After the recording session, when we registered our names, they refused to pay me under my own name. They had to send a check to Ralph. When I went to the ACLU, they weren't much help. After that, the radio program was canceled. I don't know if it was related to my complaint or not.[64]

IN HIS 1955 MEMOIR *False Witness*, People's Songs member turned HUAC witness Harvey Matusow recalls fingering the Weavers to the anti-Communist magazine *Counterattack*:[65]

> It was here I got my first training in how to use the names of well-known people in the theatrical world to my advantage, as a money-making witness. We discussed the careers of a well-known quartet, who at the time had the top-selling phonograph record in the United States. One of its members was listed in *Red Channels*; there was nothing could be pinned on the group specifically. Having known all four of them, not as Communists, but as friends, I triumphantly said, "I know them, and they are Communists." Both the editors gave me rewarding glances, as if saying, "Keep that up and you'll make out all right."

Oscar Brand, on being named by Harvey Matusow: I knew Harvey because he was always at [People's Songs] offices. And one day afterwards, he'd just got out of jail I think, or was just going. He came to me and he said, "Oscar, I want to apologize to you."

I said, "What for?"

He said, "Because I was the one that told the FBI that you were a Communist and I tried to tell them that it wasn't so, but they wouldn't accept that." So he says, "Will you forgive me?"

I said, "I never got angry with you; you were doing what you were doing to save your life. But I don't think it's going to do you any good." Of course it didn't.[66]

MATUSOW RECANTED HIS ACCUSATIONS against People's Songs and the Weavers, but it was too late. By the end of 1952, the group who had brought the nation "Goodnight Irene," the fastest selling song of its day, disbanded. Or, as Lee Hays put it, "We took a Sabbatical, which turned into a Mondayical and a Tuesdayical."[67]

Not all of HUAC's witnesses were as malicious as Harvey Matusow. The pressure to comply with investigations was powerful indeed. But it was a two-way gauntlet: those who resisted risked professional ruin; those who cooperated risked alienation from the community of their radical friends and colleagues. Oscar Brand, who was approached by the FBI and agreed to speak, describes himself as having been blacklisted by both Conservatives and Irwin Silber, who accused Brand of testifying.[68]

Oscar Brand, on reactions to his cooperation with the FBI: No. No. [There was no quid pro quo.] I just had nothing to give them. But the fact that I was supported by a good bank account makes a big difference.... I had the money. I mean I had the number one song in the world.... You see the people who gave in, Jerome Robbins, Josh [White] and these others. They'd have no work if they didn't say something. Maybe they didn't say everything or they said too much, or whatever. But I didn't have that problem.

So I didn't do what I was accused of doing by Irwin Silber. Irwin decided that since he knew that the FBI had been after me—he knew that—and I was not being called up or anything like that. Oh, yes, and also at the Cooper Union and other concerts I had already opened my mouth about my feelings on the Soviet Union and about Stalin and as a consequence he was sure that I was going to give them trouble. He'd been sure all the time, even though he worked for me. (We worked together running shows for People's Songs.) So he wrote a big article for the *Daily Worker*, with photographs and all that stuff about—it was a lot of publicity, I can tell you. The quote I remember is "Oscar Brand is joining the Truman War Bandwagon." Well, the fact that I was doing things for Truman also was a problem.

But all of a sudden I would do a concert and someone would get up from the audience and call me a "goddamn sonofabitch." And I had a standard response. I said, "Why are you calling me a sonofabitch? Which particular thing that I do troubles you the most?" And it practically always was the statement by the *Daily Worker* that I was joining Truman and giving in to the FBI and that bunch.

Yeah. I don't think anybody *didn't* know [that I had talked to the FBI]. But Irwin knew that I didn't say anything. He knew me very well. At [the 1991 Dick Reuss Folklore Conference in] Indianapolis, he was there and we went out to lunch together. Irwin was in the group. I said, "You know, Irwin? The thing that got me the most—that really got me and my family too—it was very bad for my father because he was so proud of me." I said, "Your article in the *Worker*. All right the *Worker* can attack me for not being this and not being that. But not for cooperating." They expected that I would give them names of all my friends, et cetera, et cetera. And I said, "I didn't have any names to give."

He said, "Oscar, in those days we were fighting for our lives, and I apologize."

And I said, "In that case you can pay the check."[69]

Pete Seeger, on betrayals during the blacklist: A fellow, Felix Landau, who used to be an editor with People's Songs in '46, called up some woman and was chatting away and said, "Can I see you next week?"

She says, "Felix, haven't you heard?"

He says, "What happened? What haven't I heard?"

She says, "Don't you know the terrible things that happen to people these days?"

She suddenly started crying and hung up on him.

The next day he reads in the paper that she and her husband have been testifying for the Committee. She was suddenly faced with a man talking very friendly to her, when she'd assumed that she would never speak to this man again. Here he was chatting on in a real friendly way. She said, "Felix, haven't you heard?" She couldn't stand it. She and her husband had been employed by the FBI to become members of the Communist Party and join this and that organization and then go and list them as fronts. Fronts for this and fronts for that, fronts for fronts.[70]

Historian Ron Radosh, on Pete Seeger's return to New York's left-wing community: In the period after the Weavers, he gave a concert at Yugoslav Hall, on West Forty-second [Street] between Tenth and Eleventh Ave[nues], the Communist Party had control of that hall, but it was also used for concerts. Pete gave a concert there. I remember his opening words at that concert; he came out and said, "I haven't been as far away as you think." At that kind of thing he sang a lot of the old radical songs. He had a close tie to the Party. I didn't know if he was a member—I assumed he was. I've never been satisfied with his public explanations, it was really copping out.[71]

Earl Robinson, on how musicians ducked the blacklist: Bob DeCormier, well, he directed a chorus, and both he and Ernie Lieberman [once a member of the Limeliters] broke through into the sort of establishment setup. Ernie became a singer. And Bob got his own chorus and he worked with Belafonte for a while. So—I'll have to make up names here—they both met as old friends out in San Francisco. Bob was touring; Ernie was with a respectable nightclub there for a while—the hungry i. And they embraced each other, being together in New York and from the left-wing days, and as they're embracing Bob whispers, "The name is Corman," and Ernie whispers, "The name is [Sheldon]."[72]

FOLK MUSIC HAD INDEED been propelled into the popular sphere by radical thinkers and union organizers during the 1930s. But the theory that the folk music world was a front in the Communist takeover of America was, of course, absurd. For one thing, the "Old Left" had all but disintegrated by the late 1950s, as news of Stalin's brutality tarnished utopian notions. But folk music remained a propaganda medium, one that held strong appeal for new radicals, whose influence would be felt in the social upheavals of the 1960s.

Insurgent or not, folk music could not be silenced. In 1961, the year *Webster's Third New International Dictionary* first included the word "hootenanny," Pete Seeger was standing trial for contempt of Congress, and folk music lovers were rioting in Washington Square Park.

Ronnie Gilbert, on coming through the blacklist: There were two processes. And I keep going back to this. There was the music and then there was the other thing. The music process was its own process and the other process was the political, philosophical, personal, emotional part. This is obvious. What affected us was our own individual lack of connection, or whatever you want to call it, to what was going on: personal, interior and the collective thing. It wasn't because somebody asked a question, it wasn't because a reporter was dogging us, it wasn't because of that. It was what was going on for us around the question on whether we should keep going. That was the thing.

And I remember reading, maybe it was in Lee's writings, Pete saying, "If we can't do this, what is the point of doing it?" and it was a very good question. And yet there was something about hanging in there. Hanging in there was part of it. Pete's relationship to all this is hugely different from mine. His goes back a generation, to his father. It goes back to the Almanacs. The historical part that enters into his feelings on all this is way, way different from mine. I can't speak for Freddy; Freddy had his own thing. And Lee was endlessly interesting, and endlessly problematic.

The experience that was the most extraordinary was coming out on the stage *after* the blacklist [at the Weavers' Carnegie Hall reunion concert in December 1955], a breathless feeling, coming onto the stage and feeling what was going on with the audience before they even started applauding.[73] The minute we got out, there was a split second where you felt the "Ahh!" and then the applause. I think that experience is the one that I remember most vividly.[74]

GRADUALLY, THE BLACKLIST began to lift. But many effects of the anti-Communist scourge were lasting: the Red Scare and its blacklist shattered and washed away much of the Old Left and its supporting culture; but the folk music movement would recover and flourish in the aftermath. Folk musicians began to find venues to perform. Folk music was ceasing to be associated with bearded and leotarded beatniks and moving out into a do-it-yourself nation's parlor. And as Americans in the 1960s became comfortable once more with dissent (at least until the Vietnam War), they would pick up their instruments and get back to singing out.

6

FOLK BOOM

PETE SEEGER NOTED IN 1956 that an "American folksong revival [is] in full force, with 500,000 guitars sold last year, and millions more having fun singing folk songs together."[1] Little did Seeger imagine what "full force" would look like for the folk revival in the near future.

Scholars have debated the many impulses behind revivalism: why and at what point does a community look back and realize the importance of its past? The answers to such a question, usually involving movements for nationalism and patriotism, are complex ones, involving specific historical circumstances.

In the United States in the 1950s, amid hula hoops, telephone-booth-stuffing, and images of Marilyn Monroe, folk music rose again. McCarthyism gradually came under check as the decade progressed. Meanwhile, emergent recording and distribution technology, including 45s and transistor radios, meant that ever-widening audiences had access to, and generated a demand for, commercially recorded folk music. Small, independent record companies multiplied to fill demand niches, as did local AM radio and TV stations. Throughout the decade, music was breaking with cultural strictures, but it was also returning to its roots.

Ironically, this redirection of folk music was partly the result of the blacklist; first-revival performers including Guy Carawan and Pete Seeger, cut off from commercial gigs, began teaching their songs to kids at schools and summer camps, places where no one had thought to blacklist them. These youngsters' connection to folk music assured its continuation and the formation of a second folk music revival as many of these middle-class children grew up, attended college, and kept singing.

The Lomax-Seeger revival of the thirties and forties had focused on uncovering and publishing important songs for singers and scholars; in the next revival, many of the same songs were performed to live audiences of millions. For audiences of the earlier, Washington-based revival of the 1930s, folk music was nostalgic and antiquarian, until Greenwich Villagers became attracted to vernacular music and its applications. Interest in folk music waned in the forties, as rhythm and blues turned to rock and roll, and then, by the mid-1950s, rock's newness also began to fade: Elvis turned to pop; Buddy Holly and Ritchie Valens died in a plane crash; the British invasion of the Beatles and the Rolling Stones lay a few years off. In the meantime, folk music became immensely attractive.

The difference between these generations of folklorists has to do with their explicit intent, the purpose for which they were trying to "revive" folk songs. In the first generation, this meant finding obscure and forgotten texts and tunes and documenting their content and function. For a second generation of folk music revivalists, spanning the years between the Weavers' reunion album and the end of the Vietnam War (1956–72), this meant turning to treasures already unearthed, re-versioning them, and performing them in the hope of furthering social change. Woody Guthrie, Pete Seeger, and their many associates appreciated how the songs of the past informed the present and shaped the future. This difference in intent might be the biggest difference between these two generations, but what they had in common was a deep and profound love and respect for songs that were anonymous, re-created, and still sung.

The first performers to achieve popularity in the second revival were old-school concert performers of folk music—song stylists, really—such as John Jacob Niles and Richard Dyer-Bennet. Then came the citybillies: Burl Ives, Pete Seeger, and Josh White. These prominent in the first revival rode the crest of the second; though John Lomax was dead and Alan had moved to England to collect songs (and probably to avoid a HUAC subpoena). Lead Belly had died; Woody was hospitalized. Newer folk acts emerged at the beginning of the 1960s, such as Cynthia Gooding, Susan Reed, Theo Bikel, and others. But the folk music movement, as it was initially called (the term "revival" was controversial and difficult to defend), did not originate solely with performers.

Composer Earl Robinson, comparing folk music revivals: The one in the thirties or early forties was, for us present on the scene, a natural discovery that we could use this beautiful, basic American words and music to help people in a very important struggle. And we were kind of like pioneers, because [this] music was known then, to only a few.

Now, in the late fifties and sixties the same thing happened, probably, to this new generation. They just discovered this music. The Kingston Trio discovered it and many, many others. But it was complicated by the fact that immediately it became commercial... You discover that you can say something, and you can celebrate, in a way that is not obvious to the Establishment.[2]

Protest songwriter Malvina Reynolds, on the beginnings of the folk boom: There was a tremendous blood transfusion of the folk strength and beauty into American popular music. And it transformed that pallid, yucky stuff we had been getting in the twenties and the thirties. Here comes "Tom Dooley" and "I Wonder as I Wander" and Woody Guthrie stuff. And suddenly it put such a vitamin shot into American popular music. And [the Weavers] were there. They had all this material, nobody pushed them there, just the history of popular music stuck them right out in front.[3]

Singer-songwriter Arlo Guthrie, on the second folk music revival: Music styles are the first indigenous American thing that we have in the country. Music was not strictly English, not strictly Irish, French, or Italian, or African—it was all of them. Musicians are all easygoing enough, hungry enough to adapt to any circumstance. Whatever works is what they went after.

Folk music became commercial in the early and middle sixties, but it happened back in ragtime. It happened back in blues, and ragtime, and ballads from Appalachia, and banjo and fiddle contests in Texas, a long time ago....

In 1961, '62, folk music certainly struck a lot of bewildered record companies, and bewildered radio stations. A lot of people didn't know what to make of stuff like that. It was just one of those times that you have in the world when a lot of people get the same idea because they recognize something in it. It speaks to them, about them, for them, by them. There have been other times that haven't been limited to music, but music's time in this century, in terms of striking a chord if you want to put it that way, happens then.[4]

Protest singer Phil Ochs, on the reemergence of popularized folk music: There is a general pattern that happens with the music industry. There is an historical precedent for what happened in, let's say, 1955 with the Elvis Presley–Buddy Holly–Everly Brothers–Chuck Berry success story. That is, certain unique individuals, usually from country backgrounds, created a music so vital and so exciting that they essentially destroyed the big-band, big-city commercialization that was happening then and took over the market. When it became quite apparent that you could make literally a million dollars by finding a guy, or marketing a man who had a sound, the profiteers came in around 1958 and took over and literally destroyed this music. Anything like Fabian and Frankie Avalon got them on television, made the deals. The agencies were involved, the radio stations were involved, the TV networks, and a whole business pattern emerged where they just sold prefabricated products which looked like the real thing and made the same amount of money, usually temporarily; but it didn't matter because you'd manufactured your hit and sent your performer around. So the radio, which was the music teacher to a lot of people, you know, died. I think this is one of the factors that led to folk music becoming so big around 1958, because everything became so rank and so ridiculous so fast that people just turned away from all that, subconsciously. So folk music provided the perfect antidote, in terms of very human, very simple, very real contact.[5]

LAUNCHING THE FOLK BOOM

Though the Weavers' introduction of folk songs to the radio waves was cut short when they were blacklisted, that first taste of popularized folk songs had changed popular music. The Weavers had hit a nerve, and audiences wanted more. In December 1955, the blacklist was not over, but enough people were over the blacklist to sell out New York's Carnegie Hall for a Christmastime Weavers reunion concert. (The subsequent Vanguard album *The Weavers at Carnegie Hall* sold phenomenally.) The group never again approached their previous success, but their return to the stage signaled the start of the new, popular folk music revival of the fifties and sixties.

Sing Out! **editor Mark Moss, on Pete Seeger and the Weavers' role in the second revival:** There was a point in time that the work [Pete Seeger] did, particularly in the late forties and early fifties with the Weavers, gave birth to the folk revival as we know it. He saw a way of being able to present folk music—by folk music I mean traditional music—in a way that was commercial. The Weavers were a pop group, who happened to use folk music. I think that had it not been for the HUAC hearings that drove Pete in this other direction—who knows?[6]

Folksinger Pete Seeger, on inspiring future folk stars: I was being asked to sing for the Democratic Club of Palo Alto. Well, I went and sang in the Palo Alto Junior High School for about three, four hundred people. The place wasn't packed, but they made a little money.

And at that one concert, both Dave Guard, who started the Kingston Trio, and Joan Baez heard me [for the first time]. Dave got a copy of my banjo book, which at that time was still mimeographed, so it must have been quite early, 1955, something like that ('56 at the latest; it might have been '54). Joan was about twelve, thirteen, fourteen years old at that time; and she said it made a big impression upon her that someone can make a living singing these songs.[7]

Guitarist Happy Traum, on Pete Seeger's role in developing and inspiring folk boom artists: Let's say I was very influenced by Pete. In my day if Pete Seeger didn't sing a song, it wasn't a folk song. When I was first starting in the fifties, Pete was my yardstick of what songs to sing. My repertoire was based on his records. I went to all his concerts. As you get older you change and see things in a different perspective.[8]

Folksinger Michael Cooney, on inspiration: [Pete Seeger] came to Tucson when I was still playing the ukulele in high school and a friend of mine took me to see him at the Jewish Community Center. I wrote to Pete Seeger to ask him about a couple of songs and about how to play the long-neck banjo.

"Dear Mr. Seeger, what do you do to be a folksinger?"

And he wrote back a letter, actually at the bottom of my letter, I think. A little something, sent back about "sing for as many different kinds of audiences as you can for free."

And of course that's what the aspiring folksinger doesn't want to hear. I don't remember what my immediate reaction to that was because at the time I could barely play the guitar, if at all, and I was mostly playing a four-string banjo tuned like a ukulele. I was just hoping to move on to a five-string and get a guitar and move along. I was forming a high school trio to be like the Kingston Trio, but his letter did have an effect upon me....

You might say virtually every banjo player from the whole folk movement began as Pete Seeger, and some survived or recovered and went on to be themselves and others never did.[9]

Arlo Guthrie, on learning to make music powerful: Here's my theory. If you want to know something about this kind of stuff, you really don't want to take a course on it. You really don't even want to read a book on it. What you really want to do is go and hang out with the guy who's doing it and pay attention. If you do that and you're doing whatever he happens to be doing, it doesn't matter if you're performing, it's not in that, it's in being present with the person whose tricks you want to learn. It's not saying, "Now show me this trick." If you want to know how I do my stuff, you're not going to take a course on me in some college or high school. You have to go and hang out.

I started playing in 1965, and it wasn't until the midseventies that I knew what I was doing. One of the things I was doing before I hung out with Pete was doing the same kind of tinkering from set to set, from night to night and I was doing it for the songs because I was creating a kind of tale. I wasn't just singing the song.

To sing the song you have to generally stick to the words; you can't make up your own words to "John Henry" every night. The song is already written. You pay attention to how you say it, you pay attention to how you play it, how you emphasize it, where you breathe, where you don't. All these little things you don't think of. If you do the same three minutes of your life every day, after a decade, that three minutes is like a half hour because you know every part of it. It gives you room to tinker and play in a field that goes by quickly in most people's minds, but in your experience it is a much bigger playing field.[10]

Singer-songwriter John McCutcheon, on his folk music education: The [1963] March on Washington on television was my introduction to folk music. That was the beginning of my musical education. Here was this old music that was dynamic, that had roots, that was deep. Deep not only historically, but spiritually. It moved people. Plus you had these people like Bob Dylan and Peter, Paul and Mary—and they were the least interesting music I saw that day. I just thought it was for me. That I wanted to do this.

I skirted the whole collegiate folk song part of the revival. I had no idea who the Kingston Trio were. What I call the button-down part of the folk song world. I went right to Pete and Woody.

It was like you heard people like Peter, Paul and Mary, and you thought that something had to come before that. Then as you learned about Pete, you thought, what? He didn't grow up doing this so what came before him? That led me to Woody. When I got to Woody it exploded. Woody, he could write about anything.[11]

Arlo Guthrie, on the roots of his music: Well, I just remember sitting in the seats with my brother and sister and probably other kids, listening to the Weavers sing. I loved Lee Hays's stories, I used to love to hear him talk and I loved the way he sang.

Just straight out, straight ahead, a few embellishments here and there, just to make things funny, or something like that. I think our band is like that. The kind of music that we play is the direct son of the Weavers in a sense, because it comes from that same kind of attitude. It's basically songs and it's basically stories and it's basically communication that's not a lot of hype. It's real close to being the root of it, without being the root of it.

It's somebody who can interpret the root of it for somebody who can't interpret the root of it. A lot of people can't listen to blues, the old blues guys. A lot of people can't listen to jazz, or a lot of people can't listen to orchestras, but that doesn't mean that somebody can't reinterpret that for them, and maybe even inspire them to get interested, to be able to listen to some of that.[12]

Old-timey musician John Cohen, on the role of the Weavers: I remember a conversation with Freddy Hellerman. We were at a party, and he had a crowd around him. He said, "The Weavers sold so many records and we reached so many millions of people." I said, "He's right, we [the New Lost City Ramblers] didn't do anything." Then I started thinking that there was one group that sounds like the Weavers: Peter, Paul and Mary. Hundreds of groups have picked up on the music the Weavers started.

Then recently I called the Leventhal office and Freddy picked up the phone. We started talking. I told him I have always been curious about the chord arrangements from the Weavers. I told him I thought a lot of it came from him. He told me he loves jazz. That told me a lot about the Weavers. That is worth talking about because it helped shape folk.[13]

IN ADDITION TO PETE SEEGER and Lee Hays of the Weavers, an-other crucial crossover figure from the first to the second revival was Alan Lomax. Lomax had been working with New Deal folklorists and ethno-musicologists who expanded the notion of folk music to include textual and contextual elements such as performance and style; this development brought scholarly attention to performers as well as texts. In 1942, when Alan Lomax compiled his "List of American Folk Songs on Commercial Records" for the Library of Congress, he explained that his criteria for inclu-sion were based not only on the classic concepts of folklore (anonymity, age, and nonprint transmission) but on factors such as context, authentic-ity of performance, recurrent and traditional texts or melodies, or "typi-cal contemporary deviations from rural singing and playing styles of fifty years ago."[14] His very conscious efforts to perpetuate a folk song revival had led him to collect songs and promote singers; yet it was through his redefinition of folk music to include topical song and song styling that he opened the door for the next revival and the commercial dissemination of what he considered a "democratic American art."[15]

Pete Seeger, on Alan Lomax's vision for expanding folk music's audi-ence: I used to use the term "incestuous" to describe the sectarian life in New York: the same people raising money from each other; reading each other's books and criticizing each other; having the same circle of friends. In other words, the [topical/folk music] movement was their home. I felt then, and I feel now, that this is a real weakness. Now, there are times when you do want to get together with your friends. But you know that your big job is to reach out to the unconverted. Whereas in New York, I was preaching to the converted all the time, even though I wasn't as aware of it as Alan Lomax was. Alan felt that I was still pretty limited in my outlook, I guess.

He was trying to get on radio all the time. I could agree with him. I said, "We've got to reach a broad mass of people." But I didn't want to water down the content that much. Alan was willing to water it down in order for it to get on radio. Since I didn't want to water down the content, I was much more limited in my audiences. But I didn't want to be so limited. I wanted to reach people outside New York.[16]

BESIDES HIS MANY DIRECT ROLES in bringing about the folk boom, Alan Lomax played an indirect one in 1947 when he published a song called "Tom Dooley." A decade later, the version of this song sung by the Kingston Trio—Dave Guard, Bob Shane, and Nick Reynolds—hit number one on the charts. "They were cute," recalled Gateway Singer Lou Gottlieb; "These kids really had something different. There was a magic about that act that was hard to explain."[17] Within four years, the first six of the Kingston Trio's albums had gone gold. Their arranging and copyrighting of traditional songs, however, reinvigorated debate over folk music authenticity and raised issues inherent to folk music as a commodity.

Earl Robinson, on the Kingston Trio: Well part of [the reason for the boom in folk music] is we'd been through the McCarthy period—the silent generation thing where people could not speak out, or were afraid to speak out. So they saw a way through the music to speak out, to say what had to be said. That's how I would view it. And they did say it: Kingstons didn't say it as powerfully as the Weavers did in the period before, but they said it. And they celebrated.

People want to celebrate, you know? If you start looking around, you find ways to celebrate. And I think they celebrated the fact that McCarthy was beaten back, and we were starting to open up and win, and be able to love each other. Maybe those are part of the story.[18]

Phil Ochs, on the Kingston Trio's role in the folk boom: The emergence of certain key individuals, like in an early stage the Kingston Trio, served as the gurus of folk music for the college crowd; they were the translators that took the folk idiom and wore their striped shirts and went to the college crowd and made the collegiate jokes but then sang the songs. They broached it that way. [Later] Joan Baez (having the unique and great voice) came up and served as the translator of a more traditional idiom with a very almost surreal beauty, unearthly, very ancient quality in her voice.[19]

THE SLICK QUALITY of pop-folk arrangements sounded ersatz, even saccharine, to musicians steeped in tradition. Was this envy, when veteran performers from the 1950s, such as Dave Van Ronk, earned in a year what the Kingston Trio did in a week? Was it sacrilege, when centuries-old tunes were jacked into the Top Forty? Perhaps there was such a thing as too much popularization.

Redbook described the Kingston Trio as "wholesome"; *Life* deemed their sound "bright." But criticism of the group abounded. According to folksinger Don McLean, "people like the Kingston Trio who came along later just boldly and shamelessly mined the gold of the Weavers and then later took the concert audience as well."[20]

Those who opposed popularizers like the Kingston Trio cultivated an all but religious fervor about what constituted "real" folk music. For example, musicians such as Mike Seeger and John Cohen (who would insist on calling themselves "old-timey musicians" because they were not, in their own opinion, legitimate folksingers) enacted this fervor for authenticity in both scholarship and performance. The New Lost City Ramblers, of which Seeger and Cohen were founding members, researched the original recordings they updated, sometimes even seeking out source singers; they were determinedly not pop singers like the Kingston Trio or the Brothers Four.

Happy Traum, on rejecting popularizers at the beginning of the revival: The Kingston Trio came out in the fifties, and Harry Belafonte came out in the fifties. He was the guy who was the first manifestation of folk music being put onto the marketplace. Being the snob that I was at the time, I didn't give him very much credit. I thought he was really horrible. I've changed my opinion. I didn't have any idea that he had roots in music at all. I was attracted to him because I did buy his records.

The Kingston Trio I totally disowned. I thought it was a big bunch of bullshit. I never liked those groups but it was the first indication I had that [the revival] was going to go beyond the small, interconnected groups in New York and San Francisco and Boston. This is still in the fifties and being interested in folk music was a real elite kind of thing for us. If you were on the subway and you saw a guy carrying a guitar you knew him probably. Especially in the Village.[21]

Folksinger Ramblin' Jack Elliott, on the Kingston Trio and pop music: In general I just didn't like the pop music—Frank Sinatra and Perry Como; they were the pure borscht circuit, in New York, the pop scene in Las Vegas. They wore black suits, a lot of diamonds, and shiny shoes. I hated the Kingston Trio too. They were too collegiate—button-down collar, tennis racket approach to folk music. It was a whole Pepsi generation image.[22]

REGARDLESS OF CRITICISM, the Kingston Trio is broadly seen as the group that brought mass audiences to folk music. Performing groups such as the Weavers, the Kingston Trio, the Limeliters, the aptly named Gateway Singers, and others were musical translators. Middle-class suburbanites who might never have heard a traditional singer or a hillbilly band were suddenly seeking out their songs because of what they heard on the radio. Record producer and folklorist Kenneth Goldstein argued that folk stars like the Kingston Trio "were important because they introduced people like me to folk music who could then listen to traditional singers, who could then listen to hillbilly music, which they otherwise wouldn't have."[23]

Clearly, this revival of folk music revived the anthropological debate about authenticity and authority. After all, the Kingston Trio had little access to the experience of Tom Dula, the man on whose life (and execution) their murder ballad "Tom Dooley" was based. "You can't write a good song about a dust storm unless you been in one," Woody Guthrie used to argue. "You can't write a good song about a whorehouse unless you been in one." But Sis Cunningham of the Almanac Singers justified writing and singing about subjects outside of one's own experience using the example of nuclear annihilation: "The threat of an atomic holocaust," Cunningham contended, "directly and personally involves every single human being in the world."[24] And if one waited until the explosion, few songs would be left to offer a warning.

Despite the disagreement between purists and popularizers about their music, the Kingston Trio's success expanded what people meant by "folk music" beyond anything the early folk music collectors or revivalists had imagined.

POLITICAL MUSIC DURING THE FOLK BOOM

Another link between the revival of the fifties and sixties and its predecessor of the thirties and early forties was the prevalence of topical, often highly political song.

The writing of topical and protest songs had obviously diminished during the McCarthy era. Songwriters such as Malvina Reynolds and Ernie Marrs did publish new topical songs in the "Folk Process" column of *Sing Out!*—but other would-be protest songwriters were discouraged. Some of this censorship was self-inflicted and some overt: Vern Partlow's "Old Man Atom," written the year Hiroshima and Nagasaki were bombed, contained the lines

We hold these truths to be self-evident,
that all men can be cremated equal.

Columbia Records withdrew it from distribution because of charges that it preached a peace-oriented, Communist agenda.[25]

People's songster Leo Christiansen, on improvisation in protest song: The whole tradition of American folk song, and of protest in American folk song, was the taking-over of existing, well-established folk tunes and then imposing upon them new words. The original tunes that came out of the folk song movement are few and far between. I can't think of very many outstanding songs that come from that period that were original offerings. Woody Guthrie. He was a writer and a poet and a musician all wrapped up in one.

I always felt that you needed both [a message and a good musical base]. I also reacted very strongly to any attempt to simply put polemic to music. It's like setting the [IRS] Form 1040 to music. Some nut did it. It can be done.

I can't give a person a formula. Except that we know that you need repetition. And you need the simplicity that enables people to quickly grasp the melody. And with the inspiration of the words, the combination of the two will hold it together. It has to be a perfect wedding. It's a wedding between two forms. And the music has to give. The words will never yield.

Woody Guthrie had the happy facility of being able to combine two characteristics: the ballad or the love song. The ballad is a narrative; you carry your audience along willy-nilly. Like "Tom Joad." You forget about the music; the music becomes a vehicle to hear the story. Contrast that with "Goodnight Irene." There you're caught up with the whole sentiment. And those words fit.[26]

Malvina Reynolds, on politics and the folk revival: The folk song revival wasn't a movement. It was a reflection of the politics of the time. And it was really a lot of individuals expressing themselves very well, doing a beautiful job. Comparing this to a movement, the way that in Europe they have movements of workers' songs, is just not understanding it at all.

The song is an auxiliary. The song is a tool of a movement. It can't lead a movement. If there is a change, it will be because there is a new growth of political understanding and activity in this country that will reflect the problems of the people and their hopes to change things.

And it will probably be a whole new generation of songwriters that will come forward, a little more class-conscious than these people. So to expect any political clarity even on the part of those people—Pete, or me, or whomever—is asking that two things should happen together that have no logical reason to happen together: that we're able to write songs, and we have a pretty good attitude towards world problems; and that we should be up front, politically alert, and know what's going on.[27]

IN THE EARLY SIXTIES, as the paranoia of the previous decade receded and the conflict in Vietnam escalated, topical songs made an astounding comeback. In February 1962, the first issue of *Broadside*—a mimeographed collection of five songs—came out; it included "Talking John Birch Blues," the first published song by the young singer-songwriter who called himself Bob Dylan.[28] *New York Times* critic Bob Shelton called *Broadside* "a nucleus of stimulation for putting substance into song."[29]

By the beginning of the notorious 1960s, folk music was no longer the mouthpiece of the radical Left but a popular medium in which young people expressed their rejection of the restrictive, vapid conventions of the 1950s. "Why are so many young Americans today writing and singing these songs called topical? And why are so many other Americans listening, and demanding more of them?" asked Gordon Friesen in the first issue of *Broadside*. "Phil Ochs has said of the songwriters, 'we're trying to crystallize the thoughts of young people who have stopped accepting things as they are.' "[30] Or, as Ochs sang:

> *I've got something to say,*
> *And I'm going to say it now.*

Broadside editor Gordon Friesen, on starting the magazine: Looking back on it, American writers had been so scared by the McCarthyism period, they were not writing protest songs. The fifties were more or less a vacant period. Even the Weavers, the bulk of their stuff is not political because they were working for a commercial company. They wouldn't even let them sing Woody's "So Long (It's Been Good To Know Yuh)" the way he wrote it. They rewrote that whole thing. And they made hits out of "Goodnight Irene."

[We started *Broadside*] because there was dissatisfaction with *Sing Out!* and they were not printing (or at least not printing enough) topical/protest songs as they had started out to do. You know they started in the early fifties with [Irwin] Silber and I think Betty Sanders, who were both called before HUAC....There had been a correspondence in *Sing Out!*—Malvina Reynolds thought there should be a new magazine which would print nothing but protest songs. And that had been going on for about a year. And she had been urging *Sing Out!* to print more of them. *Sing Out!* didn't do it. So she was going to start a magazine. And then she decided she couldn't do it.

So then Sis said, "Well, let's us try it."

Pete and Toshi [Seeger], they gave us some financial help. There wasn't too much involved because the first issue only cost us forty dollars. We had it mimeographed. And most of that I think went for postage.

Hays, I guess, had lost his interest in protest material. In fact, when we started *Broadside*, he sent us a letter, saying to the effect, "what fools you are. Nobody's writing protest songs in America. You won't get any material. What in the hell do you think you're going to publish?"

I guess it was more or less a coincidence that at that very time all these young people emerged like Bob Dylan, Phil Ochs, Len Chandler—I can't even remember them all anymore. These young folksingers were from all over the country.[31]

Old-timey musician Mike Seeger, on topical versus folk songs: To me the music and connection to tradition were the first and most important things: whether it worked as music. I feel in order for a topical song to work it should be good music to start with. I think some other people on the Newport [Folk Festival] Board tended to consider the person's politics before the sheer musical value.[32]

Arlo Guthrie, critiquing the leftist view of folk songs: The theory of folk is that the music has the power to move people to action concerning their own practical, everyday reality. How do you change somebody's everyday circumstance and still remain an individual? They had come to a conclusion—Pete and Lee Hays and my dad, all these guys—that the songs of the average people, normal Americans, the power of singing their songs was a way to elevate the "workin' man" to a place of authority and a place of dignity and a place of respect. All of that combined. That was a good theory and they tested it out with the books that were generally called "Struggle" or something like that. As good as the theory was, it doesn't mean that everybody can make you feel, in the audience, as if you were all in it together.

I learned all kinds of little things that had to do with giving people enough; not making them necessarily sing along with you, but have you sing along with them, together. It *seems* like the same thing. There are a lot of people that get up there and sing their songs and if the audience sings along, that's great. It's not something that's unique to folk, there's probably a dozen glam-rock singers who understand the same principle. When you get a couple hundred thousand kids out there waving lighters in the air—they're all in it together. How do you keep that and have that feeling and also sing a song that's more than in the key of me.

When you combine all those things, it's very powerful.[33]

Mary Travers of Peter, Paul and Mary, on how timelessness affects political songs: [We recorded "If I Had a Hammer" because of] the whole civil rights thing. It seemed so very, very appropriate. It's hard to find good songs that have social connotations.... We also sang "Blowin' in the Wind." That for instance is a perfect example of a perfect song. It will always be relevant no matter what the problem is because it is ambiguous enough. It says there is a problem. It doesn't say what the problem is. It basically deals with the fact that there is an issue at hand, and if you're singing it at a moment when there is an issue everybody knows what the issue is.[34]

Pete Seeger, on opposition to politics in folk song: Many of the folk song lovers were actually rather outraged by Alan's and my inclusion of so many left-wing sentiments. Alan's father was outraged. When Alan introduced the Golden Gate Quartet and Lead Belly and Josh White in the Coolidge Auditorium of the Library of Congress for the program of Southern Negro Folk Music, he gave it a very hard-hitting analysis. His father turned beet red listening to his upstart of a son. During intermission he went up to him and said, "Alan, you're a disgrace to the South!" And he stomped off.

[Philanthropist] Lulabelle Pitts agreed to be one of the sponsors of People's Songs in '46; three or four months later, when she heard the kinds of songs I was singing, she angrily wrote in, resigning. She said, "I will not be part of any Communist front."[35]

Arlo Guthrie, on topical song: Basically, it's looking at reality, pointing out parts of it that are so absurd, yet true, that they make you laugh at the thing you fear the most. I think that's the strength of the people we're talking about. That's what they have to do to survive. They have to be able to laugh at the thing they fear the most, in a good-humored sense of way.[36]

FOLK MUSIC VENUES AND PROMOTION

Folk clubs sprouted like mushrooms in the early 1960s: the hungry i and the Purple Onion in San Francisco, Club 47 in Boston, the Gate of Horn in Chicago, Gerdes Folk City, the Bitter End, Café Wha? and the Gaslight in New York. Los Angeles had coffeehouses, too: the Unicorn and McCabe's. This revival did not originate in the hollows of Appalachia or with the chain gangs of the Deep South but in cities, particularly in the Northeast, and then it radiated out, via radio and record sales, to the rest of the nation.

As clubs, coffeehouses, and folk music radio programing proliferated across the United States, folk magazines multiplied: *Sing Out!* and *Broadside* were joined by *Caravan* and the *Little Sandy Review.* All the while, would-be folksingers were trickling in to Greenwich Village, hanging out at the Folklore Center, and joining the open-air performances in New York's Washington Square, hoping to land a booking at one of the clubs and, eventually, a record contract with Folkways, Vanguard, Elektra, or Columbia Records.

Promoter Izzy Young, on opening the Folklore Center in Greenwich Village: I opened up my store in 1957 in the Village, and it was sort of a last-ditch maneuver with my life. I didn't know what I was going to do with my life.

Who came into the Folklore Center in Greenwich Village? Everybody. There was a secondhand bookshop there. I was getting in when everything was cheap, and it wasn't that commercial yet. I sold the only insurance policy I had and got a thousand dollars. I paid that for the store and started selling the records that were coming out at that time. Stinson records, Elektra records, and Folkways records. Shortly after that, everything was going from ten-inch to twelve-inch just when I got in, so I made a killing buying these ten-inch records for fifty cents and selling them for a dollar. I would buy a hundred dollars' worth and then come back and buy another batch.

The American Square Dance Group: that was completely forgotten at the time. People's Artists was forgotten, and *Sing Out!* was struggling. There was a need for my store. There was no place else for people in the folk movement to appear.

So, innocently enough, I open this store, March '57, in the Village. It gets a lot of attention. I was selling old, musty books on folklore from my mail-order business. No one in the Village could possibly be interested in books on the history of John Henry, the old sea songs from New England, Texas folk songs, the whole shebang from these university presses. No one could possibly be interested, except individuals. Burl Ives and just a few other individuals bought books from me. I had one wall that was basically scholarly studies. A lot of songbooks. Pete Seeger's, Jerry Silverman's. At the time it wasn't "acoustic guitar," it was just "guitar." I was selling some jazz. I was selling *Sing Out!*

The night my store opened there was a picture in the *Village Voice*, literally hundreds of people came in. I never sold very much. I could hardly ever make a living. It was a gathering place.

The Folklore Center. I picked the name. I remember talking to some of my friends about that. Everyone thought that was the wrong name. I think Pete Seeger at the time said it should be called Folk Music Center or Folk Dance Center, but I felt under the strict term "folklore," I had complete freedom. I could do whatever I wanted.[37]

Michael Cooney, on the superficiality of the folk scene: When I first got to New York, I did get invited to a get-together at Tom Paxton's house with all these people, Phil Ochs and Carolyn Hestor and some others talking about going down to help the miners in Harlan County, Kentucky.

Phil Ochs once wrote an article I think for *Broadside* of New York about getting your "folk points" by going to Harlan County or Mississippi or whatever and it seemed like they were all jostling each other for folk points, and I was really put off by the whole scene and so I never hung out with it.[38]

Izzy Young, on promoting folksingers: June '57, Al Grossman calls me one day; I didn't even know who he was. He said, "Listen. Peggy Seeger's at the Gate of Horn in Chicago. How about putting on a concert with her?"

I started putting on concerts with people like Reverend Gary Davis, Brownie McGhee, Sonny Terry; and I put on a tremendous series of concerts. All the young, up-and-coming folksingers. I remember we became the center of information. Everyone can meet anyone through me almost instantly.

I became a noncommercial step in a commercial culture. Everybody was on the make except me. The only thing I was interested in was meeting people. I became the place where everyone could be heard. I had a little newsletter and three or four hundred subscribers. I could never make money on those concerts. Now I look back and realize that no one could make money on those concerts. The singers could not make a living on my terms, my idealistic terms. I put on more than a thousand concerts without a contract.

I worked out my own rules. A traditional singer would get a guarantee. A city singer, John Cohen, Mike Seeger, I was like "Fuck it. He's in a commercial boat." I was more concerned about the traditional singers; they got a one-hundred-dollar or seventy-five-dollar guarantee.

The audience was a group of people. Most of them didn't know about People's Songs. None of them knew about the American Square Dance Group. Now I would say it was a bunch of clean, scrubbed middle-class kids that probably went to private schools, like Little Red School House. Maybe half of them came from Brooklyn College like myself. I can't say that there were many ordinary working people coming to my concerts.[39]

Gordon Friesen, on finding "Woody's Children": Pete and Toshi [Seeger] also introduced us to Gil Turner who at that time was emcee at Gerdes Folk City, where, remember, young folksingers in the folk medium were called "Woody's Children." When they hit New York, they would go to Gerdes Folk City, and Turner would bring them up to our apartment. He would audition them if they wanted to do a gig there. In that course of events he brought up Bob Dylan, who was just a kid in Minnesota....

It was at *Broadside*. We were living on 104th Street in the low-income project. We had a tape we made at that time, which we turned into a record at *Broadside*, in which Pete questions Dylan. He'd met him almost for the first time and that was in '62 and Dylan already starts his career of put-ons: Pete asked him, "Where were you born?" and Dylan said, "In Albuquerque, New Mexico." That's Dylan.

Oh, I'm sure Pete had heard of Dylan. There is the story that when Dylan first came to New York, he went to Folkways and to *Sing Out!* and they both threw him out. They thought he was some snotty Jewish kid trying to be something. Pete was connected with both of those institutions. Pete encouraged Dylan greatly.

Well, [at the magazine] we'd been having regular monthly sessions [at the Village Gate]—sort of a cooperative. We'd have a date set, and Pete would then come and sing new songs and sort of pass judgment on them. Pete's original judgment of Dylan was that he thought he was *way* up there—that he was a great young singer and a great young songwriter. Of course he was writing very strong protest songs in that period. We've got some of that on tapes.

Gil Turner would generally bring Dylan. In fact, in later years Dylan gave an interview to some newspaper in which he said: "No one else was interested in me—there was this place in Greenwich Village called *Broadside* which printed my stuff." So apparently when Dylan was up on 104th Street, he thought he was still in Greenwich Village![40]

Izzy Young, on promoting an unknown Bob Dylan: One day, Bob Dylan walks into the store and introduces himself. He starts playing songs for me and uses my typewriter. I thought he was great. I had never been turned on by anyone like that. I heard his songs, and I told him that his were the first songs written in the folk song genre that took into account modern psychological currents and feelings.

He looked soft. Not a strong personality. Very ordinary clothes. Might even say like a kid. When I met interesting people in the store I started writing in my notebook about it. He told me a story and I bought it hook, line, and sinker. He's telling me he's meeting Arvella Gray, this singer here and this singer there. Later I understand he had never met any of these people. He was telling me about California, and later I realize he wasn't there at all. He's almost pushing me to write it all down. I tell him I want to manage him. He said he didn't know what he was doing. I realize later that Al Grossman had let him loose in the Village. He was hanging around and playing with everyone. He was *already* managed.

Then I did something that I do very rarely in my life. I took somebody and said I wanted to push someone. I really wanted to be part of a historical process. I took him to Oscar Brand and recorded him. That session was really lousy. Dylan started putting on this bumbling voice, and I was embarrassed.

I take Bob Dylan to Moe Asch who by this time is my idol. He said no. Then I brought him to Vanguard Records and they turned him down flat.

Then I took him to Elektra and I introduced him to Jac Holzman. In other words, me with my uneconomic position, I still could just call up anybody and walk in. Well, Jac Holzman turns him down....

I say, "Let's put on a concert." The agreement in this case was unusual because all the other concerts were half the gate. I had to get seventy-five, one hundred people to break even. The artists would always make more money than me. The audience was paying two dollars. I felt it was an honest situation. Instead of putting on at the Seventh Avenue South Theater, I said we would put it on at the Carnegie Recital Hall. I had only put on three concerts there.

Our agreement was that we would share the gate after expenses. I printed a program, which cost me forty dollars to print. I did that rather than mimeograph. Nobody was there. None of the pros, none of the half-pros, none of the people from the recording companies. It was just Bob Dylan and me. As the history books say now, only fifty-two people came, so it was a total loss. And the concert, as far as I'm concerned, was a total mess. He was trying to be relaxed and he was really just imitating Jack Elliott. It was very boring. We lost money and I gave him twenty dollars.[41]

Happy Traum, on first hearing "Blowin' in the Wind": We were in New York with the New World Singers around '62 in the basement dressing room. Gil Turner had heard the song before. He was one of the founders of the group. He said, "Hey Bob. I heard you were working on a song the other day. Why don't you play it for us?"

He said, "Sure" and pulled out his guitar and sang "Blowin' in the Wind." It blew us away. I can visualize the moment.

We went into the studio, the first time I was ever in a recording studio, and made a record called *Broadside*. It was the first volume we did with Pete Seeger and Phil Ochs and Bob Dylan [listed as Blind Boy Grunt] and one or two other people. We did the first recorded version.

After making that record for Moe Asch, the New World Singers were signed by Atlantic Records. And Ahmet Ertegun, who was one of the geniuses of American popular music who was responsible for Ray Charles and Aretha Franklin and others, took an interest in us. It was quite unsuccessful for a number of reasons. We sang him "Blowin' in the Wind" and told him we thought it would be a great single. He listened to the song very thoughtfully and he said, "It's a great song but you have to change the words and make it a love song or it will never sell."

Of course we as folk music purists were appalled and never brought it up again. It was probably one of the only times he was embarrassed by a decision like that because not long after Peter, Paul and Mary had the enormous success with it. I don't want to imply we would have had the success that Peter, Paul and Mary had because they brought their own thing to that song.[42]

Gordon Friesen, on record companies signing up singers: These record companies saw a demand for this kind of music. I guess Bob Dylan's sudden rocket-like rise carried that. So they began making LPs. Seeger got a contract with Columbia. I think it was a part of the rise of Dylan; that they were looking for more material that had now become marketable. In fact, [Phil] Ochs, after several records by Elektra, Columbia offered him a contract. He didn't take it because he said they'd already got enough folksingers. They'd got Seeger and they'd got Dylan.[43]

Phil Ochs, on the record companies Elektra, Vanguard, A & M, and Folkways: Elektra records were the only company who would record me when I came out, therefore I have great respect for them, because they would put out controversial records, whereas Vanguard was very snobbish and very standoffish in their whole outlook. Because Vanguard had Baez and the Weavers, they went through their arrogance thing. Everyone has gone through their arrogance number in some form. Now, I left Elektra after three albums and went with A & M, on the West Coast, which is super commercial and which is totally removed from the New York scene. To me, A & M has been like an island away from this jungle.

Let's put it this way: Folkways existed and Vanguard existed, but I look back at Folkways with great respect because Folkways did in fact document a lot of vitally important music, and overall Moe Asch has to emerge a great man, in spite of all his failings. He did the important things, ultimately the moral things; he preserved a lot of music and I think he should be able to look back at everything as a total victory.

[The Solomon brothers at] Vanguard step out as one extension away from it and say, "Well, we have the Weavers; we'll do what Moe Asch did but we're a lot hipper than him, so we'll sell it better and still keep our standards up and still put out classical music." Classical music is like a shield against commercialism, it seems. They did that and they did it beautifully. And they stumbled on Baez, and they put out the first two Joan Baez albums which were great and were valid. So everybody who came to New York wanted to be on Vanguard. Dylan wanted to be on. I wanted to be on. And Vanguard, being incredibly falsely aristocratic—because being aristocratic means that you really must have the knowledge and breeding and education to do that. Vanguard really doesn't have that. They just had success, and a certain amount of knowledge. So they looked down their nose at everybody and were totally patronizing toward everybody.

So Elektra, which had been around, slightly one step out again on a more commercial level, was sitting there. And they got other people, Judy Collins and so forth, and so at a certain point, Elektra passed Vanguard. At a certain point, Vanguard was so much locked in the shell of success, at their level, that they froze and got very old very fast and died, died right in their successful tracks. So, Elektra came in and literally copped the scene around '63. Jac Holzman copped the scene from Maynard Solomon in New York.[44]

THE NEWPORT FOLK FESTIVAL

Vanguard Records was best known in the folk boom for issuing live recordings of the Newport Folk Festival. Starting in 1959 and continuing into the twenty-first century (in spite of a very long hiatus), the Newport Folk

Festival has been both a representation and product of the popularity of folk music in the United States. In its first three years, guitar sales increased 500 percent, and in folk music's heyday of the midsixties, the Newport Folk Festival staged pinnacle folk music popularizers (a.k.a. citybillies) such as Bob Dylan and Joan Baez (whose career was more or less launched at Newport) alongside protest groups like the Freedom Singers and traditional acts like Doc Watson and Maybelle Carter.[45] For the increasing numbers of folk aficionados, the Newport Festival became a mecca. For those who concerned themselves with defining and shaping folk music, Newport became a hall of contention, echoing earlier conflicts about folk music.

Folklorist Archie Green, on Newport: One of the conflicts at Newport was whether Newport should just be a staging ground for Dylan, Baez, for Peter, Paul and Mary—for the stars. One of the inner conflicts at Newport was what to do about traditional performers; with Glenn Ohrlin, with Sarah Gunning, with Robert Pete Williams.

One of the rationales was this: if you bring the stars and get the mass audiences, they will hear the traditional performers. You would help educate great numbers of youngsters to traditional performers.

At the evening concerts, there was always bedlam because someone would bring a traditional performer on who was hoarse or atonal or lacking in musicality or whatever and the hip audience and the freak audience would go mad; and they would scream for Dylan or Baez. This was always embarrassing to people like Mike Seeger who tried to push the traditional performers.

There were many responses. One was to just have small, traditional festivals. Don't try to have Sarah Gunning and Joan Baez on the same platform. That was never resolved. Newport just went until it went broke or went out of fashion. The Seegers—Pete and Toshi and Mike—put a lot of energy and effort into Newport....

I think Pete was very active at the beginning of Newport and Mike at the end. Mike was dedicated to traditional performance at every level. He issued recordings. He brought people on tour. He helped edit songbooks that were faithful in transcription.

The hard question is still the question of mass culture and popularization. Because Mike was a purist in this regard. If Mike had a choice between a large audience screaming to hear Dylan and disrespectful to Dorsey Dixon on the one hand—and a small respectful audience for Dorsey Dixon, he would take the second.[46]

Happy Traum, on the gap between the traditional and the popular at Newport: That was a major problem. There was always the balance between having the big names that would bring in all the people and the people who were really the folks that should be featured. I can remember distinctly in '68—the first time I played at that festival—the old guy who played the banjo. No one was listening to this guy. There must have been thirty thousand people in this field and Joan Baez or Joni Mitchell or someone had played. On comes this guy whom I really wanted to hear. Suddenly, no one was listening. He was very upset.[47]

Pete Seeger, rethinking Newport's balance of traditional singers and citybillies: One of the things I think I would do is bring more of the original singers out…and not have people like me trying to sing them for them. And maybe they aren't such fabulous singers, but I like to get them out.... Now, it's hard at a folk festival. Newport tried, but we were only just learning how to present these workshops right. I remember one day, in Newport, hearing Henry Crow Dog singing in his high clear voice, and it just made everything else at Newport pale by comparison. I mean, this was music that was born out under the sun. And there was grass underfoot and sun overhead, and there was this Sioux Indian song, it was perfect.[48]

COMMERCIALISM: FOLKSTARDOM AND PARADOX

In 1955, early chronicler of folk music Russell Ames predicted that "perhaps 'folk' song will not long be an accurate name for the roving, changing, people's songs of the atomic age. But if we listen for what is honest, truthful, and human, in the songs being made today, we need not worry much about the name we attach to them."[49] But people did worry about the name attached; throughout the folk boom of the fifties and sixties, as folk music became increasingly eclectic, concerns about authenticity and cultural authority persisted.

"From the beginning of my years as a performer there had been heated squabbles among singers of folk songs," recalls folksinger Ellen Stekert. "I watched people put one another down or approve of a performance using charged (but never defined) terms such as 'authentic,' 'popular,' or 'ethnic.'"[50] "Folk music" meant "urban folk" to those trying to distinguish this from the more exclusively traditional music from which it evolved. The Weavers sang folk songs backed up by orchestras; the Kingston Trio had little in common with the Carter Family. As folk music began to make real money and be heard on the airwaves, folk music purists found themselves swimming upstream.

That a commercial market had now formed for traditional music, rearranged and spiced up, was undeniable. The market orientation of folk music in the second revival might in fact be its defining characteristic. The first revival brought collectors and texts to the fore; the second brought out hits and stars, via mediated popular culture. In the 1960s, the problem became one of distinguishing between three primary groupings: folksingers, who sang in a traditional style songs they learned in a mostly traditional context; performers of folk songs, such as John Cohen or Pete Seeger, who were sometimes scholars of ethnomusicology and skilled at musical adaptation; and commercial entertainers, musicians who were mining the country's treasury of old songs in that brief period when folk topped the charts.

Purists collected, persevered, and even achieved success they may not have been seeking—the New Lost City Ramblers, for example, played "old-timey" music, refusing to polish or update the rustic styles they imitated; yet they proved to be one of the most enduring bands of the revival.

Mike Seeger, on the New Lost City Ramblers' relationship with commercial success: We never reached for it. In the early sixties, people said we were going to be the next commercial thing, and why didn't we just add a bass and polish up a little bit here, maybe try to get a commercial or two, and go that route. I just say, "Well, you live that way, you die that way." And I didn't want to live that way or die that way. So, I just never thought there's any sense in trying to reach for a mass market, because all you do is try to sound more and more like everybody else. And do violence to the music to boot....

From the very start [I've been asked to play popular folk songs]. People were familiar with the Weavers then. Some people asked me to sing Burl Ives or the Kingston Trio. More recently, the John Denver music. Yes, people ask for that all the time. People don't differentiate; they don't think.[51]

John Cohen, on the mission of the New Lost City Ramblers: First of all we didn't have a big following. We didn't even look for a following initially. One of the things we were doing was hammering out this philosophy....In a strange way we felt there was a need that other people didn't, the need to be conscious of the rich sources for this music. Music that wasn't translated in city terms. Then we had a mission. I laugh when I think about *Sing Out!* writing an article on us, "Crusaders for old-time music." I never thought of the word "crusaders" or thought of us as being on a crusade. We rose to the occasion in a way. That's very different from the Kingston Trio, Limeliters, or the Weavers.[52]

Archie Green, on making folk music palatable to mainstream audiences: Folk style in its pure form, it's valuable; it's treasured because it is the people's music. One might even say it's the purest form of people's music. It's genuinely the music of rural people, of poor people, of exploited people, of miners. In that sense it's platonic. But it's also music that isn't in the mainstream, that is difficult for many people to assimilate. So that Pete [Seeger], say, in his presentation of an Appalachian song will make sometimes subtle and sometimes dramatic changes in style to make the music palatable to large numbers of people.

At one level pop music is democratic and open and the music of the majority of our people. But at another level it contradicts or cheapens the pure folk music of the separate groups who make up society. And I think Pete has struggled with his feeling about pop music. He mostly acts it out by performance. In performance, he has a tendency to flatten out, to even out, to popularize...he doesn't come out of folk culture but functionally he's close to Bob Wills and Elvis Presley and Louis Armstrong, people who have helped to broaden and popularize folk music.[53]

John Cohen, on playing other people's music: I remember even into the sixties that Pete in the reviews of his concerts would often be referred to as "only a bridesmaid, never a bride." (I think it's a statement of Bob Shelton [*New York Times* folk music critic].) [The Seegers] always present other people's music and introduce other people, never asserting themselves. In the process, all the others have died away and, for instance, Pete sounds like Pete. He always sounded like Pete, but people weren't aware of that because he was so busy pointing to other people. It's an interesting phenomenon. It's not just for Pete. I think it's endemic with the people we're talking about who were not trying to assert themselves as the central artist, the creator. They're drawing your attention to other people who have inspired them and in the process they're coming up with their own unique identity.[54]

Folksinger Peggy Seeger, on class consciousness in traditional folk music: One of the best ways I think I can put it is; do you know the song "The Ballad of the Carpenter"?

> *Jesus was a working man, a hero you shall hear.*
> *Born in the slums of Bethlehem, at the turning of the year.*

That's a song that Ewan [MacColl] made up and he made it up for a Christmas program in England in 1953, '54. It's full of terms like "working man," "working masses." True, they are jargon words; but they are words which, in England, you are proud of, if you are working class. There's a tremendous sense of belonging to the class that makes the wealth of the country.

Phil Ochs sang this song—or was it Tom Paxton?—recorded it and he excised every single reference to working class, to violence...the song was about the death of Jesus Christ. I could sing it to you and you would see exactly what would be excised by a middle-class person who feels that these words are too loaded and therefore takes them out. When you do that the song doesn't mean anything anymore. The song was made out of anger; it was made out of the experience of people who live in poverty, who live without, who live on the edge of death, starvation, and we middle-class people, we don't understand this. We may have an intellectual concept of it, but it's not gut.

It's as if you were taking Beethoven, and performing it on a bongo drum and an electric guitar and two flutes, a quartet. It's no longer Beethoven. And it's the same way when you take one of these working-class songs and you perform it in a middle-class manner, with middle-class ethics, middle-class values, middle-class—well, I won't say tone of voice because we don't have a tone of voice; but without that working-class anger, the song changes. It doesn't become better or worse, it just loses its intention. This is what has happened with a lot of the songs that a lot of revival singers sing.[55]

Charles Seeger, on "low-grade" folk music: Now, people like Peggy [Seeger] and Ewan [MacColl] think that Peter's songs are sometimes pretty low grade. He shouldn't sing them; they're too far from the ballads. They will tolerate a watering down of the ballad style just so far and then they begin to draw the line. It's pandering. It's debauching. . . . And a lot of people can't stand for that.[56]

Peggy Seeger, on the cultural dilution of folk songs: Pete [Seeger] was under some congressional litigation and came over [to England]. Now how he got over there at that point. I don't know. But he came over and did something in the Albert Hall, and Ewan [MacColl] helped to organize that. I wasn't there. Ewan just said that he didn't find it very interesting singing. He said it was very interesting watching the audience. Ewan said it frightened him. He says, "You could have gotten that audience to do anything." He did find that the audience wanted to hear only songs they could sing to, clap to, or that they knew already.

This is a precept that goes entirely counter to the revival that's happening in England now. The attempt is not to make a whole number of favorite songs, but have each area celebrate the songs that come from that area and to delve more and more into the folklore of the area until they have a kind of identity that keeps that area's songs not pure, but just distinctive.

Once you have a song from Scotland, like "I'm a Rover and Seldom Sober" being sung in Tanzania it tends to lose its Scotchness. Purity's the wrong word; it tends to lose its internal truth as a song.[57]

John Cohen, on the difference between revivalist and traditional musicians: One of the first serious talks I had with Woody Guthrie was about

Pete Seeger. I asked him how he saw the difference between what Pete Seeger does and Earl Scruggs. He said that there's a little valley and two musicians that live there and they play together their whole life. And that's what they know. But Pete, he can play anything. That was Woody's view of Pete.[58]

Pete Seeger, on the value of popularizers: [When] Lead Belly sang, people couldn't understand his words. So, I sing them and they can understand them; this was the function of the Weavers and to a certain extent the Kingston Trio and perhaps even of the Brothers Four. I think I draw the line at the *Hootenanny Show*. I don't think that was necessary. I don't know.

In the long run, you have to sing your own songs. You can be given assistance in learning how to sing your own songs. But I think one of the great musical achievements of this decade is David Bromberg: [at first] he was singing self-humorous songs: "How can a Jewish boy from Brooklyn sing the blues?" Now he knows damn well what he can do and he's doing it beautifully. He doesn't mind singing and playing an Irish song or a Jewish song. He does it. He's David Bromberg; he's himself.

This is why I've joked all the time. I've said, "Of course I'm not authentic—all I can be is authentically myself. That's all anybody can be in this world."[59]

Singer-songwriter Si Kahn, on the relation between the revivals and roots of folk music: I believe that because of Mike and Pete Seeger more people have been led back to the roots music than otherwise would have. Pete has always said, "go back and listen to the original."

So for everyone who sings "lay down your head Tom Dooley" the way the Kingston Trio did it, there is probably as many who went back and found Frank Profitt, as far as we know, the earliest version recorded, and sing it exactly the way he does. So revivalism circles back to the roots and my guess is the music will survive all this.[60]

Mary Travers, on the connectedness of the folk music community: I first heard ["If I Had a Hammer"] sung by the Weavers in concert when I was a teenager, in the early fifties. I'd been very involved in folk music as a hobby. I thought it was a wonderful song and they sang it, I thought, very excitingly. It had a good message. It's a very direct song. It's a song about brotherhood. It's about a community of caring, and vocalizing of caring. And I think for the Weavers (as for Peter, Paul and Mary) it was a song that was like a tool. It was literally "If I Had a Hammer" in the sense that the song became The Hammer and The Bell and The Song. Tools to talk about caring. I think that that is the essence of most folk performers' background. That music can bind a community together....

For me, folk music was always a very inclusive form of music as opposed to exclusive. You didn't have to sing well. You didn't have to play well. You just had to come on with a lot of enthusiasm. It was a very giving form of music in that way. You'd go to Washington Square Park and sing and nobody really cared how well you played. There were always a couple of technocrats. Eric Weisberg was always very concerned that he played the "Foggy Mountain Breakdown" best and more cleanly.[61]

Pete Seeger, on definitions of "folksinger" during the second revival: If Woody [Guthrie]'s a folksinger, Tom [Paxton]'s a folksinger. I would say that right up front: "No two people really agree on what folksinger is. Let's see if we can find some kind of a midway course." This is the folk song revival.[62]

THE NEW, URBAN AUDIENCES attracted to folk music may not have been as nuanced in their tastes as the early collectors or as purist performers would have them be; but their numbers and their enthusiasm took the music world by surprise, catapulting Joan Baez with guitar and bare feet to the cover of *Time* in November 1962. Bob Dylan was hailed as the voice of his generation. This success was paradoxical; could a folksinger be a "star"?

To the thirteen thousand cheering fans that summer of 1963, Dylan certainly was a star. But for folk music performers, the contradiction between self-seeking commercial success and disinterested promotion of traditional culture had never been sharper. The singer of folk songs Sam Hinton articulated this dilemma:

> A professional entertainer who allows himself to become known as a singer of folk songs is bound to have trouble with his conscience—provided, of course, that he possesses one. As a performing artist, he will pride himself on timing and other techniques designed to keep the audience in his control; these techniques often require slight changes to be made in his songs. On the other hand, his respect for genuine folklore reminds him that these changes, and these techniques, may give the audience a false picture of folk music.[63]

The dedicated amateurism and down-home styles carried over from the first revival was fading in favor of careerism. Now the country was awash in folk music popularizers. Traditionalists castigated entertainers for having commercialized what was thought to be properly the product of *des Volkes*, but once begun, there was no stopping this boom.

Charles Seeger, on the historical precedents for commercial folk music: [Folk revivalists] seized upon the potential in the culture to advance their social-political-cultural feeling of change, gradual for some people, abrupt for others. It is a great, mass movement. It was a real renaissance for music in Western culture. Western culture had really suppressed any kind of music that tried to push culture in some direction. Music was concert music. The rest of it was bad, and people don't know it, but we just won't encourage them to make it.

Then business came along, found they could make money out of it, from about the early part of the nineteenth century with the hymns, which were popular music and around in the 1840s and '50s with the popular, minstrel show, and the popular songs of Stephen Foster and like that. So that it gradually had a momentum, using the vernacular for making money.

Now the dialect of folk music was mostly forgotten or repressed in the city, but it was still existing in the country, and then this revival comes along and so many people buy the records of the revival. Commercial success meant that the music...the people could make for themselves became profitable. So people made music in that style. And it is a regular music renaissance. It's fantastic, and all to my thinking, one of the best things that's happened. In the world *now*, what is the great music? American music.[64]

Mary Travers, on the surprise of success: We never thought of any songs as being hits. Nobody was more surprised that we were fashionable to begin with, than us. We were majorly amused in the beginning because it just was ridiculous. Whoever would have thought? That in itself was bizarre. Then on top of it—to be able to say some of the [political] things, Peter [Yarrow] and I had long been concerned about, and be accepted![65]

Ramblin' Jack Elliott, on the process of commercializing folk music: I know that when I hear Judy Collins singing, I feel like I can see [producer] Harold Leventhal standing in the background: "Now sing one for the people out in Long Island." Judy doesn't sound like a Colorado girl; she's been New York-ized. That's Harold's commercialization of folk music. I think it was a smart way to get folk music on the map, to get people earning money who were singing folk music. Years ago people weren't ready for raw folk music.[66]

Folksinger Judy Collins, on the unpredictability of commercial success: There are a lot of people like [Joan] Baez and Joni Mitchell and Jackson Browne. A lot of these people who are identified with this movement and have come along with it haven't ever had a hit record. (I mean singles.) They've had records, long-playing records which were terrific successes. I haven't really had hit singles, I mean I've had a couple of nice things that helped a lot. But I think somewhere in there, there's a grain of truth about fear of commerciality. And I don't even know what I mean when I say it, because record companies don't know. I mean they say one thing is commercial and one thing isn't; the next thing you know, Dylan's got a hit with the song that's seven minutes long. I mean, they don't know.[67]

Malvina Reynolds, on the two sides to commercial success: "Commercial," that's a funny word. You mean because people like someone and will buy his albums? The company is just a purveyor; and sometimes we have to battle our way through that thing, because it doesn't realize the people like it. The only reason we're interested in the fact that it will sell is that people get to hear our stuff.

So there are two sides to this commercial thing. We have to reach those millions of people out there. We want to, we know they want it, and the company happens to be the machine. The company won't do it unless they can make money, but they can make money because the people out there like what we do. Now the company will try to warp what we do because they think they know better than we do what the people want. Many times they're wrong.

It's not as simple as commercial versus noncommercial. To become a big commercial property, will you be cut off at the roots from the very thing that made you special? You become surrounded by this complex of grabbing people.[68]

Phil Ochs, on the destructive effects of manufacturing success: Now in the sixties, the folk music came and colored everything toward a more pure and toward a more basic approach. Which evolved into folk-rock and up to [Bob Dylan's] "Desolation Row," where a truly brilliant writer was involved with all these different crosscurrents, including Buddy Holly and so forth, and it all came together in his *Bringing It All Back Home* [1965], or *Highway 61* [1965]. It got together with the communication of very lucid ideas and beautiful imagery allied to a pop music or folk music.... What's happened since then is so ugly; I mean it's hard for the mind to fathom. How could you take a cast of characters so exciting and so scintillating and so fantastically creative, and how could you just destroy them? But it happened.[69]

Happy Traum, on rationalizing commercialization and folk music: Once people start making music for a living, it doesn't matter if it's folk music or rock or jazz, you strive for commercial success because that's the way you eat. It satisfies many things including egotistical things. One of the reasons people become performers is for ego. I don't really differentiate folksingers from anybody else. As much as there was this myth of the

Woody Guthrie type of people who are spurning all commercial gain and putting down the wealthy and all these stories of the folk heroes walking out of lucrative jobs; I feel that musicians make music first of all, and they make music to make money out of it as well.[70]

Arlo Guthrie, on the risks of commercializing folk music: We saw a separation between what was exciting and new and speaking to everybody; and...the old traditional cultural habits. I remember even Pete [Seeger] himself was very concerned about country music, which before it was country music was country-western, and before it was country-western it was country and western. Before it was western, it was hillbilly and western, et cetera. It goes back...there were all these different styles. I remember Pete saying to me years ago: "Well, you know one of the problems is that you go to Houston and turn on the radio and you hear the same kind of music that you hear in Atlanta and the same kind of music you hear in Atlanta, you hear in Oshkosh."

In other words, the local idioms were dying out because record companies and radio stations were playing the same kind of music. To some extent, Pete was right in being concerned about that, but I think other people were overconcerned, thought it was all going to die and that's not what you call faith in people's music for sure. People who had been proclaiming faith in people's music didn't have any anymore.[71]

EARLY REVIVALISTS HAD UNCOVERED, studied, and imitated folk music styles and played them back to the people from whom these styles had originated. The next generation of revivalists translated—or transformed—folk music for mainstream music listeners. Most had not worked in coal mines or survived the Dust Bowl, but plenty of folk enthusiasts wanted to experience the "folk" (usually referring to an imagined rural worker) of the music. So this folk music revival became associated with rough-hewn fashions; it evolved as a cultural aesthetic as well as a musical genre: Seeger drove a VW bug and lived in a cabin he'd built with friends and family. Bob Dylan channeled Woody Guthrie in old dungarees. Joan Baez became famous for performing in bare feet. And their fans followed suit.

Charles Seeger, on the folk aesthetic of the 1960s: It goes with the rough clothes. Later on in the sixties, all the young people began to wear patched overalls. But in those old days, you wore patched overalls, because your overalls gave out and your wife put patches on them. You didn't buy them patched! Or worn. So [folk musicians] came by a lot of the affectations of the sixties by force of necessity in the forties.[72]

Judy Collins, on the cultural aesthetics of folk music: It used to be, in the sixties, that there was a certain kind of attitude that money and the outward trappings of success were not something that should easily be confessed to. I remember the funny story about Joanie Baez, when she had a lot of money, walking into a car showroom (now this may be hearsay, because I don't think I ever asked her if this was true)—the idea of having the cash for something big and being barefoot. There was a contradiction between success, making money, but not wanting to use it or flaunt it in the way that society had done so much of before.

The folk music revival in the sixties period had a lot to do with confronting power and wealth as used in showy ways. And I think one of the essential ingredients was the struggle. Youth struggling against power. Young people confronting middle-class wealth, middle-class standards, middle-class acceptable modes of behavior.[73]

JUST AS IN THE FORTIES, when black leather jackets for men and leotards for women signaled proletarianism, folk music in the sixties was about more than style. And like the updraft of a fire, shooting out sparks, the second folk music revival coincided with and ignited that decade's social movements. Folk music's balancing act between tradition and popularity and its heyday in popular culture could not last; its relevance was its topicality, and the newly inclusive notion of folk music was nothing if not topical: ban the bomb, march for freedom, protest a stealth war over in Southeast Asia—there were songs for every cause. "We are the folk-song army," mathematician and nightclub satirist Tom Lehrer would sing on TV, "every one of us cares. We don't like poverty, war, or injustice—unlike the rest of you squares.... ready, aim, sing!"[74]

The best was yet to come for true believers in the folk process: the folk making up their own protest songs, from music they had sung all their lives, as they sat-in, ate-in, taught-in, and in every other way found their way into remembering and asserting their civil rights.

MOVEMENT MUSIC

IN URBAN COFFEEHOUSES and on the radio were not the only places where folk music could be heard by the late 1950s and 1960s. As the nation regained the democratic voice long censored during the period of the anti-Communist excesses, people were singing out loud everywhere: in jails, in lecture halls, in the street. And there were plenty of causes, but none so immediate, authentic, and musical as civil rights. On the road to Selma and in segregated bus stations, and in churches across the South, the sounds of freedom rang out.

Unlike earlier singing movements, such as the Almanacs' union singing and People's Songs' work on the picket lines, the civil rights movement's musicians did not bring in music from outside activist communities (except to generate publicity for particular protest events). Civil rights song burst out of the churches that had nourished a community of Sunday singers with a gospel and spiritual tradition rooted in Africa and made subversive under slavery. As the quest for civil rights became a social movement, its songs got louder, as people started to sing the same words together, with a particular intent.

Activist-singer Jimmy Collier, on why music was so important to the civil rights movement: There were people getting shot and beat up and those three ministers had gotten killed, so there was a lot of violence going on and that's what people felt. You know what happens when people are really scareder than shit? You know what I mean? They sing like they're not going to ever be able to sing again. And they eat, and it was that kind of an atmosphere. People were really scared but they felt that they had to carry on. So the music was very important to making people feel good.[1]

ON AUGUST 28, 1963, a quarter of a million people heard Martin Luther King, Jr., at the Lincoln Memorial ask the nation to dream of "that day when all of God's children, black men and white men, Jews and Gentiles, Protestants and Catholics, will be able to join hands and sing in the words of the old Negro spiritual, 'Free at last! Free at last! Thank God Almighty, we are free at last!'" It was not just a call to arm but a radical call to song. The civil rights movement answered that call; from the pews in Albany, Georgia, and the sit-ins in Nashville to the marches on Selma, Birmingham, and Washington—and the festival stages at Newport— freedom music was in the air.

Never has music been so integral to a political movement as it was to the civil rights movement during the 1950s and 1960s. As *Newsweek* put it, "history has never known a protest movement so rich in song as the civil rights movement. Nor a movement in which songs are as important."[2]

CIVIL RIGHTS AND FOLK MUSIC

Bernice Johnson Reagon, a Freedom Singer and prominent historian, grew up in Albany, Georgia, where the "singing movement" began in 1961. The Albany Movement was a broad campaign targeting segregation wholesale, rather than addressing specific grievances, such as demanding the right to sit at Woolworth's lunch counters or ride on interstate buses as permitted by federal law, which were known as freedom rides. The breadth of the Albany Movement's scope made its success difficult to measure, but according to marcher Josh Dunson, "the Albany Movement made the non-violent army a singing army all the way from its minister generals to six-year-old buck-privates."[3]

Across the civil rights movement, local singing groups stepped forward to lead their communities in song. The Montgomery Bus Boycott of 1955–56 was led by the Montgomery Gospel Trio; the songs of the Nashville sit-ins in 1960 and the Congress of Racial Equality (CORE) freedom rides in 1961 were led by the Nashville Quartet and the CORE Singers, respectively. Albany, on the other hand, helped produce a singing group that represented the community to the larger movement and the rest of the country. The Freedom Singers, which formed as part of the Student Nonviolent Coordinating Committee (SNCC), did more than sing its community's songs back to that community. With Toshi Ohta Seeger as their first manager, they carried songs of the struggle in the Deep South to the ears of America.

Bernice Johnson Reagon, on the origins of the Freedom Singers: After the Albany, Georgia, Movement, and articles being written about the singing movement, Cordell Reagon and Jim Foreman of SNCC began to talk about the idea of actually having a singing group. They had tested it out at a benefit in Chicago, where Cordell had gotten together a whole group of sit-in, freedom-rider singing people, and had formed a choir, and had sung as a part of that benefit, a whole series of civil rights movement songs. I had not been given permission to go to Chicago by Spellman [College]— they thought I should just focus on my studies—then on November 11th, what was then the Freedom Singers (which had about seven members: me, Rutha Harris, Cordell Reagon, Chuck Neblet, a woman named Dorothy Vales, who came out of Talladega, Alabama, a high soprano, and Charles Sherrod); and we did civil rights movement songs. Afterwards we went over to Andy Young's house and talked about the music. Pete [Seeger] had said to us that he thought it was a good idea, it would really go, and then he left town. At Andy Young's house, Guy Carawan was there, who taped a lot of the songs.

We sang songs like "We Shall Overcome," and we ended the concert with it. We did "Ain't Gonna Let Nobody Turn Me Round," "Ballad of the Sit-In"—that was a ballad written by Guy Carawan. "Freedom's Coming and It Won't Be Long," which is the tune of "Banana Boat Song." "This Little Light of Mine," "We Shall Not Be Moved," "Which Side Are You On?"

Those songs came out of the movement. The songs came out of very specific movements. If you'd begin back at the Montgomery bus boycott, they were doing things like "Onward, Christian Soldiers," and they did "Freedom." They did "Lift Them Up Higher." It was a heavy church, and slightly educated church; their songs came out of the hymn books.

The Nashville sit-in movement pulled songs from rhythm and blues, and the tight, black spiritual stuff, so you get things like "Get on Board, Children," which is in a very arranged Negro spiritual base. Also in Nashville they did a lot "Battle Hymn of the Republic" and "Negro National Anthem." In Nashville they did "Freedom," which was based on "Amen."

When the Nashville sit-in students came, they were given that song ["We Shall Overcome"]. Freedom riders picked up another; "Which Side Are You On?," a union song, was brought into that experience through James Farmer, who was the head of CORE, and who had all of those union songs in his repertoire. "Freedom's Coming and It Won't Be Long," these are freedom-rider songs, but from Nashville. "Woke Up This Morning with My Mind Set on Freedom" is a gospel that comes out of the Jackson [Mississippi] State Pen where the freedom riders were held in jail; they were there from six weeks to six months, I think.

Albany brings in a wider range of traditional forms, like "Come and Go with Me to That Land," "I'm on My Way to Freedom Land," "Ain't Gonna Let Nobody Turn Me Round." These were the call-and-response songs that you'd find in every Baptist church. Every song that was slightly religious at all also went into Albany and came out in a new form in terms of the way it was sung. "We Shall Overcome" in Albany loosened way up with lots of space for improvisations, lots of antiphony and answering and calling, and it stayed that way in terms of the black movement in the South wherever it went after that. So Albany to a large extent took all the music that had been done up to that point, and transformed it.[4]

IN THE SOUTH, "the mass culture of the civil rights movement was shaped by its central participants: Afro-American Southerners steeped in oral tradition," writes Bernice Johnson Reagon. "The freedom songs…[their] power…came from the linking of traditional oral expression to the everyday experiences of the movement."[5]

The music was neither academic nor commercial; it was not generated simply to make a point. Nor was the singing of civil rights music intended for an audience so much as for those who sang it. In contrast to the anti-establishment music of white radicals, which was top-down and carefully constructed to sway an audience, the music of the civil rights movement was rooted in spirituals and slave songs; it came out of tradition, common experience, and generations of resistance. There was no party line, no need to teach the activists what to feel or think. Freedom song had no audience: the songs were songs that everybody knew and everybody sang.

Pete Seeger, on the successful creation of freedom music: Well, I think [the freedom movement's success creating songs] points up the value of a good strong tradition. The South has been full of music because it has had the strong traditions of Africa and the strong traditions of Ireland, I think, more than England (although different people disagree with me, they feel the English is just as important as the Irish). My father feels that the Germans had an important part too; they probably all blended.

But for one reason or another, perhaps because the South was agricultural, the South has had this tremendously strong tradition of music. It's no accident that Music City is Nashville, and that when people like myself try to recapture a sense of American music, we find ourselves just gravitating to southern music. And it's not just string music, but New Orleans, jazz, the blues, and in this particular case it was the vocal tradition of the black people more than anything else.…

"We Shall Overcome" got down South—it didn't go directly from Highlander to civil rights workers; it came up here, circulated around up North here—and then went back there.

Well, this is an ancient African tradition, that of continually recreating songs. A song is not a set of long verses, certainly not in a set order, and it's kind of a base for improvisation. The major credit has to be given to the Afro-American tradition. It's true that it's using English language and European harmony, but it's the African tradition of continual improvisation and recreation which took over.[6]

Mary Travers of Peter, Paul and Mary, on the folk process behind civil rights music: It's very much like the folk process. "Go Tell It on the Mountain" that Peter, Paul and Mary sang was a rather up-tempo version of the traditional hymn with a lyric change at the bottom where it went "Let my people go"—which is a borrowing of the last line of another traditional song which we welded together because it was appropriate for the political moment. The civil rights people picked the song up down South, took the marriage of the two lyrics but slowed it back down to its original tempo and it was sung in many, many churches.[7]

WE SHALL OVERCOME

Though it was first recorded in 1950 by the Congress of Industrial Organizations, "We Shall Overcome" was not widely commercially available until 1963; but by then thousands of Americans already knew it well, particularly in the South. A *New York Times* article about the 1963 release quotes Reverend Wyatt Tee Walker, executive assistant to Reverend Martin Luther King, Jr., describing the sheer resonance of "We Shall Overcome":

> One cannot describe the vitality and emotion this hymn evokes across the Southland. I have heard it sung in great mass meetings with a thousand voices singing as one. I've heard a half dozen sing it softly behind the bars of the Hinds County prison in Mississippi. I've heard old women singing it on the way to work in Albany, Georgia. I've heard the students singing it as they were being dragged away to jail. It generates power that is indescribable. It manifests a rich legacy of musical literature that serves to keep body and soul together for that better day which is not far off.[8]

The evolution of "We Shall Overcome" from a religious folk song to the anthem of the integration movement is a case study of folk process, far different from efforts of the Composers' Collective three decades earlier. Originally copyrighted in 1901 as "I'll Overcome Some Day," the song was sung in 1947 by striking members of the Food and Tobacco Workers' Association.[9] Two of those union workers, remembered only as Anna Lee and Evelyn, sang the song for the labor movement's Highlander Folk School in Monteagle, Tennessee, where Zilphia Horton taught it as a folk song.

Civil rights singer Guy Carawan, on the origins of "We Shall Overcome": [Frank Hamilton and Pete Seeger and my] names were on the copyright at that time; so we took the money and put it in a fund. I was the only one working down there for about five years spreading that song. Frank's name is on the copyright because he first taught me that song out in California. He'd heard it from Zilphia Horton, who had worked in the South and in the labor movement and died in 1954. She learned that song from black people.

The old words were:

I'll overcome someday, I'll be all right
I'll wear the cross, I'll wear the crown
I'll be like him, I'll sing my song someday.

It got switched around to "We'll" in 1945 for the Food and Tobacco Workers strike.[10]

Bernice Johnson Reagon, on "We Shall Overcome": The Nashville sit-in leaders were taken to Highlander, and there they met Guy Carawan, who taught them one of the songs that Highlander always used in their workshops, which was "We Shall Overcome," and that song had come to Highlander in the thirties, while Zilphia Horton was the music director there. In the thirties, Highlander was mostly doing workshops with labor organizers, and in this particular case, the group that brought the song in was not the group that sang the song. The group that brought the song in was the white component of the radical Tobacco Workers' movement, who were trying to sing for Zilphia what the blacks were singing in the strike lines. Zilphia took that song, and got it singable, and began to use it, and it went from Zilphia, to Pete, and it was in *The People's Songbook.* Pete sang it around a little in the North but it didn't catch on. He taught it to Frank Hamilton, then went out to California, and taught it to Guy Carawan. Guy Carawan became music director at Highlander, and it was already in Highlander's repertoire.[11]

Pete Seeger, on changes *not* made to "We Shall Overcome": I did a concert on Martha's Vineyard, around '67 I guess it was, and Lillian Hellman invited me over to her house for a drink, and there were some others there, and she said, "We Shall Overcome," what kind of a revolutionary song is that? 'One day, some day': That's not what I call a revolutionary song!" And I wrote her criticism to Bernice [Reagon] and she gave a very thoughtful reply. She says, "It's true, but what would we say if we said next week, and next week came and we didn't overcome next week?"[12]

THE SOUTH ALREADY KNEW how to sing for its soul. Though northern white middle-class performers helped spread the word about desegregation, they were not leading songs as they had with union organizing and Communist rallies in earlier years. The folk music of the civil rights movement was generated differently from back when the Almanacs gathered in their Village loft to fit new words to an old tune for their song "Jim Crow," which was designed to outrage a northern liberal audience. Put another way, no one in a black church in Georgia or Mississippi in the 1960s needed a middle-aged radical to help them sing.

Pete Seeger, on performing in Albany, Georgia, in 1963: My little concert [in Albany] didn't really work out that well. It was only of peripheral value to them. Well, the black people in Albany had their own music. Why'd they need some Yankee come down and sing to them? And I didn't do the kind of program that would have done them most good. It would have been better if a group of union people from New York had gone down, because I, as an older intellectual, wasn't able really to do the job for them that they needed. I'm sorry.

[I couldn't connect] as well as I should have. Well, they had a crisis on, and they were very much wrapped in it. Now I think I could do a better job than I did then. I tried to give too wide a picture of music, instead of zeroing in on crisis songs.

I remember I was singing some ballad, and Bernice's husband, Cordell, told me that a woman leaned over to him and said, "If this is white folks' music; I don't think much of it." And he said, "Hush, if we expect them to understand us, I've got to try to understand them."[13]

Mary Travers, on performing at "Ole Miss" (the University of Mississippi) in 1962: I think the only time we ever really had a problem with "If I Had a Hammer" was when we sang it at Ole Miss, when [James] Meredith was there. It was in the process of being very well received, and this terrible thought dawned on me that the audience en masse was interpreting it totally differently than I was meaning it. I think they were enchanted by the life and vitality of the song, but [were] deliberately oblivious to the fact that we were talking about brothers and anybody else.... There they were with half of the National Guard on their campus. I couldn't imagine how they could receive "If I Had a Hammer" from us with such enthusiasm unless they were just blocking our intention.[14]

Pete Seeger, on writing civil rights songs: The guy who wrote "I Woke Up This Morning with My Mind Set on Freedom" was a SNCC organizer, a white man, white college student, and he heard somebody singing the old "Woke Up This Morning with My Mind on Us." And he said, "That wouldn't be hard to change." And it wasn't. It spread all around. So I don't think you can say, this is this, that is that.[15]

Broadside editor Gordon Friesen, on the radicalism within folk music in the 1960s: The writers of the protest songs that *Broadside* had, even Dylan, they were kids in the fifties, middle-class kids. McCarthyism didn't touch them. And their songs mainly appeal for reformism. We've had two songs really, calling for extreme radicalism that I can think of quickly. One was Phil Ochs's "The Ringing of Revolution," which we consider his most beautiful song. That's maybe because we're biased. We'd like to see the bourgeois trapped in their tuxedos in their last holdout. And Jimmy Collier's "With a Pickaxe and a Stone" which was the first American guerilla song:

> I'll fight your tanks and all your armies if I have to
> with a pickaxe and a stone.

You know, like the Viet Cong; they started out with bamboo spears.[16]

Bernice Johnson Reagon, on white folksingers in the civil rights movement: [The SNCC benefit in Greenwood, Mississippi] was a festival. It was July. Pete [Seeger] was there, Dylan was there, Theo Bikel was there. Dylan had just written "Medgar Evers" ["Only a Pawn in Their Game"]. One thing I remember, we were standing in a church in Mississippi, Fanny Lou Hamer was there, Pete was there, and the sheriff walked in.[17] And Fanny Lou Hamer started to talk directly to the sheriff. And then people would sing, and then the kind of moaning we do in the black church. And Pete was doing that kind of moaning, and I thought it was real strange, that there was this white man singing.

The major impression I have is the song from Dylan, the fact that it was a festival out in the field, that the people that owned that land were real strong people who said that it was their land, and we could be on that land.... And those particular gatherings did not focus on individuals a lot. You got up and you led freedom songs if you were effective. If you could lead a freedom song, you were all right; and if you couldn't, you could be forgotten very quickly.[18]

FREEDOM SONG AND DISCORD

At the 1963 March on Washington, Bob Dylan sang "Only a Pawn in Their Game," and the Newport Folk Festival "turned into one big freedom sing," according to Cordell Reagon of the Freedom Singers, who stood on stage for the festival finale as Peter, Paul and Mary, Joan Baez, Bob Dylan, Pete Seeger, and Theo Bikel all joined hands and sang "We Shall Overcome."[19] But as the integrationist dream began to disintegrate and blacks within the movement began to shake off white leadership for the sake of self-determination, the situation became more complex.

Starting in the spring of 1965, and increasingly through the following summer, regional and racial differences—actually class differences in most cases—separated white and black civil rights activists.[20] This split mirrored another in national politics, as Martin Luther King, Jr., and other activists began to challenge the war in Vietnam. The gentle, idealistic world of folk music and the integrationist world of civil rights cratered at the same time.

Civil rights activist Irene Paull, on shifting race relations within the movement: There was a lot of anger from the blacks because the whites were the leaders [of the local SNCC chapter]. The whites took over the leadership naturally, but the blacks fought them like hell. The whites were used to making the blacks subordinate to them. And the blacks for the first time in their lives said, "We will not be subordinate. You will listen to us."

When we came back, it was interesting. One guy said, "There's a big change going on in the world. It would be nice if we could give you all big badges that say 'I was in Mississippi. I am a good white.' We can't do it. Our people are angry and you may be killed and hurt along with the guilty ones. We can't say these are innocent and these are guilty. You may be hurt and killed along with the guilty because our people are that mad."

And here are all these white people...who were told to shut their damn mouths and get the hell out. This is a black movement. And they had no place to go. But you see, they had mixed motives too. Part of it was concern for the blacks. Part of it was the feeling of doing something for somebody. Being useful. Part of it was sense of adventure.[21]

Bernice Johnson Reagon, on the period when SNCC decided to expel white members: When SNCC went black, I was talking to Pete Seeger about it, and I said I was real nervous about it; I didn't know what was going on, because I was traveling in the North and it was going on in the South. And he said, well he felt like it was not going to be until black people focused and identified and spoke up, and did whatever they were going do that there was really going to be some real change. (I'm certainly terribly paraphrasing him now.) Basically what I felt he was saying was that he thought it was all right.

I don't think the resentment was toward the singers as much as it was toward the media and the organizers. Because I think people were fairly clear that when they saw these performers; they were very glad to see them.

When I saw Peter, Paul and Mary, or Joan Baez, or Pete Seeger, it was real good to have them there. And I think that was fairly well consistent throughout the movement. There were intense problems with the organizers who would set up a star system, the civil rights movement organizers. If you've got a rally, the person who's organizing the rally sets up who sings, how long they have, and stuff of that sort. They would feature what they considered the stars, and then the news media comes. So there was incredible resentment around the coverage and around the people who ended up organizing those mass rallies. But I don't feel that that was directed against the specific performers. Though some of those performers, like Bikel, later got real righteous about what they had done for us.

He said, "You know me well," listen, I never quoted the letter before, but I remember it. "You know me well, I've slept with you in shacks in Mississippi." He stayed in Mississippi one night, right? Shacks in Mississippi, my brothers and all of this shit, right? And I was really incensed; I didn't get angry with anybody until I heard that.

Up until that point, I felt like people were there to be used in whatever way somebody could figure out to use them. But if anybody tried to tell me in any way that they were down there to save me, then I'm still angry at anybody who did that. I just felt that anybody who went down there went to save themselves, and they got more out of it than the movement got out of them.[22]

AT THE SAME TIME that white involvement was called into question, the civil rights movement debated the efficacy of singing. Advocates of black power argued that the singing had gone on long enough and there were too few changes to show for it; it was time for action. Those who remained committed to nonviolence contended that music had indeed paved the way for change in America. Folksinger and SNCC organizer Julius Lester wrote of this new mood:[23]

> Now it is over. America has had chance after chance to show that it really meant "that all men are endowed with certain inalienable rights."... Now it is over. The days of singing freedom songs and the days of combating bullets and billy clubs with love.... Love is fragile and gentle and seeks a like response. They used to sing "I Love Everybody" as they ducked bricks and bottles. Now they sing:

Too much love, too much love,
Nothing kills a nigger like too much love.

Jimmy Collier, on the disintegration of the civil rights movement: The movement was starting to get to be an old person. It was at this point that people were starting to have to make decisions about the war; people were going off living on farms. The feeling that goodness and truth and light would somehow win over was starting not to be believed by a lot of people. Guys in the ghettos that we tried to get to go do marches would go tear up buildings and shit. By that time, our organization completely fell apart. Completely. Just dissolved. I think it was a very pessimistic and depressing period.[24]

Pete Seeger, on the influence of civil rights music: I wouldn't be a bit surprised if the song "We Shall Overcome" didn't have a big influence in the sixties, even to the point where President Johnson intoned it. He didn't sing it, but he ended his famous civil rights speech saying, "We shall overcome." And I wouldn't put it beyond the range of possibility [that] some of his people had heard me broaden the meaning of that.

See, every time I sang, I pointed out that it wasn't just the black people of Alabama who were going to overcome, but, I said, you and I are going to overcome, all of us in this world are going to overcome someday. And this is the kind of poetic extension of an idea that a sharp politician like Johnson could seize on. That's what he did in his famous speech.[25]

IN 1968, MARTIN LUTHER KING, JR., was assassinated. Malcolm X had risen and likewise been shot down. Across the nation, blacks were being brutalized and killed in race riots in the Watts neighborhood of Los Angeles, in Chicago, in Newark, and in Detroit. Amid this turmoil, the civil rights movement shed its principles of nonviolence and with these went freedom songs. One protestor suggested in 1966 that "We Shall Overcome" ought to be replaced with "We Shall Overrun."[26]

In spite of rising frustration, some civil rights activists kept singing. Among these were Jimmy Collier and Reverend Frederick Douglass Kirkpatrick, song leaders of the Southern Christian Leadership Conference, who organized musical programs to sustain protestors' spirits in Resurrection City, the "live-in" that the Poor People's Campaign established on the Mall in Washington in 1968.

Jimmy Collier, on Resurrection City: Logistically, the movement had gotten itself together, with all the early union help. So we knew how to organize portable showers and stuff. We usually got those things donated from unions. So there was running water and hot water, and we had facilities to feed thousands of people at once and a medical tent. Kirkpatrick and I ran what was called the Cultural Tent. (I was also the assistant sheriff of Resurrection City.) Mainly what we tried to do was to create a cultural feeling so that the Appalachian people and the Indian people and the black people from Washington, D.C., and all of these people would sort of get along and exchange stories.

There were a lot of Indians. There was the feeling of a lot of different movements in this country: the Indian movement, the poor white people's movement, the civil rights movement, the inner-city kind of movement. There were Mexicans from Colorado and Mexico; Puerto Ricans from New York; and there was just really a big coalition of cultures. People were suffering great hardships, and we were in the nation's capital. It was a real serious feeling.

Kirk and I had a good-sized tent and it had a stage in it and a PA system, and I think it was every night or almost every night, we ran programs for most of the night. You know, impromptu kind of hootenannies. Then people would have later things at their campfires.

Well, we had a sizeable Indian delegation there, and I just felt that in deference to that—all of us sitting around singing "This Land Is Your Land," was sort of insulting in a sense. You know? This all sort of sounds like one of those things that you stage but it did happen sort of innocently. This guy named Henry Crow Dog just happened to be there. And you have to understand, these are guys sitting around drinking in the hot sun, and the cops are surrounding the place and all of that, and I think I asked Henry Crow Dog if it was all right for us to sing that song; and he of course said yeah and had some comment.

Resurrection City was another one of those projects that, had King not been assassinated, would have been a tremendous success. Because it was a success; we did something that hadn't been done in a long, long time.[27]

Earl Robinson, on the antiwar movement: Remember the period when it felt like the Vietnam War was winding down, when all of a sudden Nixon has us over into Cambodia? And the country was very much divided on this subject? The working class, which I always felt had to lead the revolution, if there ever was one, was acting badly.

The hardhats had marched in New York City and beaten up on the young peace demonstrators and the hippies and the flower children. Why? Because they were threatening jobs, jobs. This war was giving jobs. A backward, shortsighted way of looking at things, but that was a lot of the working class then.[28]

Folksinger Holly Near, on the responsibilities of a protest singer: I think the difference between being a working artist and one adding to that the social change, activism, political—whatever words we want to use; we've never come up with really great words to describe this—is that you're not just doing a show, you're holding the weight of the human experience; and you're helping people to do that. So you're really more of a heart surgeon than an entertainer.

And it's one of the things that makes me sad about our training programs in this country around social change/activism. Because, if I was going to get heart surgery, I would definitely do research and make sure that I went to a doctor who had some skill and some experience.

But a lot of times, people just get up there and think, "Okay, I'm a folksinger. I like political songs. I can sing and you ought to listen to me"— without having gone through any training, without having any sense of what their craft is.

And then you have an audience member who walks away from having seen something like that, and they go, "Oh, I don't ever want to go hear folk music again or political music. It's boring." So they got a bad taste in their mouth for it.

But when you hear it done right, when you hear it done well, when you hear it done by people who've done their homework and understand where they're coming from; there's nothing as spectacular as a political artist that can not only entertain you, but can challenge you, inspire you, lift you up, give you a sense of direction, remind who you are in this world, remind you that you are part of community, remind you that there's a job for you to do in order to have this planet keep spinning through the world at an unimaginable rate of speed.

Those artists—and that's not to say once in a while there's a bad day— but those artists who do that really well can't be in a hurry. They can't leave the stage until they've done their job. And so they're not just going to run away and go get the beer. They have a job to do. And until they open up the heart and then seal it back up so it's intact when people walk out, they're not done yet.[29]

HOLDING HANDS AND SINGING "We Shall Overcome" had given way to the raised fists of black power; but as the civil rights movement fragmented, having accomplished much, other movements for social and political change learned from its tactics. Sexism, wars, and the mistreatment of the environment became the stuff of protest songs.

In music, the British invasion had taken place, with the Beatles, the Rolling Stones, and the Kinks bringing new luster and a counterculture edge to rock and roll. But that was not the only invasion: shortly after the New Year in 1965, President Johnson ordered air strikes in North Vietnam. On March 7, civil rights protestors marching on Selma clashed with state and local police armed with billy clubs and tear gas. Throughout that spring, protestors burned draft cards, and the nonviolent activist organization Students for a Democratic Society (SDS) held its first "teach-ins" against the Vietnam War. As the war escalated, so did a dramatic, mass antiwar movement. All across the country, young people were resisting the draft and "turning on, tuning in, and dropping out" in more ways than one—and they were singing in the process.

Civil rights, environmentalism, and the new sloop *Clearwater*, peace marches—everything seemed to happen at once. Images of racial harmony—as in the classic tableau of the Freedom Singers on stage with Baez, Dylan, and Pete Seeger at the close of Newport '63—belonged to a different era. From New York City to Los Angeles, scenes of ghettoes on fire filled TV screens just now turning to color, and news of increasing American casualties in Southeast Asia was reported on FM radios just changing to stereo sound. The world had become a more complex place, and right and wrong had become, to many, less absolute. Or, as Bob Dylan sang in "My Back Pages":

> *"Equality," I spoke the word as if a wedding vow*
> *Ah, but I was so much older then, I'm younger than that now.*

Protest music was moving away from rallying cries and toward more abstract, broader critiques of society, as in Dylan's "Mr. Tambourine Man" and Paul Simon's "Sounds of Silence," or toward thoughtful antiwar songs such as Sioux Indian Buffy Sainte-Marie's "Universal Soldier."[30] By 1965, the times they were a-changin,' all right, and soon that prophecy's singer would be singing a different tune.

8

FOLK-ROCK

IN JULY 1965, the Newport Folk Festival was surprised by Bob Dylan's appearing in black leather while playing electric guitar, with which he shattered the festival's calm with a high-volume rendition of "Maggie's Farm," backed by the electric Butterfield Blues Band. He performed only a short set before returning alone with an acoustic guitar to play "It's All Over Now, Baby Blue." Of course, Dylan's first (and largely unknown) electrically backed recording—a 45 of the rockabilly tune "Mixed-Up Confusion," briefly released in 1962—would also have surprised his more traditionally oriented fans if they had heard it.[1] (Dylan's initial work in folk-rock went unacknowledged before his dramatic concert at Newport.) It is generally conceded that this moment represents a tectonic shift in the landscape of folk music, but what that shift was—what was "all over now" and what was just beginning for folk music—is open to debate.

In his review of the concert, Paul Nelson (one of the editors of *Sing Out!*) declared:

> Like it or not, the audience had to choose. Whether, on one hand, to take the word of [Pete Seeger]...or whether to accept as truth the...world of Bob Dylan, where things aren't often pretty, where there isn't often hope, where man isn't always noble, but where, most importantly, there exists a reality that coincides with that of this planet.[2]

That day, the boos suggested that the audience chose Pete Seeger. But Nelson staked his reputation on Dylan's art: "Maybe he didn't put it in the best way. Maybe he was rude. But [Dylan] shook us. And that is why we have poets and artists."[3]

1965 was a year of tumult and transition. The Vietnam War was costing American lives, and the draft doubled in size. The Voting Rights Act, civil rights, and race riots dominated the nation's TV viewing and conversations. Yet one of the most remembered events of the summer was one singer's change of genre. In September 1965, Dylan told *Newsweek*: "I've never written a political song," and in a direct hit on folk music's idealism, he added, "Songs can't save the world. I've gone through that."[4]

Singer-songwriter Bob Dylan, on his initial interest in folk music:
I became interested in folk music because I had to make it somehow.
Obviously I'm not a hard-working cat. I played the guitar; that was all
I did. I thought it was great music. Certainly I haven't turned my back on
it or anything like that. There is—and I'm sure nobody realizes this, all the
authorities who write about what it is and what it should be, when they
say "keep things simple, they should be easily understood"—folk music
is the only music where it isn't simple. It's never been simple. It's weird,
man, full of legend, myth, Bible, and ghosts. I've never written anything
hard to understand, not in my head anyway, and nothing as far out as
some of the old songs. They were out of sight.[5]

Freedom Singer Bernice Johnson Reagon, on Newport in 1965: I was
there [backstage]. I read a lot of stuff about Dylan going on with the
band, and having people yell at him from the audience, and him coming
offstage and going back on with his acoustical guitar. And I did not feel,
first, that the audience did that—that rejection of him. And I did not connect his going back with his acoustical guitar with him making a choice,
except that he was very insecure to be going out there in the first place
with the band.

From a personal standpoint, I've been in a lot of situations singing
where I had to try something new, and if I had to do one extra thing, I did
it the way I always understood inside of myself it would work out. Dylan
came backstage, and Dylan's really insecure. I remember the first time he
did Newport, he goes, "Did they like me?"

So every time Dylan sings on stage, he says, "Did they like me?"

I say, "Yeah, they liked you."

Irwin Silber talks about tears in his eyes, and I didn't see them. Like he
came off stage, and we were together, and so I totally reject that analysis.

I've had problems with lots of the stuff that people have created that
came out of Newport. I went the year that ('68, '67) Irwin Silber said the
only good thing was me, Kirkpatrick, and Jimmy Collier. But Jimmy Collier never showed up! So I felt that there were a lot of political people at
Newport creating levels of analysis.

I wouldn't call [Pete Seeger's reaction in 1965] freaking out. He felt he
was real upset, but I just felt he was real upset because it was a major decision. He felt Dylan was going the wrong way. I felt like Grossman was real
commercially oriented in terms of Dylan. I felt real bad about that. I felt
that Pete was feeling real bad about that. They were really crazy men, all
of them.[6]

Folksinger Ramblin' Jack Elliott, on Dylan's influence: I think the folk
song revival finally got through, thanks to Bob Dylan mostly. Bob's appreci-

ation and knack for borrowing sounds is amazing. He'll try everything and anything. Bob Dylan is a beachcomber for material. I admire his great guitar style, his great singing style, his marvelous choice of words, and his poetry. I think that Bob is one of the greatest poets that ever lived.[7]

Protest singer Phil Ochs recalls criticizing Dylan: Now I had a fight with Dylan I never talked about before, I might as well mention [it] now. I went to a photographic session, when he was a god. Dylan used to come around to the Kettle of Fish, and he was beautiful then, and he was super arrogant then, and he used to walk around and try to categorize all the other writers in terms of himself, of how really good he was. He used to say, "Eric Andersen, you're not really a writer," or he'd say, "Phil, you're not really a writer, you're a journalist, and you shouldn't try to write." He just went through this whole fantastic riff of how we shouldn't even write and that he was the writer. (Which on straight aesthetics, I would admit was true: he was the best writer.)

A whole bunch of riffs went down then. But one day he was being photographed by Jerry Schatzberg, and he was playing one of his new singles and he was asked me what I thought and I said that I didn't like it, and he said, "What? What do you mean you don't like it?"

I said, "Well, it's not as good as your old stuff."

Speaking commercially, I said it wouldn't sell. And he got furious. David Blue was there and I was there in this limousine, and he said, "Get out of the car." So I got out of the car and that's the last time I saw Dylan.[8]

Bob Dylan, on classifying his work in 1965: What I'm doing now—it's a whole other thing. We're not playing rock music. It's not a hard sound. These people call it folk-rock—if they want to call it that, something that simple, it's good for selling records. As far as it being what it is, I don't know what it is. I can't call it folk-rock. It's a whole way of doing things. It has been picked up on; I've heard songs on the radio that have picked it up. I'm not talking about words. It's a certain feeling, and it's been on every single record I've ever made. That has not changed.[9]

WITH DYLAN'S EPOCHAL APPEARANCE at Newport, the already tenuous agreement on a definition of folk music fractured. A genre (and a community) characterized by its traditionalism, pluralism, and conviction now became introspective and even more slippery to define. This was a split between the esoteric, purist side of folk music versus its light industry, as *Time* put it.[10] Now critics labeled urban performers "nonfolksingers of non–folk songs" and described their music as the "new pop music for intellectuals."[11]

Confronted with Dylan's supposed renunciation, or evolution, or treason (depending on whom one asked), folklorists and ethnomusicologists reopened the debate about folklore versus what was now called "fakelore," as folklorist Richard Dorson called it, or, another favorite term among skeptics, "folkum."

In 1966, folksinger-turned-folklorist Ellen Stekert delineated four categories of folk music: traditional singers (Lead Belly, for example); imitators, or emulators (New Lost City Ramblers); utilizers, or "singers of folk songs" (Peter, Paul and Mary, Joan Baez); and the "new aesthetic" performers (Bob Dylan, post–Newport 1965, followed by Paul Simon, Neil Young, and other singer-songwriters of folk and folk rock).[12] This typology has its uses, but for many musicians, what mattered most was the music itself: post–Newport 1965, folksingers/singers of folk songs broke free of a folk orthodoxy, or, mainly, felt free to experiment.

Guitarist Happy Traum, on the fading of folk revival music: All these people started out loving folk music and loving traditional music and felt it was a natural shift. John Sebastian [of the Lovin' Spoonful] used to play his autoharp in Washington Square and his harmonica. He used to hang around Washington Square and was a part of the jug band Izzy [Young] put together, the Even Dozen Jug Band. I don't think you put him in the group of doing it to make money. The only people I would put in the third category you are talking about are people like Trini Lopez, people who had no root connection with that. Some group or some solo individual who never had anything to do with folk music and jumped on the bandwagon and put out a record of America's favorite folk songs.

It was in late '64, '65, when the Beatles were starting to influence. My experience is from New York; I don't know about the rest of the country. Suddenly, there was an incredible amount of activity around the Village. Most of it was around electric music or what we would have considered two years earlier heresy. Folksingers were using backup bands, sometime in late '65; I remember there was a period in the Village.

The Lovin' Spoonful were very powerful for me; Frank Zappa [and the Mothers of Invention] was starting to play around New York; a lot of the folksingers started to get backup bands.

During that time that whole mass folk music thing started to drop. Not that people weren't still carrying it on. When Marc Silber, who was always very acoustic, started playing electric bass, we formed our group. We then started hearing all this stuff about the San Francisco sound. Suddenly clubs started to sell liquor. (Obviously there were clubs that always sold liquor.) The first place I ever heard Peter, Paul and Mary was at the

Blue Angel nightclub. The folk clubs were always coffeehouses. Liquor just didn't go along with the whole ambiance.[13]

FOLK-ROCK

The year 1965 was nowhere near the end of the second folk revival, but it marked its transformation. Many folk music fans still listened to old-timey, traditional, and vernacular music, including bluegrass and ethnic music. But others were drawn to the hybrid genre of folk-rock. As folk music branched out further, many wondered whether it had lost its connection with its roots. *Sing Out!* panned folk-rock as derivative; Izzy Young went so far as to call it racist—a generic way to privilege white imitators over black rock groups; but *New York Times* folk music critic Robert Shelton deemed the new movement a healthy one.[14]

By the end of the 1960s, some argued that the rock revolution had trumped the folk revival, or that folk music had been absorbed into pop music and rock and roll.[15] Still others argued that it was rock and roll that was emerging from folk music. Chicken-or-egg debates aside, the very term "folk-rock" illuminated the fact that the two genres were related within the American music tradition, and, as rock and roll matured, were coming to serve the same function; by the seventies, even Pete Seeger was recording folk-rock.[16]

Ethnomusicologist Charles Seeger, on folk music's foundational shift in the mid-1960s: The evolution is a little rapid; that's all. We're a little bit too fast for our own ability to digest what is going on these days. Sometimes we'll leave something very worthwhile behind, simply because we're going on to the next so fast. We're moving now in ten years, what they used to move in two centuries, musically. I told you about the rock group, the Youngbloods, that I was listening to in the big hall at Berkeley.

I made a point of sitting in the front row, next to some nice, pretty teenage girls. Who were excited about it, you know. So I sat there and at the end of a few of the pieces, I turned to the girl on one side and the other and said, "Can you hear the singer?"

"Oh, no."

It was a terrible din. Well, I went part way back in the audience, about halfway for the next song, and I began to be able, by adjusting my hearing aid, putting it very low, so to keep the reverberation down, just as I do at a cocktail party.

I went outside and listened through the swinging doors. And what do you suppose I hear? "Go tell Aunt Rhody, go tell Aunt Rhody," over and over again. From one of the parts. Only three instruments. As far as I could see, that was a bass part to which two counterpoints were added. They were different, as far as I could make out, a little different each stanza, but "Aunt Rhody" kept on. I inquired about the group. And, oh, yes, several of them had been very active in the folk music revival. Oh, yes, lots of the rock players were in the folk music revival. That's just beautiful for me because it's historic change happening quickly in a few years instead of a hundred years.[17]

Phil Ochs, on folk-rock: So [the stage was set] for all the New York folk writers, for lack of a better term, the midwestern, New York folk writers who came together which brings in the birth of *Broadside*, the protest song movement, and then Dylan with the shift to more lyrical songs, more philosophical, self-searching songs, but always a high regard for words, for songs as words plus music, not just music, and then merging with folk-rock and trying to find ways to communicate the combination of sounds—instrumental sounds, rhythms, and words.

This culminated in 1965. And again, it seems to me the second time in a row, history repeating itself very rapidly, is seeing the fantastic success of a Dylan, or of the Byrds, specifically, in terms of doing a good and logical musical step, immediately the companies have stepped in and done them one better, went out to find or create their guys and make their deals and market it off at the expense of the radio again.

So this brings in the new people that, to me, don't give off a sense of lasting value in the sense that the older people did. I don't think they are the real creative individuals. There were exciting bands that temporarily came together. And on a certain cut, you could find it, like Grace Slick singing "White Rabbit" in the Jefferson Airplane is a cut that will last, or them singing "Don't You Want Somebody to Love," will last, but their new album, and the whole new direction of the Grateful Dead: so many of these groups just don't have a real artistic leg to stand on. Their own standards are lower, and therefore what they try to put out when they get right down to it and say, "We've got a new album to make" and then they've got to say, "Okay, what songs are we going to sing and what words are we going to sing and how are we going to do it?"

They face the limitations that should have been solved in the first place, before they became famous. This is a very common problem in America to become very successful and have no talent and then try to find a way to salvage your fame by other means. I get this view of America, that America has become quite fat and quite alienated from life, and from a sense of struggle and a sense of conflict.[18]

Folksinger Judy Collins, comparing her transition to electric backup to Pete Seeger's: He is a superb entertainer, but I don't think he sees the ensemble backing as part of his expression. Pete [Seeger]'s work, music is in some ways a tool for a social movement. You see, he sees himself in an entirely different role [from me]. My goal as a performer is to keep becoming more and more focused as an entertainer. I think he sees himself as a storyteller, and therefore he focuses much better as a storyteller. And I see myself as a storyteller too, but in another kind of tradition. I see myself more in the French tradition, let's say, of Jacques Brel, or Édith Piaf. I want the freedom of movement, for instance; I don't want to be stuck behind a guitar or piano. I want to have a different kind of freedom. And so it involves different kinds of tools.[19]

Guitarist Danny Kalb, on Pete Seeger's first album with electrical backup in 1973: John Hammond was the producer. It was a very uptight session. Pete was so weird. He came over to my house to go over things a couple of weeks before the session. Any remark I made to him, he wouldn't reply. He would just say, "Uh huh." Yeah, one piece I failed to do right, he didn't criticize me on that. He sat on the floor and played the banjo. I asked if he wanted anything to eat or drink—no. I had trained with him at other times. There was this kind of detachment of a fundamental type. He's crazy in a way.

As soon as Hammond came into the room, they made the electronic part go down, and I think it was John Hammond. I felt that right away. The whole session was just so unjoyous, unfun. It was tight. Pete didn't seem to have the magic, the recording studio smarts, to do certain things which perhaps loosened us up and confronted the producer on the silly low [mix], so low there was nothing happening there. If you want joyous sounds from electric music you have to have it sort of loud. It was ridiculous the level we were at....We all thought it was going to be a thrill to play with Pete and a black choir; that we could play as the band. But there was no firm hand on the direction of the session. There weren't many takes.[20]

Folksinger Arlo Guthrie, on the relationship of tradition and style: You can argue about who felt bad about it or what, but I think once you begin to understand what folk music is, what the tradition is, people cannot consciously bend and shape what is going to happen. You have to do your own part. Do what you think you can do, say the things you have to say, and let the rest alone. If your songs have meaning and if your songs have value; if your style is a good medium for what you have to say, that will last.[21]

NEWSWEEK CALLED FOLK-ROCK "big-beat music with big-message lyrics," noting that "the folky rollers protest—against being put down, being hung up, being drafted, Vietnam, Selma, the FBI, the Bomb."[22] But plenty of aficionados also felt that late-revival folk music, and folk-rock in particular, had moved away not only from its traditional roots but from protest music, too.

Some attributed this shift to the crises of the times: conservative Richard Nixon had won the presidency in 1968, and his vice president, Spiro Agnew, called the youth of the day "overprivileged, underdisciplined, irresponsible children of the blasé well-to-do permissivists."[23] Many folk music fans were running short on hope and optimism and were coming to the new protest music not motivated by their consciences or their zeal for traditional sounds but largely by their need for community, entertainment, and escape—as Woodstock demonstrated.[24]

If some people insisted that folk music was now no more than mass entertainment, its message diluted, others argued that folk music encompassed far more than Francis Child's conception of "folk"-as-reminder-of-tradition; folk music and the folk process now drew from "roots" music of all kinds; it became boundless and divergent, its limits porous.

In other words, rather than dissolving, facets of the folk worldview were absorbed into many forms of music; nowhere did this happen as continuously as in the music opposed the Vietnam War the source of the greatest social division of the late sixties and early seventies in the United States.

THE VIETNAM WAR

As Dylan's dramatic Newport performance did, the Vietnam War split the folk music revival community. A new direction was emerging, one alienated from the earlier Popular Front patriotism, as American musicians resisted the country's disastrous military intervention in Southeast Asia. This alienation coincided with the psychedelia movement, which began in California in 1965 and grew stronger across the country. Political musicians—for example, Joe McDonald's psychedelic band Country Joe and the Fish—lashed out against the war with songs like the "Fish Cheer" ("1, 2, 3, what are we fighting for?"), recorded in 1967 when there were nearly five hundred thousand U.S. troops in Vietnam. This transformation is evident even in the few right-wing songs that remain from the era, such as the way the theme of noble sacrifice in Barry Sadler's "Ballad of the Green Berets," a tune honoring Special Forces fighters, was given a nihilistic twist in Barry McGuire's "Eve of Destruction" and Phil Ochs's later recordings.

Phil Ochs, on the departure from topical song in folk music: I'm talking about "Eve of Destruction" being a hit, and how I thought that was a negative effect: because that was used as a symbol of the songwriting movement when it was really an imitative and a weak song. It made a point but you have to differentiate between songs that really make a point like "[The Lonesome Death of] Hattie Carroll" and songs that make vague philosophical points that can be taken anyway by anybody. A soldier could hear "Eve of Destruction" and not think anything of it and say, "Yeah, well, I guess things are pretty bad," and go on fighting.[25]

Composer Earl Robinson, on the sixties: The sixties. Some of you participated, I am sure, in the grand, exciting rebel years, where we stood against this unwanted war in Vietnam, as long as we could; and finally, people really got up in arms, and brought it to a stop. Finally. I think you have to credit us, in mass, the American people with doing this, although we were helped by the Vietnamese fighting back and beating the shit out of us in the process occasionally, too.[26]

Folksinger Holly Near, on seeking a feminist perspective on war: Music was taking me into the world, but I didn't envision myself that I was going to become a political folksinger. Until I kept being pulled that way. One of the reasons I started writing was the only songs that I knew to find were coming from a man's point of view on war. So, as I was becoming an early feminist, and I thought, "Well, what does this mean to women? What is the feminist perspective on war?"

As Country Joe MacDonald, or Phil Ochs, or Pete [Seeger], or these different people who had written antiwar songs were writing them sort of from their point of view. So that question, of "Where are the women's songs?" got me writing more.[27]

Singer-songwriter Country Joe McDonald, on how his music changed from Pete Seeger to psychedelics: I started singing folk music and protesting. At the same time I was big on jazz and instrumental and blues. Blues and Pete Seeger probably affected me more than anything. He's responsible for me doing that song ["I Feel-Like-I'm-Fixin'-to-Die Rag"]. He's the one that turned me on to audience participation. I went from him to James Brown. James Brown is like another black Pete Seeger. He yells out something and they yell back. There's a certain style that goes into that.[28]

Folksinger Pete Seeger, on Joe MacDonald's antiwar songs: I was singing in the town of Hudson, [New York,] and I'd been singing "Waist Deep in the Big Muddy," and it caused a lot of tension.

And one of my friends said, "Look Pete, Hudson is a real conservative town, please don't sing any of the anti-Vietnam songs while you're up there."

So I said, "Okay, okay," and I was a good boy, and I didn't sing "Waist Deep in the Big Muddy." But after I'm all through singing, some high school kids were walking past me singing, "1, 2, 3, what are we fighting for?" at the top of their lungs.

It was foolish of me to be so goddamn polite; the kids all know that song.

And I learnt the song, and I started singing it, and I decided it was a lot better than "Waist Deep in the Big Muddy," and I sang it everywhere, all around that year.[29]

Clearwater **volunteer David O'Reilly, on opposing the war:** A lot of the Hudson River Valley, where we sailed, is fairly conservative. So we were seen as sort of a leftist group at a time when the country was very divided, about the Vietnam War—I can remember being at a concert one time that Pete [Seeger] was doing and there were members of the John Birch Society handing out pamphlets: "Don't Listen to Stalin's Canary" I think was how the thing went. So we were often perceived as troublemakers. People who didn't stand four-square for America and that sort of thing. It gradually softened over time. . . .

But these were confusing times for young people. You were apart from the prevailing culture that was oppressing black people and the culture that had created the Vietnam War and was prosecuting it with a sort of zeal that didn't seem to be right. Seeing the exploitation of workers, you tried to make sense of it all, and the clothing and the hair was a way of signaling, well, I'm not part of the dominant ethic. I'm trying to find my way out of that into something new but I'm not sure what that is. So the clothing and the long-hair ponytails and stuff like that were an offense to people of a more traditional worldview.[30]

Pete Seeger, on performing during the antiwar era: Sometimes a few boos just serve to make the rest more united. That used to happen back in the mid-sixties when I was singing songs about Vietnam and I think when I first sang "Teacher Uncle Ho," got a few boos, or:

> *If you love your Uncle Sam,*
> *bring 'em home, bring 'em home.*

A few people would boo, but the rest would just sing it all the stronger.

It's amusing now, I've forgotten what exact year, but there came a point when they realized how outnumbered they were. In the mid-sixties there were some who couldn't believe that anybody but an out-and-out Commie traitor would sing a song against the Vietnam War. And they were surprised themselves at the fact that no one joined them in the booing. Here were a thousand people, fifty of them booed. But when they heard the 950 come crashing down on them, they suddenly realized, "Gee, we're in the minority here!"

And it was a very thrilling thing. The majority suddenly realized, "Yeah, we are the majority of people." And it was quite a revelation. To both sides.[31]

Country Joe McDonald, on performing at demonstrations in the 1970s: I don't get to play long enough. It's terrible. I want to play for an hour and a half. I've got something to say and it takes an hour and a half to say it. There's no other way I can say it. I can't edit it down. The experience doesn't translate in ten minutes.[32]

Holly Near, on the Free The Army (FTA) tour: It was a three-week tour where my whole life changed. I learned about imperialism in a really direct way; I learned about feminism in a really direct way; I learned about the relationship of soldier to military authority in a really big way....I came back from that trip and I wrote a lot of songs....and I thought, "How are these soldiers going to like these songs?"

Well, they were on their feet screaming because they felt the same way about the military that women felt about sexism and the patriarchy. So there was this kind of bonding around this material that I thought was actually going to be received in a hostile way....

There was something like twelve thousand soldiers in stockades at that time for resisting war and racism from in the military. I hadn't known that; I didn't know soldiers were resisting.[33]

WOODY AND PETE'S CHILDREN: A NEW GENERATION OF FOLKSINGERS

Folk music was not only branching out to take on new issues and experiment with disparate modes and styles of music, it was passing down its traditions to a new generation. "Woody's Children," as the folk revivalists were sometimes called, gave rise to a generation raised on folk music as a living entity, not just dusty collectibles held in the Library of Congress or excavated from the memories of old-timers in the hills and hollers.

There was a generational transfer. Ronnie Gilbert of the Weavers inspired Holly Near as a political singer. Mike Seeger's New Deal tunes stimulated Ry Cooder's songs. But it did not stop there. The "revival" of the 1960s was over, and it had accomplished what its name implies: folk music was alive and well in America, if changed, and another generation of musicians dated their lives from when they encountered folk music.

Broadside **editor Gordon Friesen, on "Woody's Children":** There was one thing that struck me: their inspiration came through Seeger but went back to Guthrie. Their main influence was not Seeger but Guthrie. You can just go down the list: Paxton, Ochs, Dylan…They saw something in Guthrie that attracted them and motivated and directed them much more than anything about Pete Seeger. In fact, Pete invented the phrase "Woody's Children." He didn't call them "Seeger's Children."[34]

Folklorist Archie Green, on schools and protégés: Pete got thousands of people to sing along on the choruses of songs. Mike [Seeger] got hundreds of people, whether this is good or bad, college intellectuals, to form hillbilly bands.

You have to remember that the New Lost City Ramblers left a trail of college youngsters who became proficient in Appalachian music. Now many of those then became city youngsters in bluegrass bands. You began to have college kids performing with Bill Monroe. Ry Cooder in a sense is in part a child of Mike Seeger. Although Ry personally is also progressive politically. A lot of people don't know that.

I did suggest that Mike, at one time, was somewhat off-base on his attempts to identify himself as a folksinger. Mike in his heart of hearts knows that he is an interpreter of folk song. But he has a burning conviction that this is important culturally; he just doesn't use political language, but I think Mike could say that it is important to relations between people, and respect and self-esteem, to the polity, to the society, that whole chunks of culture be preserved and represented in pristine form.

I could say that there is a political dimension to Mike's work. It's just wrong to think of him as limited or an elitist. I might even be willing, if I had to develop an argument, to say that ultimately Mike's political message, as hidden as it is, is more important that Pete's.[35]

Sing Out! **editor Mark Moss, on Pete Seeger as a folksinger:** I've heard people talk about Pete [Seeger]'s repertoire as not being traditional enough. I think he's got a natural musicianship; he's making music with these instruments even if not in a true folkloric way, but to me that makes it more folk music. Perhaps the way that Pete is not a true folk musician is that he intentionally makes changes to things. Other people would be doing it by accident.[36]

The Weavers' Lee Hays, on politics and the folk music revival: Jesus, when you look at the number of people that were singing, you can't have an "ism" that would encompass this number of people.…It [started out] just a left-wing, popular movement. This is the kind of question that bugs me, because the assumption is perilously close to the assumption that [R. Serge] Denisoff is working out of, and I don't think that Pete [Seeger] would deny any left-wing bias on his part, and I wouldn't, but you can't lump a thing as broad as this.[37] In fact I think that may have been the thing that killed it in the end. [The revival] got so broad and aimless in a way that it lacked any kind of special focus.[38]

Holly Near, on singing across generations: Embarrassing as it is to say today, I didn't know where Ronnie [Gilbert] was, or even if she were alive; but my second album I dedicated to her. Because, when I first started thinking about it, I listed all these women whom I had sung with in my life growing up, to their records.... And, you know, when you make a list, all you do is think about who is left out of the list. So I said, "I can't really do that. Gotta pick one."

And of all those singers, I picked Ronnie because, it says in the dedication, "Who knew how to sing and knew what to sing about"; so it must have been in those early to midseventies that I really did identify with the fact that the Weavers were outspoken. I think the story of the Weavers and the way they were rejected, during the blacklisting, became more potent to me than it might have even been in my childhood.

Her daughter saw the record and said to Ronnie, "Do you know this gal Holly Near?" And Ronnie said "No," and she [the daughter] said, "Well she's gone and dedicated her record to you." And Ronnie, as she will tell you, probably, when you talk to her, got a little snarky about it and said "How dare she do that without talking to me first?"

I think Ronnie had gotten frustrated by the music of the sixties. She felt like a lot of the sixties singers, women singers, had gotten kind of flower child–like and soft-spoken. And she wasn't really interested in it. She'd lost track of whether there were any singers that had edge to them.

And so, Ronnie kept putting off listening to the record; her daughter had given her a copy. And then one day, she said, "Okay, I'll listen to this."

So, she put on the record and decided she'd listen to it while she was vacuuming. (You can understand how much respect she intended to give this presentation.) But somewhere, I guess, between plugging it in from one wall to another, she heard this voice that was quite big and was not a flower child voice at all. And she sat down and listened to it several times over, and wept and was very moved by it; and called me up and said, "Can I meet you?" and she came to my parents' house in Ukiah and I was just so proud to invite one of the Weavers into my parents' house, you know, to say "Look! Look what ordering all those records and having them in our lives did! And here they are in our living room."

We had a lovely day, and then I asked Ronnie if she would sing a song or two with me on something. And she said yes. So, we became quite a duo, and there were three, four generations of people coming to our concerts together.[39]

Singer-songwriter Si Kahn, on discovering folk music during the revival:
I became really aware of folk music, it's a very specific incident, right after
I moved to Bethesda, [Maryland,] just outside of Washington in 1959, I was
fifteen years old. Ms. Casey, our English teacher, sent us all down to the
Library of Congress to learn how to do research.

I'm walking down the hall and I see a sign that says, "Archive of Folk
Music." I knew there was folk music, because the Kingston Trio was out
there and Judy Collins, Joan Baez. I went in and said, "What do you do?"
They said, "We are the national depository for traditional folk music."
I said, "What does that mean?" They said, "We do field recordings." I said,
"What are those?" They said, "Well, we go out and record people." They
said, "Here," and handed me the translucent red vinyl record. It's got Pete
Steele playing "Cold Creek March"; it's got somebody tooting their fiddle
for three minutes; it's got McKinley Morganfield before he became Muddy
Waters doing "The Delta Blues"; it's got Texas Gladden singing "The House
Carpenter."

They sent me to a listening booth, this raggedy plywood structure with
a turntable and an arm you put down by hand, and the little headphones
like you see in submarine movies where they say, "Captain, Captain we've
been hit, we're sinking!" I put on the headphones and dropped the needle
and it was just a magical moment. I felt like I had never heard music like
this before in my whole life.

So I bought it for ninety-nine cents, and I took it home. I got all excited
and I made my classically trained parents sit down at the table and I said,
"I've just discovered the most beautiful music in the world!" and there is
Pete Steele playing "Cold Creek March." I can still remember the look of
pain and anguish on their faces. They were very nice and said, "We're so
glad you found something that interests you."

I became a complete fanatic at the age of fifteen in 1959. But a fanatic
for roots music which, thinking back, is not that I didn't know that Kingston Trio was out there and Joan Baez. I had respect for all those artists,
but what I was fanatical about was the roots recordings. There wasn't a
lot in those days, but you had Folkways and Stinson (also in translucent
red plastic), you had the Library of Congress. I must have at one point
had forty Library of Congress records. I had a paper route, I was working as a collator at a print shop, and I would save up my money and
I would buy these things. That reshaped my musical consciousness.
Later I discovered the revival at a different level, but that is really where
it came from.[40]

THERE WERE, OF COURSE, members of the old guard in left-wing
music who were unimpressed with the new generation.

Activist Margaret Gelder Frantz, on the music of the Old Left versus the New: I think there's something terrible about the way this generation, this culture, doesn't sing songs. I went to an International Women's Day meeting, and there were a whole bunch of performers up on the platform who sang songs that they had written, and there was never any effort to get the audience to join in. They weren't the kind of songs that people could possibly join in with anyway. They were arty songs that were stupid, most of them, as far as I was concerned.

If they'd just dittoed some words and handed them to everybody, it would have changed the whole character of that meeting. It really would have made a difference in what people took home with them from that meeting, a sense of solidarity and feeling and participation and engagement that people would have had at the meeting. But they didn't have it at that meeting. People all went home singly or in couples instead of feeling that they had shared a real group experience. Nobody sang. There were five or six of us Old Left types at that meeting, and we all had the same reaction. We all said the same thing to each other spontaneously, because we missed something.

We sat through these lengthy songs in which people were expressing their own single individual consciousness in their own agonizing ways. Some of that poetry really leaves me cold. You couldn't hear the words half the time. They were the antithesis, at the total other end from the kind of singing experiences we used to have.[41]

Anthropologist Bess Lomax Hawes, on topical song and American identity: Folks move very slowly in cultural movements. They hang on to their old stuff. The pop people did it much better; I think they were faster at it.

It's interesting. I see what's happening now in terms of increased demand. We've got a national repertoire; and we're not very interested in it anymore. We would like to develop our own specialties: local, cultural, regional, racial, whatever. We want to get back into our own little groups and stop worrying about all this other stuff. We've got to act now, that's settled. Americans can all get together in the same place and sing the same songs. When it turns out to be the Coca-Cola song, we don't like it very much![42]

Earl Robinson, on the new generation departing from the old: In the sixties when all of the revolutionary upsurge occurred, black power and everything else, I passed through a sad period because all these young people were not trusting anybody over thirty. At the College [University of California, Santa Barbara] they gave me a reason and that is that songs like "The House I Live In" and "Ballads for Americans" were too patriotic for them. In other words, the stuff that got attacked by reactionaries in the thirties, forties, and fifties gets attacked by the Left, ha! The New Left, you know? That's really something.[43]

THE FOLK BOOM, or revival, or rerevival, or arrival, was considered over by the end of the 1960s. The 1969 Newport festival had been a flop, while Woodstock had attracted well over a quarter of a million attendees.[44] A community was disintegrating. Woody Guthrie had wasted away in a hospital (1967). Phil Ochs "had run out of words" and entered into a downward spiral that would culminate with his suicide in 1976.[45]

Critics charged that the second folk revival was not only romantic and naïve but also opportunist, even colonialistic.[46] Some were more positive, claiming that the revival accomplished what it set out to do, to bring American traditional musical forms back into the national musical vernacular: "By gosh, it revived," said Charles Seeger. "And it revived with such speed that it nearly exploded and seeded itself all over the place!"[47] Yet a question lingered in the minds of those who had helped bring folk music to international prominence: was folk music—were the songs— better off for being interpreted for and presented to mass audiences?

Mark Moss, on the heterogeneity of folk music: I would blame the heterogeneity of folk music a lot more on the people that [Pete Seeger] influenced, the Kingston Trio, Peter, Paul and Mary—that kind of stuff—than I would Pete. When you listen to some of those solo records he made in the late fifties you can still hear some of that crookedness to the music. He understood what made those songs those songs. The orchestrated Weaver stuff—yeah, not my cup of tea. Had that stuff not happened where would the real stuff be?[48]

Si Kahn, on the existence of a folk "revival": Okay, now we are in the questions of whether there really are historical periods. My read of music in American history, with a very broad definition of folk, is that it's always there. (There is a separate question of who is paying attention to it and why.)

So I would say, what do you mean the thirties were the first folk revival? What about the Wobblies? What about the IWW, where you had hundreds of people who were writing songs? We had thousands of people singing them. We had the *Little Red Songbook*, printed by the hundreds of thousands, which people carried in their back pockets. Why is that not a folk music revival?

We have the complication that, well, almost all those songs were set to Tin Pan Alley songs. As were so many of our folk classics. My favorite example is Charlie Poole and the North Carolina Ramblers. Great traditional band right? Almost all their stuff is Tin Pan Alley. "Moving Day, Moving Day"—that's a Tin Pan Alley song.

These folks in the thirties, they bought records. They went to New York. They heard music; they were like, "That's cool, let's do that." When the Hawaiian band in 1912 goes to the mountains, everybody is like, "Wow, we could turn these guitars flat and raise the nut, and play like that."

So I don't believe that music itself in the context of community flows quite as dramatically as the idea of folk revivals would have us believe.[49]

Arlo Guthrie, on the folk music revival: Well, I think the folk revival movement was real good; it was an important thing. First of all, everybody went out and bought a guitar: that was the first good thing. So that even if you didn't play it, you could appreciate somebody else playing it; that was real good. It was like a hundred years ago everybody had a banjo; that's a good thing for a country to go through. These days everybody's got a Fender: that's okay too. I think it marks an interest in the culture. But not only that because of the kind of music it was, it marks an interest in the contributions to the culture by a lot of different and various groups.[50]

ALL THIS CHANGE was anticipated by one of the revival folklorists, Ben Botkin, in his essay "The Folksong Revival: Cult or Culture?" (1964): "Every revival contains within itself the seed not only of its own destruction (in our mass entertainment the destruction proceeds from repetition and dullness as much as from catering to the lowest common denominator) but also of the new revivals."[51]

In 1971, there was no Newport Folk Festival. Diehard folk fans and performers returned to their enclaves, but the music's vast audiences had moved on to the rising disco fad or to rock and roll. By the mid-1970s, the general thinking was that folk music's day as popular music was over. Again.

But rumors of folk music's death were premature. For one thing, the conflation in the public's mind of "folk" with "singer-songwriter" ensured that the form continued to be popular. On an even more elemental level, the cultural tidal wave that swept folk music left acoustic instruments in millions of living rooms. Folk music has never needed stars or high-tech equipment; all it has ever needed is a few people who could sing it to one another. Ultimately, the nonrevivability of what never died finally emerged; a new generation, and a new folk revival—more worldly, yet dedicatedly down-home—began.

9

NU FOLK

The Music Changes, but the Beat Goes On

GRADUALLY, AS THE CHASM between traditional and popularized (singer-songwriter) music broadened, the two sides went their own ways. Or, rather, many ways.

On the surface, folk music seemed to revert to its earlier state, when the early collectors had feared it might be forgotten. The old guard of folk music performers had largely stopped touring by the 1990s, and without tours, the major record companies—now mostly subsidiaries of large entertainment conglomerates—hesitated to issue new product. Nevertheless, two subsets of folk music remained popular: songs of social protest and songs of introspective singer-songwriters.

By the 1980s, young people interested in antiestablishment song were drawn to the anyone-can-do-this ethos of new wave and punk music or to hip-hop or rap, born of dire ghetto politics. Public Enemy's song "Fight the Power" (1989) is as incendiary as anything Paul Robeson sang; NWA's "Fuck tha Police" (1988) earned the performers an investigation by the FBI.[1] Young people in the 1990s were more likely to encounter Lead Belly not through folk musicians, but through the grunge band Nirvana. And some Woody Guthrie songs may be better remembered in versions by the alternative country-rock band Wilco or the Navajo punk band Blackfire than by Pete Seeger.

Singer-songwriters exploring their personal experiences, rather than traditional songs, came to dominate the folk music produced. Work by Joni Mitchell and Neil Young set the stage for wider audiences and paved the way for folk-rockers like the Indigo Girls, Ani DiFranco, and Ben Harper. This shift opened a gateway through which musicians and younger audiences later discovered more traditional styles and instrumentation, amid a third folk music revival.

The signs are many, though any such survey must be unscientific. To begin with, an increasing number of new national labels are devoted to folk, such as Appleseed and Waterbug, while many folk labels of the seventies and eighties, such as Rounder, Shanachie, Green Linnet, Sugar Hill, and Alligator, are still producing music. Unconstrained by geography, new folk music enclaves are forming online, including what *Rolling Stone*'s Hot List called "the YouTube folk revival."[2] Folk music perseveres at the local level as well: since the year 2000, more folk festivals have taken place annually than during the folk boom's commercial peak in the 1960s.[3] Today nearly every state has a state folklorist, and local and regional festivals abound. Banjo contests and blues jams are mainstream, and even if the pickers do not identify themselves as "folk," by traditional standards their music often is. And this is occurring internationally—for example, at a "folk session" in a Scottish pub or at a picnic in Denmark where young people sing folk-styled songs of Carl Nilsen.

To further complicate the question of what is folk music, a plethora of experimental subgenres have emerged in the decades since the folk boom. These include alternative country (a mix of folk, punk, or rock, such as Uncle Tupelo or Steve Earle), Dawg music (a jazz-grass fusion of mandolinist David Grisman), newgrass (traditional bluegrass instrumentals with original music, such as fiddler Laurie Lewis or the Charles River Valley Boys' covers of the Beatles), and many other variations. These were followed in the 1990s and the following decade by a bewildering assortment of neologisms, including psych-folk; folk noir; Americana; naturalismo, also known as "freak folk" (embodied by singer-songwriter Devendra Banhart); and free folk, which one *Village Voice* reviewer defines as "a highly recombinant style whose warp'n'weft includes threads of not just traditional music but West Coast acidrock, prog, free jazz, Dead C–style noise, musique concrète, and 'outsider' minstrels."[4] There is even antifolk, an amorphous music movement complete with an Antifolk Festival in New York's East Village, weekly "Antihoots," and a zine called *Urban Folk.*[5] With many more labels encapsulated under the "nu folk" umbrella than ever before, one reviewer complained in *Folk Roots* magazine: "It used to be so simple—either it was trad or contemporary; electric or acoustic; guitar or unaccompanied; good or bad."[6]

Yet is this blurring of lines so different from earlier hybridizations, for example, Pete Seeger playing Bach on the five-string banjo?

Folk Alliance founder Mark Moss, on people's music in the twenty-first century: There are dozens of really amazing, traditional-rooted contemporary artists that are coming on to the scene today. They are not going to be Pete Seegers because it's a different world than it was then. Pete would do a record of Appalachian ballads one time; and the next, union songs; and then an original album. People today focus on one specific area.

The politics are out there, but it's being done by Rage Against the Machine and Moby and people that are part of the pop world, not the folk world. Absolutely it wouldn't be [done by] folk music. I'm using the word "folk music" in that frozen way of that concept in 1958, when it really became the moniker of that revival period. Child ballads were originally referred to as the "popular ballads"; they were the pop music of the day.

Today we have a different paradigm. It's on MTV; it has to have a video attached to it. When you're trying to generate a political message, it's a whole different array of choices and tools that you almost have to use. You can't just be a guy with a guitar out in the picket line; because you become an anachronism to the people you're trying to get rallying. Most of the great old union songs used old pop tunes. If you wanted to do a song like that today you would have to use pop music, like Chuck D and Steve Earle and people like that.[7]

Guitarist Happy Traum, on post-sixties protest music: I'm not sure that it's really true [that there's a decreasing number of political songs being sung]. I actually think it's spread out a bit. In the sixties, all the musical protest was coming from small groups who were playing acoustic guitars and singing songs like Woody Guthrie or like Bob Dylan. Later on, that began to spread. Now, there's a whole reggae movement that's very political with the Bob Marley influence.

A lot of the rock musicians are very involved politically.... I think there's quite a lot of political music activity but I think it's taken different forms and isn't necessarily the "We Shall Overcome" variety.[8]

Folksinger Holly Near, on musical genres and youth culture: Hip-hop has already mobilized urban children and young people. It's definitely been the platform for speaking about the conditions of contemporary urban life. As is rap. And spoken word. This generation that has so profoundly embraced the use of words—at some point, they will come back and rediscover the extraordinary sensation one can have when expressing oneself through melody.

I don't think that everybody in the world, in the youth culture, is just into hip-hop or rap. I think there are people who are taking that experience and moving it out into all kinds of other forms. Hip-hop and rap: it's become really economically viable to be a spoken-word poet. You don't have to have a big studio; you don't have to have lots of instruments; [it's] a very accessible form to young people....

The thing about rock and roll and folk is that it keeps coming back to the fact that you can pick it up, know three chords, and you can do a song. And you can become a garage band or a folksinger with just three chords.

And as you get to know more, then you become something else. But those three chords are always available in rock and roll and folk music, as a starting point. And it makes it accessible to people in a most extraordinary way. And, of course, even more so is a cappella singing. You don't even need the guitar. You just start singing.

I have great faith in sound. I think that it always will race off here and there and there'll always be a John Cage who'll come along and challenge melody. Or there'll always be a rap band that will take it off and challenge it that way.

There's going to be challenges. But I think that just adds to the mix. But you go back—I mean, Woody was a rap artist. I mean that; he talked! And when he didn't have a guitar handy, he just chattered!

I think we reinvent ourselves again and again and again. And there's kind of a wonderful, delightful hope in that.[9]

Bagpiper Chris O'Reilly, on how it feels to be a teenaged folkie in the twenty-first century: I was probably about ten or so when I heard folk music. I never thought I liked music that much; I didn't really have any favorite artists. I must have heard my dad playing albums around the house. I think I liked it originally for its musical melody. I started listening to it, and my dad gave me some CDs. Then I started listening to the lyrics more and more, and I didn't fully understand it at first.

For a while it was pretty much all I listened to. This was when everyone else was listening to music that was pretty bad in comparison, I thought. Rap and punk, and all the other genres of music that are around that I never really went for. I wasn't really too affected by that. I listened to folk music by myself. I prefer to listen to music of someone who has something to say.[10]

Punk and traditional Navajo performer Jeneda Benally, on the folk roots of punk: Folk music is the original punk music. I say that because punk has this energy about it, this rawness, this message. We're not talking about mall punk, but I'm talking about true punk music, which really has something to say. And the energy and the emotion is so parallel to folk music. And folk music just means people. Folk—that's who we are, we're all people, and we're all expressing ourselves in a way that hopefully can create positive change in the world.[11]

ALTHOUGH FOLK MUSIC ENTHUSIASTS may not be in a hurry to include punk-rock or street rap under "folk music," these genres do share folk's functional, participatory, and people's-music qualities.

Attempting to definitively define folk music today would be brash; but all could agree that the tent is wider than ever before. The songs of the Rolling Stones (who once recorded acoustic versions of traditional blues) are now themselves passed from one generation to another, uncredited; and new singers make up words to "(I Can't Get No) Satisfaction" when they forget how it goes. At what point does one call the song "folk" the way "Home on the Range" is, despite its known author and original form?

This third revival is better organized and much larger than the revival of the People's Songs era. Unlike folklore societies of yore, the North American Folk Music and Dance Alliance has a professional staff and hosts one of the five largest music conferences in the United States each year.[12] This folk music advocacy organization, known as the Folk Alliance, seeks "to foster and promote traditional, contemporary, and multicultural folk music and dance."[13] Its mission statement sums up the consensus on North American folk music today: American roots music and world music, melding contemporary sounds, styles, and instrumentation with traditional and vernacular styles. But the world is so much smaller today; underlying this diversity is the same yearning for community (now global) that drew people to folk music during the sixties folk revival.

Of course, American revivalists have long included international material; folk music has always involved travel and trade in its transmission. In the 1940s and 1950s, nightclub audiences heard Marais and Miranda, or in the sixties, Miriam Makeba, singing songs from their native Africa. The Weavers popularized "Tzena, Tzena," "Guantanamera," and "Wimoweh." Caribbean *son* and salsa have enormous followings in the United States. Whether this is cultural appropriation or exoticism, the attraction of world music and its integration into what is called folk music has only increased.

Now, with the global interconnectedness enabled by advancing technology and travel, folk-musical tourism has emerged. Folksingers have often embellished their personal repertoires with an Irish drinking song or a South African freedom chant, thus showcasing the traditional alongside the modern, the foreign within the familiar (as Paul Simon did with Ladysmith Black Mambazo on his 1985 album *Graceland*). Today, folk musicians not only borrow folk songs from afar; they incorporate any tune into their own musical idiom. Thus, Celtic singers belt out blues, Eurasians play bluegrass fiddle, and Jewish Americans sing Macedonian folk songs at traditional weddings.

In this new revival, the evolution of folk music suggests that anyone can play traditional music from any country in any style. Of course, accepting such a statement makes untenable the classic three definitional pillars of folk song (anonymity, nonwritten transmission, and variant lyrics). With folk music learned from recordings widely, even instantly (and freely, if illegally) available, the meaning of "nonwritten transmission" has obviously changed. Even performers who inherit their traditions through oral transmission feel compelled to transform (and personalize) that music. With all of these changes comes a smorgasbord of possibility: African bands make music videos in the style of America's MTV; and rural Kentucky youngsters, whose grandparents originated claw-hammer-style banjo, perform reggae.

FOLKSINGERS OF TODAY

Around the world, young musicians turn to traditional music—hybridized and purist—as a way to identify with a particular culture and tradition, whether or not that culture is a part of their heritage. Eva Salina Primack is an example of just how international folk music has become. A young Jewish-American singer of Balkan music, Primack was raised in California, where as a young child she stumbled on unusual tunes from a region far away. Something in her responded deeply, and she has grown up to become a serious teacher and performer of Albanian and Bulgarian tunes. A critic described Primack's identity-border-crossing repertoire as an example of how music travels now "by way of the internet, amalgams of expatriates, and the local musicians who have traveled the caravan routes. Maybe just being a musician today is to be a gypsy of sorts, and the cyber world allows for wandering freely across musical perimeters."[14]

Eva Salina Primack, on becoming a folksinger in a culture not her own: Balkan music felt like the most natural way to express myself. There was something about just hearing and repeating and learning in that folk style. I had played violin for a few years and didn't find the Western classical system of learning to be anything that I was made for. I prefer to just kind of listen and observe and repeat. And because when we went to Balkan music camp [the Mendocino Balkan Music and Dance Workshops in Northern California] I met all these Bulgarian musicians who really took me under their wings. . . .

I experienced a lot of really intense isolation as a child because what the folk music had given me was this parallel life—a huge community, a huge network of people all over the world. And that was not something that I could really show to people my age. There was no frame of reference for them. And so I ended up really living these parallel lives where I was one person when I was at school. I read a lot. I kept to myself. Then when I left school, I felt like my life began.

I made a conscious effort to learn about American pop culture in high school. Because I felt like I needed some common language. . . . I had to go through the motions of being a normal American teenager. I've tried and now I think I've succeeded at being less separated. I don't have to have multiple identities. I am identified through music completely, 100 percent.

If I can renew interest within the Balkan youth immigrants in the United States, in their own culture, than that's the greatest thing for me. If I can play a show where there are as many hipsters as there are immigrants in the audience, then I know that I'm doing something productive.[15]

WHY SHOULD A YOUNG WOMAN from the United States sing centuries-old Albanian tunes? For today's revivalists, the answer may lie in finding a way to reformulate musical community, beyond its original borders and ethnicities. Put simply, this revival is about exposing old songs, styles, and instruments to new audiences and then, as Primack explains, putting "something relevant of myself into it." This last comment is what allows her to bring her personal mix of tradition and innovation to larger audience. For many third-generation revivalists, personalization coincides with a presentation of tradition. As they sing, they blend consciously and unconsciously. Primack can perform songs more or less exactly as she learned them—traditional in form and transmission, though not in context and function. She chooses not to.

Eva Salina Primack, on personalizing songs: I can't just keep singing the songs over and over and over the way I've been taught to sing them. There are many other singers who have done that. So there are questions: What is it about this music that spoke to me? How is it that I can speak to this music? What can I find in myself that will add, that will contribute, that will make this bigger? That will not try to preserve it? (Because when you preserve it you effectively kill it, you are trying to keep it like a museum piece.) But what is there that is current and contemporary in this music that can be brought out, not compromising the essence but continuing the evolution? A lot of what I've been doing now is trying to counteract this mindset of "Oh we have to find the song that nobody's sung, that nobody has the words to and it will be *our* song"—this happens a lot with especially Roma music, with gypsy music, which is kind of my big love— "Everybody's got the words. Everybody's sung it the same way for so many years, let's discard it. Let's find something new." I don't believe that....

Authenticity is a really big issue. I have come across a lot of criticism of the stuff that I do over the years. But I think the most important thing a performer can do is be honest. Because if I listen to a singer who's been studying Balkan music for fifteen years, and I can say, "Oh, they've studied with this person, this person, this person, and they're trying to sound like this person," is that authentic? Is that interesting? If I'm here merely to replicate what has been done for so many years, so *well* by so many Balkan singers, there's no point for me.

When I was growing up, when I was learning, it was all about imitation, so, like, "Sing this exactly the way your teacher taught it to you and execute it perfectly every time." That all shifted.[16]

IN THE THIRD REVIVAL, young musicians forge their identities and find community in music camps and festivals. Not all regions of the country are equally involved; but musical gatherings of both sorts abound in New England, the Mid-Atlantic states, the New South, and particularly the Bay Area, where a young fiddler like Annie Staninec finds plenty of pickers.

Like Primack, Annie Staninec fell in love with traditional music and made her way onto the festival stages. Like many rising American musicians, she was musically trained via the Suzuki or "mother-tongue" method, which replicates the learn-by-ear experience of a traditional musician. And Staninec is a devotee of tradition: she sounds like the hot fiddlers up North who played in Bill Monroe's Yankee band in the 1950s.

Annie Staninec, on her folk music world: For me, folk music is social. Not socialist, but social. I love getting together and swapping tunes at jams and someone's house or in the parking lot at the festivals. I can go from group to group and just play along.

Back in elementary and middle school, everyone was into rap; but by the time I got to high school [San Francisco's School for the Arts], I began to meet others who picked and sang. And I'd always known other kids [who played]—just not in school. Parents would bring the family to a bluegrass festival and other kids, like me, would play along with their parents. And sometimes we'd have friends over for dinner and picking parties. I learned other kinds of music, but playing folk music together is just so much fun.

Music—particularly bluegrass—is at the center of my life. I teach. I perform. I play with friends. And I play American music, as I've learned it. I'm not mixing traditions.[17]

THE FACT THAT STANINEC is only twenty-two and Eurasian—her mother is Japanese and her father Czech—does not seem to affect her musical choices. Instead of English lullabies, she heard Japanese children's songs; but what really attracted her as a musician were the old songs and that high, lonesome sound. Staninec has played fiddle in bluegrass bands since high school; her bandmates were in their thirties and beyond. Today, besides performing with a second-revival bluegrass performer, Kathy Kallick, she is in a band of her peers. She learned her repertoire listening to old recordings and playing along with her dad in the living room.

Annie Staninec, on growing up on traditional music: My dad was asked if he liked the New Lost City Ramblers, and other revival groups. "Some," he said, "but I like the guys *they* learned from: Dock Boggs, Clarence Ashley, Roscoe Holcomb." So those are the ones I grew up listening to. I grew up playing at music camps, informal jams, festivals, small clubs. Not every-body knows this music. Not everybody likes it. One time a neighbor boy was hanging around, and I didn't want him to. I put on a record of Roscoe Holcomb singing "In the Pines." He told me he had something cooking at his house. And he never came back![18]

WHAT THE STORIES of musicians like Annie Staninec and Eva Salina Primack illustrate are the disintegration of boundaries—cultural, linguistic, generational, and geographic borders—under the influence of globalization. The folk music born of this cross-pollination is as diverse and varied as its origins.

Mark Moss, on the status of folk in the Internet age: The bottom line is that, however you define [folk music], I think we're in something of a renaissance right now. For several reasons. It's not a renaissance that has been embraced or encouraged or supported by the commercial music industry. The commercial music industry is shriveling and dying right now. Where it's gaining life is in the grassroots on the Internet. It has created a way to connect with audience and build community around music in a way that was never even imagined or thought of before. If I want to reach somebody with what *Sing Out!*'s doing, I can reach anybody in any place in the globe with an Internet connection. I couldn't do that in 1950 when that first issue came out, and we had to create a chain of people passing it along to get it out there.

It's not so much that there is a lot more at the top, but it's a lot broader at the bottom—there's more community. There's a lot more interest in researching online. In folk music I think it's similar. We have an accessibility of world music which I believe very strongly is an integral part of what defines folk music.[19]

Folksinger Pete Seeger, on his own varied influences: I've heard so many different kinds of music now, from classical music and jazz, as well as different kinds of folk music, and music from Asia and Africa, and I've been influenced by them all, in exactly which way I couldn't tell. If somebody wants to untangle it, I suppose they could. I'm not sure it's worth it. And I'm not the only person this is happening to. I'm sure it's happening to thousands, hundreds of thousands of other musicians. Some of them are jazz musicians, some of them are classical musicians, whatever they are, and I think it's a rather normal process of acculturation. . . .

I sing a song, "All Mixed Up":

You know this language that we speak,
Is part German, Latin, and part Greek,
Celtic, and Arabic, all in a heap,
Well amended by the people in the street.[20]

TECHNOLOGY AND THE THIRD REVIVAL

The vast array of music available on the Internet—commercial, home-made, and everything in between—has profoundly affected American folk music. The nature of that effect is still debatable, but not the tremendous scope of technological availability. Recorded catalogues of traditional music are online: nearly the entire Folkways collection, expanded in 2009 to include the Smithsonian Global Sound collection, is hosted digitally by Smithsonian Folkways. And with playback devices such as the iPod having the memory capacity for tens of thousands of songs, the bulk of the Smithsonian Institution's massive folk music collection might fit in somebody's jeans pocket.

The steadily enhanced virtual folk world has a growing role in shaping this third folk revival. For help navigating the volume of music available, there are listservs, blogs, and chat sites such as Mudcat that help musicians and fans network. And there are web programs such as Pandora, which uses mathematical algorithms generated by the Music Genome Project to play music specifically suited to individual listeners' preferences—including traditional performances of traditional music.

In the recent past, musicians seeking commercial success needed a recording company to record, produce, edit, and manufacture their work; now, a fast laptop and good software can do the job. The same boundaries have broken down for distribution: as of 2009, nearly 275,000 musicians (some of them folk) bypass commercial record companies by using CD Baby to distribute self-made recordings.[21] For performers, "YouTube has become the new open mike," reports Nicole Frehsee for *Rolling Stone*, writing about the virtual folk music community. "It's flooded with more acoustic guitars and harmonica racks than the sidewalks of Greenwich Village in 1962."[22]

Technology has also broken down barriers of production cost and audience access for performers and opened channels of communication between musicians and fans all over the world. Accessible digital software has simplified do-it-yourself recording; never in human history has it been so easy to record and record well. Performers are no longer beholden to commercial studios full of high-tech equipment with out-of-bounds price tags.

Of course, to the music world, technology has never been solely a boon. As with the advent of the phonograph and then the radio, copyright is again a hot-button issue. In a 2008 editorial in the *New York Times*, folksinger Billy Bragg argued: "The claim that sites such as MySpace and Bebo are doing us [musicians] a favor by promoting our work is disingenuous. Radio stations also promote our work, but they pay us a royalty that recognizes our contribution to their business. Why should that not apply to the Internet, too?"[23]

Also of concern is whether the cyber flood brings the risk of musical overexposure. Joe Boyd, veteran producer of folk albums, notes:

> There is a homogenizing effect of too much information....Most things in our society have had a lot of the rough edges rubbed off them. Computers have had a big effect on culture. They provide a way to make note of how everything works, then to get it to work better. Everything gets kind of sleekly honed.[24]

The rough-and-bumpy amateur performance, with loping rhythms, spontaneous grace notes, or erratically tuned fiddle, has contributed much to folk music's charm. Are these down-home styles at risk of being drowned out by more "sleekly honed" competition? And, as scholars of folk music have long worried, is folk music—something they have defined as born of communal recreation—in danger of dilution and decontextualization?

Folklorist Archie Green, on cultural exchange: The real danger [isn't anachronism, it] is those tens of thousands of people singing along on the refrain of a Javanese lullaby and a phrase of an Israeli *hora* and a phrase of a Soviet air force song.

All the forces of technology move us in the direction of homogenization of cultural blandness. The enemies aren't a few music merchants who are profiteering by copyrighting songs. If there are enemies here, the enemies are built into all of the technological devices we have used in communication since Gutenberg. It's these little things. It's transistor radios and it's inexpensive recordings...tape recorders and inexpensive plastic discs.

In a sense this technology helped shear the people of the world of their distinctive hides. (Mass culture continually shears special groups and subordinate groups of culture.) Now when that mass culture process gets tied into nationalism or particular historic situations—the Catholic-Protestant split in Ireland, the Muslims and the Christians in Lebanon, the French Canadians and the English Canadians—it can be a very destructive and explosive fusion. So part of my concern for cultural autonomy, for cultural dignity, for cultural preservation has come out of my radical politics. In part I want discrete and subordinate groups to have a right to hang onto their culture. But I also want, to the extent that anyone can, to commit myself to defusing cultural politics when it's negative.

Years ago if a musicologist wanted to study the music of an obscure people, he had to take four or five years and go to South Africa or go to the Australian desert. Now, you can buy more traditional performances of exotic music than that musicologist could have heard in a lifetime fifty years ago. Of course, this is contradictory. The very technology that can preserve and document a lot of this stuff, also wipes it out. Because for every person who buys the music of Angola, there's a million who are still buying the Beatles.[25]

Ethnomusicologist Charles Seeger, on musical hegemony and the future of folk music: Rock and roll and other products of the United States musically are going to kill dozens of beautiful old musics. What is happening is what has always happened in music history. The million small traditions are blending in the larger tradition. Some of them, even when they get quite large, are being obliterated by a still bigger one. Because the economic, political, religious powers help that obliteration.

It happened on the island of Nias, according to Jaap Kunst. The missionaries didn't like the natives going around naked or half-naked so they got the women to wear Mother Hubbards and the men to wear pajamas. The singing (and the accompanying dancing) they thought was very immoral. There was a public freedom of sex that they didn't like. So they got together with the business people that were coming in, and with the political governor or whoever was his police, to make the island of Nias safe for European commerce. The music of Nias was practically obliterated. Now the question is, if the people of Nias are still alive, are they trying to revive their old music, now that the missionaries are weakened, the economic push is not so great, and the governor general has been thrown out, and they're part of a republic?

The only way that I can conceive of the people of Nias trying to lighten the weight of the foreign music that's been imposed on them—hymn singing and that sort of thing and then, later, ragtime and then jazz and then later rock and roll—will be to try to go back and find their own music. What will they find?

You might call that a folk music revival if you like. They will find it or try to find it, I'll bet you a thousand to one, once the pressure from outside lets up, and they realize that they've gone into this foreign music more deeply, and forgotten too much of their own music.

They won't entirely throw off the imported music, but they'll try to bring up the old music and look at it with the eyes of the hymns and the jazz and the rock and roll and they'll fuse it. That process is going on all over the world now.

If the United States keeps up its music imperialism the way it is now, I wouldn't be surprised if we had a pidgin music that almost anybody can sing, all over the world, just the same in Patagonia as in Alaska. And it will be awful. Meanwhile, our own idioms of music are getting more and more multitudinous and more and more different, more and more fragmented. It may burn out, sort of just vanish eventually, and this pidgin music would be realized....

I feel convinced that that's what's in stock for both music and language. It may happen quickly; it may happen in centuries. I don't know. It is a continual historical development.[26]

Punk and traditional Navajo performer Clayson Benally, on tensions between preserving traditions and affirming one's own voice: When we look to our father and he passes new songs on to us, when we sing them back, there's a certain amount of accuracy that has to be upheld, obviously. Everybody has their own voice, their own unique sound, how they sing it; but when it comes to either the words, or if it's a ceremonial song—they have to remain intact. You cannot change or alter them. This is something that we're going to pass on to our children and their grandchildren. That's how it's been done for our people for generations upon generations. But the most important thing is obviously finding your voice and being able to sing them, and learning, so we just try to facilitate that connection, whether we're trying to inspire youth on our own reservation, or the different tribes and regions we visit throughout the world. We're all kind of in this same situation where we're losing our language, we're losing our traditional songs. There's that threat. If it's not carried on within our generation, a lot of these cultures are going to be lost at an alarming rate.[27]

Folksinger Peggy Seeger, on singing the songs of other cultures: When I went to England [in the sixties] there was a great thing on about singing Lead Belly and Woody Guthrie. At the club I went to, this gangly youth got up and sang a Lead Belly song. I folded up. I literally folded up. I was in hysterics, I must have had one beer too many; but I was in the aisles rolling with laughter, I couldn't control it. Ewan [MacColl] said, "What is this? You sang a French song last night. If you can't put up with that you shouldn't sing French songs." And I never did; I've never, on a platform, sung a song in a language I don't understand ever since. I don't want anybody folding up....

I know that when I went to Russia, I sang a song in Russian to open up my performance, and they loved it. I cannot reconcile this with my feeling that I should not do such things. They will love you more in Russia and China and Portugal and Spain if you do this, but now I would never do it. I couldn't, ever since that experience. My sense of a performer tells me I would get more of a response that way; my sense of personal truth tells me "You're a fake."[28]

A FUTURE FOR TOPICAL SONG

With folk music so readily available, fans might wonder what became of protest and topical songs. Are they still written and sung, if rarely broadcast? With bank failures, curtailment of civil liberties in the name of the War on Terror, and military quagmires aplenty, there are no shortages of causes ripe for song. Of course the music, like the struggles, has changed with the times—just as the Composers' Collective (sympathetic, skilled, and clueless) gave way to the Almanacs (enthusiastic, skilled, and green). Antiestablishment songs have evolved from struggle to struggle: fighting union songs in the thirties; treasonable antiwar songs as World War II began; songs informally treasonable, which provoked HUAC in the fifties; songs that pushed out boundaries in the sixties and seventies; and those in the name of feminism, environmentalism, and challenging globalization and oppression in the eighties and the relatively prosperous nineties. For much of the twentieth century, topical folk music was the genre for "singing out"; but will this continue in the twenty-first century? Who, if anyone, will be singing out in the future? And what will they be singing?

One answer to these questions is embodied by the punk-rockers of the family band Blackfire: Clayson, Jeneda, and Klee Benally—Diné (Navajo) siblings who grew up on the conflict-ridden reservation in a home without electricity or running water, but with a strong sense of tradition (the trio's father, Jones Benally, is a medicine man, traditional singer, and hoop dancer). Blackfire's work moves between traditional Diné music and rage-rock. Although their distorted guitar riffs would certainly startle the Cecil Sharps and John Lomaxes of old, the chords are basically the same.

Klee Benally, on reconciling musical tradition and the modern world: I like to say that our music is a result of our desire to find balance within the contradictions that we're faced with as people who have grown up with the cultural identity and understanding of the Diné.... Part of that contradiction is a response to assimilation, colonization, the negative influences that are destroying our environment, our culture, not only for Diné people but for all peoples.

The connection between the protest music that we play (and that other artists find as a way to express themselves on issues they care deeply about) and traditional Diné music is exemplified by the album *[Silence] Is a Weapon* [2007]. That album is actually two separate discs. One is all traditional songs taught to us by our father, who is a recording artist, a traditional singer, and *hatathli* [healer]; who learned a lot of the songs that he shared with us for this album (and which we've grown up knowing) from his great-great-grandfather, who trained warriors. The songs that we chose to

place on that traditional disc for *[Silence] Is a Weapon* are all songs for warriors; not just for fighting (it doesn't glorify killing or anything like that),
it's actually about the strength, the understanding of how we always must
maintain harmony and peace, and seek that balance.

The contemporary disc in *[Silence] Is a Weapon* is all songs that we constructed. (Actually, one song is written by Peter LaFarge, a Native American
protest singer-songwriter. Unfortunately he is very little-known, but was
a very powerful inspiration for a lot of people like Johnny Cash and Bob
Dylan.) So those songs that we wrote are also a type of warrior song. And
when we utilize that term "warrior," it's not just somebody who is of a war-
like nature. It's actually someone who cares deeply about the things that are
happening to their people, or the community, or threats to their ways of life;
and who takes a stand to do something about that. For us, it's more about
seeking justice. So when we constructed that album—a concept album—we
wanted to have not only contrasts but similarities between those traditional
songs that are for seeking justice, for seeking balance.

The songs of today are for seeking justice, seeking balance; because
that's part of what's lacking, especially with today's youth, on and off the
reservations. Not just [among] indigenous Diné youth, not just the Pueblo
or the more than 560 tribes federally recognized in the so-called U.S., but
all indigenous people from all over the world.

Something that's lacking is that connection between the traditional and
the modern, because there's this understanding that people seem to have
of two separate worlds, a traditional world and a modern world. But for
us, it's always been one world. These two discs that we have on *[Silence]
Is a Weapon*, one traditional and one modern, are just different paths that
exist, and it's not separate, because we're the same people. We still carry
on our traditional ways of life as much as we can. We still have that knowledge and still have those prayers. We still have those songs and our dances
for healing. And here we are in this modern world.[29]

**Jeneda Benally, on identifying with both traditional songs and punk-
rock:** Well, when we sing a traditional song, we sing it in the traditional
style. When we incorporate a traditional song, it's incorporated, but it's
still the traditional style. We really try to keep the integrity of our tradition
because we want people to see that it still exists; our tradition, our culture,
still exists. And it's who we are, even though we're dressed differently—
we're not wearing feathers and don't have braids in our hair, all the stereo-
types that people imagine about indigenous people here in America—that
we still are cultural people, and we want to keep our culture intact. We
have our two forms of music, I guess, the punk-rock and the traditional.
They interact, they coexist, the same that we do. We're traditional people,
that's who we are, but we are also punks.[30]

Klee Benally, on Blackfire's protest music: When we first started our band, we came up with the name Blackfire because it was a response to the pollution, the threat of war, nuclear terror, and all of these things that we saw as this force—that was just like what was burning not too far from our place where we were originally from on Black Mesa: coal. Peabody Coal Company is operating this industry that is destroying our mother, the Earth, for profit, for greed; and everything that's burning from that is killing the people and the planet. So for us, our music is for addressing those issues. It's a response to those issues, but it's a way to allow us to release that anger and frustration as a natural reaction, when you see such horrendous things happening in your community, to your own family. So our music is a type of resistance, but it's not all we do.[31]

FOLK-PROTEST MUSIC TODAY

Another response to the question how folk-protest music will continue is the People's Music Network, founded by Connecticut musician Charlie King and friends in 1977; the group has nurtured political song ever since. A modern-day People's Songs, the People's Music Network unites socially active musicians who unapologetically sing for progressive causes. Other similar organizations exist, for example Riot-Folk, a nationwide musical cooperative begun in 2004 that describes itself as "an anti-profit mutual-aid collective of radical artists and musicians [who] make music to provoke, educate, heal, and inspire."[32]

Pete Seeger, on the People's Music Network: Charlie King started it. He wrote a letter to about twenty-five people he knew and he said, we often meet each other backstage at a peace rally, sometime we should get together. But we never do. Well, he said, I've rented a summer camp for the weekend of the first weekend in June and if you bring yourself and your guitar or whatever, we can have two days to talk over this and that. Politics, music, anything. Seventy-five people showed up. They had such a good time they said, "Let's meet again the same time.". . .

Well, after about four years, I remember, Charlie had Roy Brown come up from Puerto Rico one year. But he was a little disappointed. There were no Latinos there. And Luci Murphy refused to come. She said, "No, I'm not going to be your token black. You've got a problem to solve." So they had a serious discussion and decided that every January—it's usually the last weekend in January—they'd meet in some city. Right away the January meetings got to be more important than the June meetings.

Well, we have very interesting discussions. We had a long workshop one day, "So we disagree." There were pacifists there who are devout followers of

Dr. King. There were revolutionists there saying, "How are we going to get rid of this dictator? You think songs are going to do it?" It was a very basic discussion that I wish could go on all around the world, that kind of discussion. Then we had a children's workshop that became so important that they ended up splitting and now there's the Children's Music Network.

Lots of good singers have gotten their start there. They sang in the bathtub or they made up a song just for their family, but they didn't know how to get an audience to hear them, and they come to People's Music Weekend and find out there's no great mystery about singing for an audience. The next thing you know, they've quit their job and they're traveling around the country singing and making up new songs.[33]

Singer-songwriter John McCutcheon, on today's political song: Rap music started to be urban political folk music before it became a parody of itself. I think it would be impossible to avoid hip-hop. If I was twenty-two years old, I probably wouldn't know anything about Woody Guthrie or Pete Seeger. How would you except maybe if you heard this new Bruce Springsteen album? But then, that almost feels like that's a kind of skiffle band approach—it's kind of fun; maybe I'll be in a band that will do stuff like that. I really don't see a political future doing that.

You have a whole world of music out there now. I see these new groups coming up now who are doing such interesting things musically: aboriginal rock bands out of Australia; Billy Bragg and Wilco. (If I was twenty-two years old I would think of them as old guys probably.) Young kids know who Woody Guthrie is. He's iconic—he's the new Pete, in a way, because you have these hip young rockers who are taking his music. Take the Mammals: they're so retro, they're hip.[34]

Music producer Jim Musselman, on political songwriting today: When the Iraq war broke out everybody was patriotic; and when we did "Bring 'Em Home," we got so much criticism for that because they thought we weren't being patriotic. I think the Bush administration was smart in that they didn't have a draft, because that would have politicized so many young people. I think if people were more personally affected there would be more of that social awareness. There was one very progressive Democratic congressman who called for a draft because he knew that it would empower younger people.

That's why I started the label, Appleseed, to find the roots and branches of political music; there isn't a lot. Trying to find some rays of hope, I get probably a thousand tapes a year from artists, and I will listen to every one, but I don't see a lot of younger artists making really serious political statements or really writing from the depth of the Seegers or the Dylans or the people from the previous generations.

Pete wrote in this very metaphoric, timeless way. I think that's the hard thing. Malvina Reynolds was not the greatest performer in the world but she was a great writer of songs. Phil Ochs was a journalist and wrote songs. People today don't want to write about politics [in general]; it's more "me" than "we." The sixties had such great music because it was about "we." Everyone today is writing about their lives and not the bigger picture.

There are political songs in rap, hip-hop. What I've tried to address with the folk community is that they are running from their history. The music is out there, somewhat; but to me, artists have to have the ability to respond quickly. When the invasion of Iraq occurred, how many wrote songs dealing with that? I look at things that occur now—the Phil Ochs and the Guthries would have a field day today. I think a lot of music has changed: it isn't about music; it's about entertainment.[35]

Eva Salina Primack, on politics in music: In Balkan music, politics is not really a unity-building thing at all, historically. It's intensively divisive. [Yet] I can build unity by exposing a Bulgarian to some Turkish music, when they were really anti-Turk. "I'm not here to participate in all this history," I say. "It's not mine. It doesn't belong to me."

That's a way in which my outsider status has given me an advantage. I'm not beholden to any of these histories. I recognize that there are many, many atrocities that have occurred on all sides, but I'm there for the music.[36]

Klee Benally, on turning on to punk music to address social issues: When we were growing up, there was a lot of commercial, superficial crap on the radio that really was something that I could not relate to and none of us could relate to... what with these frustrations of just trying to figure out our relationship and our identity, being mixed and being from these different areas and seeing things not in this bubblegum, plastic consumer world.

So the first time we heard the Ramones, the Dead Kennedy, Subhumans, Crass, Bad Brains, we could relate not only to the energy but to the fact that there was a message there as well. It was just really empowering, actually, to find that connection and to see how that type of energy was being used by those musicians to express themselves, to address the issues and just release it. It feels good to play that kind of music and get that energy out there, that emotion out there, and to transform that.

So for me, instead of repurposing, it's about this ongoing process of transformation. Looking to find the different ways or mechanisms, really, that we can use to be good people, good people of service to our community and to the environment that we care about and values based upon where we come from. And that might sound completely diametrically opposed to what punk-rock is, but for us it's not. I think that it is an ongoing process of healing, and music is one very powerful component of that.[37]

John McCutcheon, on protest music: The thing that's different politically now is back when I started off it was about racism and the war. Race is not the tinderbox that it is for [the sixties] generation. Now it's much more about economics and globalization: you go to the IMF World Bank rallies and it's all twenty-something-year-olds.

For instance, my road manager's son plays in a punk band, and they do a big thrash version of "Not in My Name." (Actually that song has been covered a lot by young rock-and-roll bands.)

At the last IMF World Bank rally I was at, I remember running into Pat Humphries on a street corner and some young people turned around and recognized us. They were saying, "Shouldn't there be music?"[38]

Holly Near, on the challenges facing socially conscious artists: I think that the times right now are harder for socially conscious artists, harder even than when I came in. But every generation has to find their way through that.

The Weavers had to find their way through the House Un-American Activities Committee. I had to find my way through sexism and homophobia; and the transition from a music industry that actually was owned by people, to one owned by corporations. This next generation, they're going to have to find their way through this extraordinary technology that's at their fingertips. And yet even though every single person can now make a CD in their living room, they have this problem of who's going to listen to it?

Most of us had an audience developed not because we had recordings—pop artists who were promoted have that—but folk artists become well known because they're heard live. And where are the opportunities for the next generation to perform live? Well, they're going to have to look around. And if they don't find it, they're going to have to *create* it, just like we did. When feminists or lesbians didn't have a venue, they had to create a movement that made the venues happen. They would go out and find a Unitarian church that was willing to have an outspoken lesbian in them.

Every generation has to lay down the bricks before they step on them. And they can certainly be influenced by the generation before, just as I was influenced by the Weavers; but the set of problems I faced were a different set of problems. Not necessarily harder or easier, just different.

So, this next generation will have to articulate what their walls and obstacles are and decide if they want to become bricklayers.[39]

PROTEST MUSIC MAY HAVE MOVED on to other genres, but politics and folk music still intersect. On January 18, 2009, two days before his inauguration, Barack Obama spoke at the Lincoln Memorial, near where Martin Luther King, Jr., had dreamed aloud forty-six years earlier, in the company of folksingers. Sharing that hallowed stage with America's first black president was eighty-nine-year-old Pete Seeger, singing Woody Guthrie's "This Land Is Your Land"—belting out Guthrie's radical verses, rarely performed, with grandson Tao Rodriguez-Seeger and Bruce Springsteen.

FOLK MUSIC IN THE PRESENT

If Woody Guthrie or Aunt Molly Jackson or Joe Hill were to visit this new millennium and download MP3s of contemporary "folk" or "protest" songs, would they recognize them as such? Would they hear in today's music the appreciation of homemade culture, and understand its ties to social activism?

One can only wonder what Francis Child, Cecil Sharp, Olive Dame Campbell, or John Lomax would think of critic Thomas Gruning's post-modernist analysis: "Folk is no longer a type of music. Rather, it is symp-tomatic of a dynamic confluence of ideas, ideals, and ideologies within which...tradition, lived experience, community, economy, tourism (both literally and figuratively), and technology intertwine in convoluted webs of significance."[40] We have come a long way to return to the position "It's all folk music."

Eva Salina Primack, on passing down music: My father said to me, "You have to make your own ethnomusicology. If you don't like the system, make your own. Make your own folk music."

What will I give to my children? A little piece of everything. You know, I don't just listen to Balkan music. I listen to tons of American hip-hop, and I listen to bluegrass and Brazilian music. I listen to South African music, North African music, Arabic music, old and contemporary alike, because I'm so curious to listen to people who are fighting the same fight of how do we reference [the past] and how do we also grow and contribute to its evolution.[41]

Klee Benally, on performing punk-rock at the Woody Guthrie Folk Festival: I think that one of the most nervous times I ever had getting on stage was in Okemah, Oklahoma, during the Woody Guthrie Folk Festival.... Here we are, going to get up there, plug in everything, distor-tion and all, plug in all our electric amps and everything and look out in the audience. Not to offend anybody but it's all blue-haired [people] with lawn chairs and straw bale seats.

The sense was that people will probably just look at us a little bit strange and maybe after a while they'll cover their ears and start going away. But everybody stayed. At the end we had a standing ovation, and it just sort of shocked us because we could have been prejudiced and discriminated against the audience based upon what we saw and just been like, we need to change our set. But we didn't want to; we just wanted to put it out there the way we feel, the way we're doing it.

I don't know what the audience was responding to—maybe they were giving us a standing ovation because we were done!

But people came up to us and said, "You know, Woody Guthrie was a punk-rocker, and if he was around today, I think he'd like your music too." Not to say that's unique to us; that would apply to a lot of other young people out there who are writing these songs based upon their experiences and their desires, their hopes and their fears. For me that's what it's about: music is a tool for us to be able to communicate. And sometimes it can be just a commodity, but I think it's deeper than that. We look at our values—those questions of the challenges and injustices we face—and we call on people to respond to that, to either do something or just think about it.[42]

WHAT WILL THE FOLK MUSICS of the United States be in the future? So far traditional music has survived (or incorporated) efforts to commercialize and internationalize. In the United States and the British Isles, folk music as a genre is popular enough among baby boomers to support folk music venues and community-radio programs. In broad definition, folk music reseeds itself, with the public forgetting and rewording enough songs to replenish those forgotten. Just as vinyl records have survived the CD, with more issued each year, so too do old songs appear in new contexts, sometimes in new apparel.

Twelve-year-olds learning the fiddle to play in a family band; teenagers competing at bluegrass festivals; new parents singing with their children at the park; sixtysomethings gathered around the hearth for an evening of homemade music and making up words they can't remember—all these are small but persistent signs of a folk music revival in our time.

"If folk music means music of the people, then I certainly hope we play folk music," jokes Klee Benally. So in the end, the question is not one of survival; for folk music by definition is eternal, if mutable, and the power of music to renew itself is a continuing wonder. Now, the question is which music, and which folk, will once again uncover that deep flowing river of our shared musical heritage and what they will make of it.

10

THE POWER OF MUSIC

MUSIC'S POWERS HAVE BEEN USED by armies to motivate soldiers; by lovers to sway a beloved; by candidates and ministers to inspire their followers; and by people who have no other means to voice resistance. Songs may seem chimerical when compared to bullets or votes, yet music's effect on the political process is subtle and virtually impossible to measure, even in retrospect. Folk and political music most successfully evoke not the bitterness of repression but the glory of a world remade. As the poet Stephen Spender pointed out: "Music is the most powerful of idealist drugs except religion."[1] Lee Hays argued that folk music revivalism has always had religiosity, and Woody Guthrie sang:

> There's a better world a'coming—
> Don't you know,
> Where we'll all be union
> And we'll all be free.

Folksinger Arlo Guthrie, on idealism and music: I don't think people come to the music for optimism, I think they come for realism. You have to have concrete feet in order to have an idealistic mind. Otherwise it just goes above everybody's head. Woody's songs, like "The 1913 Massacre" and others anybody could understand, were understood on an idealistic level, real level, fight-it-out, duke-it-out, shoot-it-out level: which is what this culture basically has for a foundation. And if idealism doesn't have the guns and guts, it's not real. It may not be political; it may be moral.

I don't think anybody has given up on the idea of the world singing together. Although that sounds corny now; I don't think anybody's given up on it. They see that there is a chance for it, and if there is a chance for it, there are ways to make that chance survive. And the *way* is different now. That's all that's changed.[2]

Folksinger Pete Seeger, on politics and song: People often ask me, what's the history of protest songs? And I say, well, first of all they've been going on for thousands of years and the establishment has always tried to control them in some way. I must have quoted hundreds of times an old Arab proverb. It says, "When the King puts the poet on his payroll, he cuts off the tongue of the poet."

And I quote Plato who says it's very dangerous to allow the wrong kind of music in the Republic.... I hope you'll have a chapter on the responsibility of song, or the discipline of song, or the power of song, or the weakness of song. The ambiguity of song is what I'd like to get in there.[3]

Folksinger Holly Near, on how music involves politics: I happen to think that music, the right music at the right time, is probably the most powerful invitation to change that there is. I'm trying to think of anything that competes with it. People can remember what song was playing the first time they got kissed. I mean, it's so powerful. People can come to a concert and hear music that doesn't even have lyrics and walk out altered.

There is that wonderful story about a cellist in Sarajevo who went out into the town square and the bombs were dropping, and he began to play the cello. And someone from the press ran out and said, "Sir, why are you playing your cello while they're dropping bombs?" And he says, "Why are they dropping bombs while I'm playing my cello?"

And I tell that story from the stage and you can feel the audience shift. Just them imagining the music. They're not even hearing the cellist. They're imagining the cellist. And you can feel the whole room just go *ahhhh.* Imagining the cellist saying, "We're asking the wrong question. The natural thing is not the dropping of the bombs. The natural thing is my playing. Now let's get these priorities straight."[4]

Former congressman Hugh DeLacy, on political song: If I could sing, I'd sing you something with real feeling, but I'll try anyway:

> *Mine eyes have seen the glory*
> *of the coming of the Lord.*

Now, goddammit, isn't that a great piece? Listen to the beat of that thing: a simple, old-fashioned religious piece. You can translate the coming of the Lord into any kind of cause that you like: like when you end a speech and the political movement or labor movement or a strike or something is facing disaster and you're trying to conserve what you've got … and you talk about the bright new day. That's exactly what you have to do.[5]

HOWEVER PURE THE IDEALISM behind making meaningful music—music that might influence people's lives—an artist, particularly a folk musician whose work depends so heavily on its connectedness to people, does not live or work in a vacuum.

To participate in a tradition, T. S. Eliot wrote, "involves a perception not only of the pastness of the past, but of its presence."[6] Essentially, making music for *des Volkes* comes with a responsibility: for art, for the audience, for a time and place in history, for the past and the future.

Protest singer Phil Ochs, on the responsibility of artists: I think it's possible for any writer, depending on the quality of his work, to function in that way [subliminally]. Brecht faced it as a responsibility. He said to himself, here I am, a writer, and I can write things that can change people's minds, therefore do I belong in the street getting my skull cracked, which damages my writing? Or should I stay out of the way of the charging police and create my own plays? Where is the primary responsibility? To me, Phil Ochs, the answer is obvious.[7]

Holly Near, on musicians as messengers: There is something to be said for choice. If you have people all over the world who only know about music from the radio—from a very skimmed-off-the-top pop music on the radio, they don't realize that there is a song out there that speaks to the deepest part of their life; they don't get access to the support that that song will offer them.

And therefore, they become part of the sheep that are herded through the working class until they die, and they don't get access to really positive thoughts about revolution; they don't get positive thoughts about trans-formation; they don't get positive thoughts about changing the workplace; about their relationships...

They don't get access to all the things that our songs carry. We are the troubadours, the messengers, of one of the best of the ways in which we can live that would improve the world. And if you don't have access to that, that's a real tragedy.

What is sad is ... that everybody in the world didn't have access to the joy and the power of that which is so present in the singing of a political song.[8]

Punk and traditional Navajo performer Clayson Benally, on educating through music: Some people may view music as entertainment; but for us it's more of a form of education where we really have an opportunity to share with people who we are. And of course it tears down all these bridges and barriers that exist between cultures—the barriers, yeah, not the bridges, *building* bridges, tearing down barriers. But the main thing is being an educator: music is not just a form of entertainment.

Music is an intangible substance: it's not just sound waves, but emotions and the way you can affect people. That's what's powerful and profound about music; people might not listen to you if you're just talking, if you're just trying to communicate over a table like a politician. But if you put it to some beats and actually make it something that people can just absorb into their core and maybe understand on a whole other level—that's the powerful thing about using music with intentions of educating.[9]

Arlo Guthrie, on the value of song: The point is that Americans are singing and it's what they're singing and what they have to sing that has become the battleground, and rightly so. Because it can't be determined on style.

Somebody does something that catches on and a lot of people want to do it, whether it's movies that did it or ... it doesn't matter. That all disappears. All of these things are different styles of folk music and the songs that survive are not going to be surviving because of the style that they're in; they will survive on the merit of what they have to say and what they mean, no matter what style they're in.[10]

CAN MUSIC CHANGE THE WORLD?

In search of that better day in twentieth-century America, folk songs were sung by striking coal miners and union members, by those marching from Selma to Montgomery or sitting in at a Woolworth's lunch counter during the civil rights movement. Folk songs were sung during the Poor People's March on Washington and during antiwar rallies during the Vietnam War. As much as songs can, they helped tear down political barriers in East Germany, racial barriers in Birmingham, Alabama, and apartheid in South Africa. The events of the last decade of the twentieth century and the first decade of the twenty-first have inspired songs like "Bombs over Baghdad" and "Not in My Name."

But has all of this singing had an effect? Or is it just romantic windmill-chasing? Those involved believe in its potential influence—or they would be doing other things. In retrospect, though some veterans of causes are convinced music can effect change, others are unsure.

Freedom Singer Bernice Johnson Reagon, on the impact of the Freedom Singers: You know, [history] might take a sentence for each of the singers—the Almanacs, the Freedom Singers, thirty years later. The civil rights movement was more of a singing movement, and therefore the Freedom Singers may get two lines. (I don't know how much impact that particular group has had.)

There is a line from the Freedom Singers that's represented by me and the fact that I'm still singing. It's a very clear line in my work, in my music, that is rooted in the civil rights movement, and the way I came to the wedding of politics and culture in that period. As to whether that will have any influence still remains to be seen. People try to make connections between what I'm doing now and what I did then; they usually ask me that. There may be a connection there, but I'm not sure.[11]

Broadside editor Gordon Friesen, on the importance of singing: Well, there's a lot of debate, how important is singing. Singing has always been part of the struggle in America. I quoted a black leader in *Broadside* who said there would have been no civil rights movement without singing.[12]

Pete Seeger, on measuring influence: Can't say that any song I've sung got that quick a reaction. On the other hand, maybe in some individual's life, [it] had a five-second reaction. I know that I've been tremendously impressed, moved, and all that sort of thing, by hearing a certain song at a certain time. And so, did it happen to others? Well you have to go on faith a lot of the time. You assume it must do some good, or else you wouldn't do it.

Similarly, maybe years from now, it'll be common knowledge that the songs that we sang in the sixties were one reason that certain things happened. Or the songs that we sang in the eighties made certain things happen. But, there's no way of proving it. I don't see; there's no Gallup poll you can take which would really be meaningful, because even an individual doesn't know. If you asked me what songs impelled you to do what thing, I couldn't say exactly. Except that I've been very much impressed by certain kinds of music. It's deepened my understanding.[13]

MUSIC'S POWER

"What an odd thing it is to see an entire species—billions of people—playing with, listening to, meaningless tonal patterns, occupied and preoccupied for much of their time by what they call 'music,'" observes psychiatrist Oliver Sacks, from an extraterrestrial's perspective, in his book *Musicophilia*.[14] Music has been labeled inspirational, dangerous, transcendent, sinful, seditious, elevating, spiritual, and so on; but no one quite knows how or why it works on humans the way it does. Music serves no evident evolutionary purpose, yet humans share, almost universally and from birth, the capacity to experience music physically and emotionally. That music endures, etched into memories—lines "stuck in one's head," lyrics coming back verbatim after years of not hearing them, songs conjuring forgotten associations. How music operates on humans has stumped scientists for centuries. Musicians may not understand the mystery of music any better, but they have ample opportunity for observation.

Holly Near, on effecting change: If I'm sitting in the audience, and some artist doesn't bother to offer up something that invites me to a bigger self, they've actually not only done themselves a disservice; they didn't notice there might be somebody in that audience that was going to go out and really contribute something to the world because of them. The ripple effect.

I've had people write me after a concert and say, "I came to your concert all covered up and hidden, because I'm in the military, but I heard that you sang some lesbian songs. And I didn't want to get busted, but I wanted to come and hear this. But actually, what I went away with, was your asking me why I'm in the military. And I'm starting to file papers for a conscientious objector."

Wow!

Now if I'd walked up to her on the street, and said, "Excuse me, miss, are you in the military? I think you should file for conscientious objection." You know, it would *not* have been a conversation.

But she's sitting there in the dark, and everybody's singing together, "The Great Peace March" or they're singing "Why do we kill people who are killing people to show that killing people is wrong?"

And it is the music that asks her that question in a way that is way more powerful than could be asked in a simple conversation.[15]

Arlo Guthrie, on how rally music functions: There's no purpose really, to singing to people who already agree with you; it doesn't really do anything. When people who didn't come to feel a part of [some protest], suddenly *do* feel like a part of that, that's what creates the excitement, the mood, the feeling of "Wow, it's actually changing here and now. The governor's not here, so he's not going to change his mind. But the people who are here now are being drawn into one cohesive, unified group and we're all here for the same thing."

Regardless of what color you are, what you happen to believe, whether you're a lesbian from Albany, or wherever you're from. This is what we're here for; the rest has nothing to do with this. It's what we're here for and we're experiencing a unity in that, and that's a great thing.[16]

Holly Near, on the capacity of music to do harm: Not only can music do great things, it can also really mess you up.

I grew up listening to really sexist music. And it screwed up my love life for years. Telling me how I should be as a girl and who I should love, and, you know, "I can't live without you baby, baby" songs.

As smart as I was, it took me a really long time to learn that I *could* live without you, baby, baby! And there really was something about love and respect and relationship that was going to be really important.

But those songs did a lot of damage before I recovered from them. I know the power of music. I know that when I listen to Rodgers and Hammerstein, the songs that really held up, like "You've Got to Be Carefully Taught" from *South Pacific*; and then I remember that song from *Carousel*, that I sang when I was a girl:

He's your fella and you love him,
that's all there is to that...

And it's all about, he's a bad guy and he beats me, but, you know, he's *my* guy, and that's how that goes. That message went in really deep. I had to work hard to step out of that one.[17]

IN 1758, A STORY GOES, a song stopped a battle. It happened when an English brigade was attacked in Brittany, France. "Local militia advancing to battle were astounded to hear a local song. It was Welsh mountaineers, singing an old Celtic melody older than their estrangement. French officers commanded the militia to fire, but they would not."[18]

Whether or not folk music tipped the balance in any of the struggles to which it has been applied will remain open to argument. What is generally agreed on is that music has the capacity to bring people together, to forge community. Ethnomusicologist Charles Seeger cuts to the chase: "Beyond entertainment, few could cite a social-cultural function for music other than to 'pull people together.'"[19]

Activist Margaret Gelder Frantz, on songs as unifying people: During the war I worked at the Soviet Purchasing Commission in Washington. We went bicycling with the Russian engineers....About halfway through the twenty-mile bicycle trip, we stopped and rested. We all sat on the ground and sang songs. We didn't even speak the same language; we didn't know each other, but we all knew the same songs.

We had a great time. We sang international revolutionary songs, like "Whirlwinds of Danger," the "Internationale," and a lot of other songs that we knew together. The Eisler-Brecht songs, or Russian songs that we all grew up on. It was great singing those songs with the Russians. We sang them in different languages, but we all sang the same songs.

Songs matter! Songs really bring people together. They really do foster important bonds.[20]

Arlo Guthrie, on the power of singing together: When I first started singing, there were people coming to my shows because of *Alice's Restaurant*—who were singing the end of *Alice's Restaurant*—who wouldn't be seen talking to each other on the street. They were people on the right, people on the left. It was appreciated by people of all persuasions. The same could be said for songs like "Michael, Row the Boat Ashore." There's a feeling of American unity and maybe even global unity in singing songs that mean different things to different people. Allowing the guy next to you to have his meaning and you're singing along to your own.

We don't all have to mean the same thing at the same time all the time. How boring and uninteresting....As far as I can tell, the real practical benefit of seeing people sing together is if they can learn to sing together they can probably learn to do other things together.[21]

Pete Seeger, on song stopping a war: Way back, like four, five, maybe six or seven hundred years ago, a British army had some Welsh troops, and the Breton troops were commanded by their French officers to shoot, to fire on these invaders. But they said, "We can't, they're singing our song." The Welsh people were singing the same melody that the Breton people knew. "How could we shoot them? They're singing our song!"[22]

Arlo Guthrie, on listening: You can't sing together without listening. That's the great secret. Once that's successful, you learn to listen to each other in all kinds of other ways. It opens the listening door that stays open for the rest of your life....If everybody would just sing together and listen to each other then they would learn to do all these other things together. I don't see anything mistaken about that idea. I think that's perfectly right, it's been proven over and over again. It can be used in wonderful ways, it can be used in horrible ways. The Nazis all sang together too. It's not just a good thing. It's a very powerful thing. We need kids and people to grow up in a world where they understand the power of that.[23]

Singer-songwriter Si Kahn, on music's community-building properties: People fall in love with traditional music because it is a music you create for yourself. Playing music with other people creates community; it creates a sense of belonging; it creates a sense that you are not alone. Actually, playing a traditional tune sitting all by yourself on your front porch can create that sense that it is historical lineage. You hear the echoes of things that have gone before you.

When I discovered folk music, I discovered not just music but a community. My 1953 Chevy—I took a hacksaw and I sawed out the struts that kept the trunk from falling in, put in a mattress, and I would sleep with my feet in the trunk and my head in the back seat, so that I could stay up all night at the bluegrass festivals and fiddlers' festivals. And there I am surrounded by thousands of people playing the same music, going from campfire to campfire. There are many, many worlds that create that sense of belonging of community excitement. This is one of them.[24]

Folksinger Don McLean, on the artist's role: An artist knows exactly what he's put on earth to do. They know what it is that they are looking for. They are not looking for something just to turn people on. It's that sense of focus and purpose that gives a group a sense of rightness. It's right because it stems from everything that the people in that group are.

An artist starts off with twenty, thirty years of experience before he surfaces. He's drawn to this and he's drawn to that. He develops a line of communication with people and his inner self. He refines that line of communication; until the feedback starts. And that's when it all starts. When that's put through the recording industry, through the television screen, through the radio, that's when the enormous return comes from the audience. And it's that time—when you become a valuable property—when all the external, meaningless pressures start to box you in. When all the people who haven't got the slightest clue about where you're coming from start to try to mold you and fix you and aim you. It's those years that you spent in the tunnel with the light on your hat that have got to stand you in good stead. They will determine whether you will stay true to your goals as an artist or whether you're going to sell out for money.[25]

Educator Norman Studer, on the connection of songs to emotions: We have learned something important through these years of using folk songs; we have learned that folk songs can speak to people in many important ways. The language of the people, the faith, the hope, the fear, the language of the heart and the feelings is in the folk songs. Through their language we learn the lessons of the heart and mind combined. Archibald MacLeish made an important point in an article in the *New York Times*: that modern people have not developed the capacity to feel. And the capacity of the mind goes far beyond the capacity of feeling. So we have the spectacle of millions who know with their minds the consequences of the nuclear war. But in their feelings, they cannot comprehend the horrible example of Hiroshima and the reality of such warfare. Those of us especially, who are involved with the growth and development of children, are deeply concerned that the cultivation of the feelings run along with the development of the mind.[26]

Clayson Benally, on how youths grow through music: The key is obviously empowering the youth, giving them the tools they need....And what's worked for us is obviously using creative expression. That's the key: that whatever challenges somebody is faced with, you can find a way to communicate or transform that energy through whatever arts, whatever means you have, whatever access you have. Even though you might not have the resources, the way our schools didn't have arts; they didn't have music. We didn't have [music] teachers; we went out and just made it happen. We went to a garage sale, found drums, found guitars, and just started teaching ourselves, out of desire and will.[27]

Holly Near, on how to ensure future revivals: One of the things that's really important about [making music] with young people is to assume that they need an invitation to it, and not just leave it to chance. We grew up having school bands. We grew up having an invitation to pick up an instrument. That's not happening in schools today. Even in my little rural town, we had a little band in the school; we had a music program. My niece goes to public school; they don't have a music program.

So, we have to try to remember that you can't just leave young people alone and expect them to come up with all this on their own. And get back involved in programs that are going to hurl musical instruments into the public schools. And to make sure that if you can't do it on a large scale, then just look around your own neighborhood and buy a pennywhistle for some kid.

You have to start with that.

My niece was sitting in the living room playing the fiddle the other day; we had a friend come by and she played the mandolin.

And she said, "You know, the fingering for the mandolin is the same as the fiddle." And Devon's eyes got really big and she said, "It is?"

She handed her the mandolin, and the next thing she knows, she's sitting there for hours playing the mandolin. Well, I don't play stringed instruments; I never would have known that the fingering was the same; one little sentence, and this whole musical territory changed for that girl.

So, adults who are interested in having there be an ongoing folk tradition have got to be part of making it available to people. It doesn't just happen. There's a few people who say, "Well yeah, I was digging through a dumpster, and I found a guitar."

But, you know, you shouldn't have to dig through a dumpster to have a guitar. There ought to be ways to go down to the shelters, and go down to the places where kids aren't going to have access to this stuff, and give them finger cymbals. Give them a pennywhistle. Give them a recorder. Give them a keyboard. Give them whatever to keep inviting this talent out of young people.

We just can't expect it's going to drop out of the sky.[28]

Notes on the Interviews

Making history is necessarily selective; but for the oral historian, the layers of selection are negotiated at each stage of the process. Take for example the interview, a concrete but tangential representation of culture. Because we cannot transcribe an entire culture—or so broad a slice as the folk music revivals of the twentieth century—we interview to reassemble an approximation of that culture. Determining who will be interviewed and what line and style of questioning to apply affects the outcome.

The musicians and scholars in this volume were not selected by scientific sample. Folk music is the only constant that binds this broad cross-section of people active in recording, collecting, organizing, and performing folk and topical songs in America. Much like the early collectors who crisscrossed the country seeking folk songs, over the course of three decades and multiple cross-country expeditions, I have collected the interviews about folk music included here.

Among the limiting factors (time, memory, access, and so forth), my research was limited to those willing and able to participate. Some prominent figures, such as Bob Dylan, Alan Lomax, Joan Baez, and Bruce Springsteen, declined to make themselves available (Dylan appears briefly in excerpts from an interview conducted by Nora Ephron and Phil Ochs, from recorded interviews by Gordon Friesen).

Not all sources contributed equally. Some spoke at great length, such as Charles Seeger, whose transcription numbers hundreds of pages, or Pete Seeger, thousands of pages; some were able to speak only briefly. The dates of my interviews are catalogued below; the majority are deposited at the American Folklife Center of the Library of Congress in transcribed, indexed, and digitized form, as part of the David Dunaway Collection on Folk Music Revivals.

The interview itself, of course, is barely the beginning. Once "got down" on audiotape, the interviews were transcribed and edited for the purposes of this book. Yet, what do we end up transcribing: an interview as a worldview, a series of facts? When we transcribe, we as much re-create as translate. The divergence between oral and written expression is natural, for in writing we revise and reconsider. However, the distinction gives the lie to those claiming transcriptions are absolutely accurate. Accurate to what—to written or oral form? To what was *said*, or to what was *recorded*? Charles Seeger once compared transcribing music to photographing a bird in flight, its motion frozen into a gesture.

From this extreme perspective, transcriptions may seem inherently inaccurate. A false sense of participation may be created by the reader of transcripts. Readers might think they are as close as the television viewer who watches a rain forest on the screen. In the end, reading a transcript could resemble Plato's famous analogy of the cave dwellers who take the shadows on the wall for the rich three-dimensional world of direct experience. Nonetheless, it is the raw material to which we oral historians must turn.

Processing this "raw material" into the text before you, we have edited many thousands of transcribed pages for print presentation: fragments were turned into sentences and annotated; excerpts of a page were taken from interviews of hundreds of pages; the interruptions of questions were eliminated; the compression of material (as in all oral history volumes) is considerable. Re-contextualizing these fragments by framing them and situating them beside other fragments—in some cases by speakers not even alive at the same time—inevitably complicates the process of presenting oral history.

The scope of oral history (and my own view of the field) can be found in a volume I coedited in two editions, *Oral History: An Interdisciplinary Anthology*. The procedure of oral history is well documented, notably in Donald Ritchie's *Doing Oral History*.

Ultimately each oral history interview is a tangent to the world it expresses; recollection embodies culture through a combination of traditional formulae and individual memory. 95 interviews were culled to make this volume. Such multiperspectival tellings of history offer more than the sum of their parts.

INTERVIEWS

Asch, Moses: May 8, 1977
Benally, Clayson, Jeneda, and Klee: June 5, 2009
Brand, Oscar: March 15, 2008
Brown, Jim: May 18, 2006
Carawan, Guy: June 27, 1978
Casetta, Mario "Boots": September 26, 1976; January 19, 1977
Cazden, Norman: June 17, 1976
Christensen, Leo: September 22, 1976
Cohen, John: May 16, 2006; October 18, 2006
Collier, Jimmy: July 10, 1978
Collins, Judy: December 30, 1977
Cooder, Ry: October 14, 2000
Cooney, Michael: May 30, May 31, 1978
Dane, Barbara: May 26, 1977
DeLacy, Hugh: September 26, 1978
Draper, George: September 22, 1976
Dylan, Bob (by Nora Ephron and Susan Edmiston): late summer 1965
Elliott, Ramblin' Jack: August 27, 1978
Frantz, Margaret Gelder: April 28, 1977
Friesen, Gordon: April 14, 1976; December 21, 1977
Gilbert, Ronnie: January 14, 1977; December 21, 2007
Guthrie, Arlo: November 6, 1978; May 19, 2006

Haufrecht, Herbert: April 14, April 19, 1976
Hays, Lee: May 25, 1977
Hellerman, Fred: March 30, 1977
Hille, Waldemar: September 27, 1976
Horton, Myles: May, 2, 1980
Kahn, Si: November 6, 2007
Kalb, Danny: March 24, 1980
Kennedy, Stetson: March 16, 2007
Lampell, Millard: October 29, 1979
Leventhal, Harold: June 6, June 7, June 9, 1977
Lomax Hawes, Bess: May 6, 1977; August 28, 1977
Magil, A. B. and Harriet: April 3, 1976
McCutcheon, John: August 8, 2006
McDonald, Country Joe: March 30, 1978
McLean, Don: November 10, 1976
Moss, Mark D.: June 7, 2006
Musselman, Jim: June 5, 2006
Near, Holly: December 20, 2006
O'Reilly, Chris: June 4, 2006
O'Reilly, David: June 5, 2006
Ochs, Phil (by Gordon Friesen): 1976
Paull, Irene: September 7, 1976
Primack, Eva Salina: July 24, 2007
Radosh, Ron: March 24, 1980
Reagon, Bernice Johnson: December 7, 1977
Reiser, Bob: May 23, 2006
Reynolds, Malvina: September 5, 1976
Robinson, Earl: March 18, 1976; September 7–8, 1978; KUSP Interview September 1978
Seeger, Charles: April 6, April 7, April 8, 1976; January 12, 1977
Seeger, Mike: December 7, 1977; March 29, 1978
Seeger, Peggy: August 29, 1977; February 15, 2007
Seeger, Pete: March 6, 1976; April 15, April 16, 1976; July 19, 1976; October 6, October 10,
    1976; January 12, 1977; March 6, March 9, March 10, 1977; October 6, October 9,
    1977; December 14, December 15, 1977; January 12, 1977; August 8, 1978; March
    26, 1980; July 24, July 26, 2000; May 23, 2006; September 19, 2006
Seeger, Toshi Ohta (and Pete Seeger): March 6, 1977
Silber, Irwin: December 21, 1977; May 26, 1977
Staninec, Annie: February 19, 2009
Starobin, Norma: January 20, 1980
Studer, Norman: April 16, 1976
Traum, Happy: July 14, July 16, 1984
Travers, Mary: January 21, 1977
Young, Israel, July 14, July 15, July 16, July 17, 1984

Biographies of Interviewees

Asch, Moses (1905–1986) "Moe" Asch, son of the Yiddish author Sholem Asch, founded Folkways Records (with his secretary, Marian Distler) in 1948, as a successor to his Disc and Asch record labels. (Before this, Moe Asch worked for the Radio Corporation of America and as a radio repairman; he opened his own shop in Brooklyn in 1930.) Ultimately, Asch recorded a catalog of twenty-two hundred titles of folk music, jazz, and blues, including work by Woody Guthrie, Pete Seeger, Ella Jenkins, Burl Ives, Josh White, Mary Lou Williams, Art Tatum, and many others. The Folkways Collection is now available—permanently "in print"—through Smithsonian Folkways.

Benally, Jeneda (b. 1974), Klee (b. 1975), and Clayson (b. 1977) Children of Jones and Berta Benally, of Black Mesa, Navajo Nation, the Benally siblings grew up learning traditional songs and dances. In 1990, they formed their own punk band, Blackfire, in which Clayson plays drums, Jeneda bass, and Klee lead guitar. Since then, the band has toured internationally, performing traditionally infused, politically charged, "alterNative," or Rez rage-rock music, often alongside traditional Navajo music and adapted songs by protest singers such as Woody Guthrie and Peter LaFarge.

Brand, Oscar (b. 1920) is a Canadian-born singer of folk songs, songwriter, author, and, for over sixty years now, host of *Oscar Brand's Folksong Festival* on WNYC-AM. His most notable works include the folk song collections and corresponding audio series *Bawdy Songs and Backroom Ballads* (1949–56) and *The Ballad Mongers: Rise of the American Folk Song* (1962).

Brown, Jim (b. 1950) Three-time Emmy Award–winning producer-director Jim Brown has produced many documentaries on American music, including *Pete Seeger: Power of Song*. He has also produced programs on Woody Guthrie, Lead Belly, Ricky Skaggs, Alison Krauss, Harry Belafonte, and Mary Chapin Carpenter.

Carawan, Guy (b. 1927) Guy Carawan is currently music director and song leader for the Highlander Research and Education Center located in New Market, Tennessee. Before joining the Highlander in 1959, Carawan was part of the Greenwich Village scene of the 1950s and (with Peggy Seeger) a participant at the World Festival of Youth and Students in the Soviet Union in 1957. He taught the protest song "We Shall Overcome" to the civil rights movement via the Student Nonviolent Coordinating Committee (SNCC), having learned it from Pete Seeger in the 1950s.

Casetta, Mario "Boots" (1920–1996) A charismatic broadcaster of folk and ethnic music on the independent radio station KPFK–FM in Los Angeles and leader of the West Coast branch of People's Songs, Mario Casetta promoted folk music and folk dance and participated in projects such as the award-winning documentary film *Genghis Blues,* about Tuvan throat singers.

Cazden, Norman (1914–1980) A graduate of Juilliard and Harvard, pianist Norman Cazden was a member of the Composers' Collective during the 1930s. He subsequently turned to collecting folk music and became a professor of folk music at the University of Maine. He composed *Songs from the Catskills,* for band (1950) and *Woodland Valley Sketches,* for orchestra (1960). His collecting included music from the Catskills as well as recordings of Penobscot and Passamaquoddy Indian songs.

Christensen, Leo (b. 1912) Leader of the California Labor School chorus from 1946 to the early 1950s, Leo Christensen directed the San Francisco branch of People's Songs. As a union organizer, he worked to promote interaction between leftists in the Bay Area artistic community and the working class.

Cohen, John (b. 1932) A founding member of the old-timey string band the New Lost City Ramblers, John Cohen is also a well-known ethnomusicologist, filmmaker, and professor of art. He has collected mountain music in Appalachia and in Peru.

Collier, Jimmy (b. 1945) Folk, blues, and gospel singer and songwriter Jimmy Collier began his career as an aide to Martin Luther King, Jr. His album with Frederick Douglass Kirkpatrick, *Everybody's Got a Right to Live* (1968), is included in the Smithsonian Folkways Collection. He crewed aboard the first voyage of the Hudson River sloop *Clearwater.*

Collins, Judy (b. 1939) Grammy-winning folksinger Judy Collins is known for her pure soprano and for her social activism. She released her first album, *Maid of Constant Sorrow,* when she was twenty-two. She also gained a reputation for highlighting unknown singers—recording songs by Leonard Cohen, Joni Mitchell, and Randy Newman before they became names of their own.

Cooder, Ry (b. 1947) Guitarist, singer, and composer Ry Cooder was ranked eighth among *Rolling Stone*'s 100 Greatest Guitarists of All Time (2003). Unbound by genre, Cooder has collaborated with Taj Mahal, the Rolling Stones, and Van Morrison, to name only a few. His movie scores have won awards, as did his film *The Buena Vista Social Club.*

Cooney, Michael (b. 1943) Folksinger, songwriter, writer, and activist Michael Cooney has worked on the board of the Newport and National Folk Festivals and has directed and written columns for *Sing Out!* His albums include *Mike Cooney* and *Still Cooney After All These Years.*

Cunningham, Agnes "Sis" (1909–2004) Folksinger, songwriter, and publisher of *Broadside* (along with her husband, writer Gordon Friesen), Sis Cunningham was a socialist beginning in her childhood on a sharecropper farm in Blaine County, Oklahoma. She was a founding member of the Red Dust Players, and she later moved to Greenwich Village and joined the Almanac Singers.

Dane, Barbara (b. 1927) A powerful folk, blues, jazz, and (in all genres) protest singer, Barbara Dane has sung for unions, civil rights, and women's rights, and against the war in Vietnam and the Cuban embargo. Her albums include *Trouble in Mind, On My Way, I Hate the Capitalist System*, and others.

DeLacy, Hugh (1910–1986) Elected to the House of Representatives in 1945, representing the First Congressional District of Washington, Hugh DeLacy was a New Deal Democrat who took stands against the House Committee on Un-American Activities. Accused of being a Communist, DeLacy lost his bid for reelection in 1947. Following defeat, he served as state director of the Progressive Party in Ohio.

Dylan, Bob (b. 1941) Singer and phenomenal songwriter Bob Dylan has shaped a half century of American music. Ever the innovator, he remains unpredictable, though he has performed roughly a hundred shows a year from 1990 to 2009. He has been listed in *Time*'s 100 Most Important People of the Century and *Rolling Stone*'s Greatest Artists of All Time.

Elliott, "Ramblin" Jack (b. 1931) When Elliott was fifteen, he ran away from his home in Brooklyn to join the J. E. Rodeo, where he encountered his first singing cowboy. He taught himself to play the guitar and (after being retrieved home to Brooklyn) started busking. He was a friend and student of Woody Guthrie and a major influence on Arlo Guthrie and on Bob Dylan's early work. He has recorded more than a dozen albums.

Frantz, Margaret Gelders (b. 1922) Introduced to radical politics by her Communist father, Frantz joined the Young Communist League in 1935. She organized for unions, campaigned for Henry Wallace with Pete Seeger, and worked for Planned Parenthood. She then earned a Ph.D. and became a lecturer at University of California, Santa Cruz. An interview with her is included in the Voices of Feminism Oral History Project at Smith College.

Friesen, Gordon (1909–1996) Writer and Communist Party member Gordon Friesen married singer Sis Cunningham in 1941 as they fled harassment in their native Oklahoma for the Almanac House in Greenwich Village. They next moved to Detroit, where he worked for the *Detroit Times*. The pair reemerged as the editors of *Broadside*, a shoestring publication that ran for 187 issues, containing the work of political songwriters like Bob Dylan, Phil Ochs, Tom Paxton, the Freedom Singers, Len Chandler, and Malvina Reynolds.

Gilbert, Ronnie (b. 1926) Ronnie Gilbert was one of the four founding members of the Weavers (with Pete Seeger, Fred Hellerman, and Lee Hays). The group was blacklisted during the McCarthy era, but the band did not dissolve until 1963. She has continued to perform ever since, producing records with Holly Near, Pete Seeger, and Arlo Guthrie (as H.A.R.P.), as well as other performers.

Green, Archie (1917–2009) Folklorist and musicologist Archie Green specialized particularly in "laborlore," a term he coined. He was a member of the United Brotherhood of Carpenters and Joiners of America and self-described "anarcho-syndicalist" or "left-libertarian." He is credited with convincing Congress to pass the American Folklife Preservation Act of 1976, which established the American Folklife Center at the Library of Congress. His books include *Only a Miner: Studies in Recorded Coal-mining Songs* (1972) and *Songs about Work* (1993), among others. His collected materials are archived at the Southern Folklife Center at the University of North Carolina at Chapel Hill.

Guthrie, Arlo (b. 1947) Son of the famous Dust Bowl balladeer Woody Guthrie, Arlo Guthrie launched his career as a folksinger with his antidraft protest song "Alice's Restaurant Massacree." He has appeared on film and in television, starring in *Alice's Restaurant*. He performed at the 1969 Woodstock Festival, has released dozens of albums, and continues to perform internationally.

Haufrecht, Herbert (1909–1998) Trained as a composer at Juilliard and later a member of the Composers' Collective, Herbert Haufrecht was deeply influenced by his experiences collecting folk music and organizing square dances in West Virginia for the Resettlement Administration during the New Deal. He also worked as a staff composer for the Federal Theater. He later collected folk music from the Catskills with Norman Cazden and Norman Studer at Camp Woodland, a progressive summer camp with a focus on folklore.

Hays, Lee (1914–1981) Songwriter, singer, and political activist Lee Hays was born in Arkansas. The depression frustrated his hopes for college, but he educated himself while working for the Cleveland Public Library. In 1939, he moved to New York City, where he formed the Almanac Singers with Pete Seeger and Millard Lampell. After World War II, Hays worked with People's Songs as a columnist and sang in the Weavers, the first popular group to draw much of their repertoire from folk music. He authored a novel, and he wrote the words to "If I Had a Hammer" and many other moving songs.

Hellerman, Fred (b. 1927) A singer, guitarist, and songwriter, Fred Hellerman was a member of the Weavers and active in People's Artists. He later played on albums with Joan Baez, Judy Collins, and Harry Belafonte. For the last few decades, he has worked as a producer of albums and films, including *Alice's Restaurant* (1967) for Arlo Guthrie.

Hille, Waldemar (1908–1995) Pianist, composer, and folk song collector Waldemar Hille was the editor of the *People's Songs bulletin* and *Song Book* (1948). He joined the Communist Party in 1942. He was for many years a church organist in Los Angeles.

Horton, Myles (1905–1990) Myles Horton was an educator, a socialist, and a cofounder of the Highlander Folk School, which he directed until 1973. The Reverend James Bevel dubbed Horton the "father of the civil rights movement" for his teaching of and influence on the era's leaders, including Martin Luther King, Jr., and Rosa Parks.

Kahn, Si (b. 1944) Arriving in Washington, D.C., from rural Pennsylvania when he was fifteen and the civil rights movement was picking up steam, Si Kahn found folk music recordings at the Library of Congress that launched his half-century career as a musician and performer.

Kalb, Danny (b. 1942) Blues guitarist Danny Kalb has played with many of folk music's biggest names as a studio musician and was for three years a founding member of the Blues Project, the house band at the Cafe Au Go Go in Greenwich Village during the late 1960s.

Kennedy, Stetson (b. 1916) Folklorist, author, and activist Stetson Kennedy has written extensively about Floridian folklife. He also infiltrated the Ku Klux Klan, about which he wrote *Southern Exposure* and the dramatized memoir *I Rode with the Ku Klux Klan*.

Lampell, Millard (1919–1997) First known as a founding member of the Almanac Singers, Millard Lampell went on to become a movie and Emmy-winning television screenwriter, sometimes writing under the pseudonym H. Partnow, due to his blacklisting.

Leventhal, Harold (1919–2005) among the foremost managers of professional folk musicians, Harold Leventhal represented the Weavers; Woody Guthrie; Pete Seeger; Peter, Paul & Mary; Arlo Guthrie; Judy Collins; Buffy Sainte-Marie; and Joan Baez. He also represented international artists such as Ravi Shankar, Mercedes Sosa, the Clancy Brothers, and Ewan MacColl. His involvement with the civil rights movement included a benefit concert for Martin Luther King Jr., at Carnegie Hall in 1961. He wasn't the man making the music, but he was certainly the man making the music heard.

Lomax Hawes, Bess (1921-2009) The daughter of the folklorist and musicologist John Lomax and sister of the Library of Congress's Alan Lomax, Bess Lomax Hawes was a member of the Almanac Singers, during which time she supported the group on money she made with her office job. With her husband, Pete "Butch" Hawes, she left New York for Detroit in hopes of starting a sister group to the Almanac Singers there, along with Sis Cunningham and Gordon Friesen. In 1968, she became a professor of anthropology and served as the first director of the folk arts at the National Endowment for the Arts. In the 1970s, she worked for the Smithsonian Institute. She is the author of the memoir *Sing It Pretty* (2008).

Magil, Abraham Bernard (b. 1905–2003) A household name of the Left, "A. B." Magil was a crusading investigative journalist and pamphleteer. He graduated from the University of Pennsylvania in 1926 and promptly moved to New York City, where he joined the Communist Party and the staff of the *Daily Worker*. Sent to Detroit during the depression, his reporting breakthrough was an exposé of Father Coughlin, a vitriolic anti-Semite with a regular Sunday broadcast; Magil's pamphlets sold in the hundreds of thousands, and Coughlin was forced from the airwaves. Magil's books include *The Peril of Fascism: The Crisis of American Democracy* (1938), *Battle for America, 1776–1861–1941* (1943), *Socialism: What's in It for You* (1946), *Israel in Crisis* (1950), and many others.

McCutcheon, John (b. 1952) Multi-instrumentalist (hammered and mountain dulcimers, guitar, banjo, fiddle), singer, and songwriter John McCutcheon is known for his politically conscious repertoire.

McDonald, Country Joe (b. 1942) Founder of the prominent psychedelic band Country Joe and the Fish, a Woodstock Festival favorite, Country Joe McDonald in his forty-year career has produced thirty-three albums and hundreds of original songs. He is still protesting—for example, collaborating with Cindy Sheehan against the Iraq War.

McLean, Don (b. 1945) Singer-songwriter Don McLean was launched from the Greenwich Village club scene to international stardom by his 1971 song "American Pie." He continues to record and perform.

Moss, Mark D. (b. 1955) A trained folklorist and one of the founders of the North American Folk Music and Dance Alliance (Folk Alliance), Mark Moss has served as editor and executive director of *Sing Out!* (now the oldest continuous folk music publication in the world) since 1983.

Musselman, Jim (b. 1957) Attorney, social activist (a former "Nader raider"), and Grammy-winning music producer Jim Musselman founded the folk music label

Appleseed Records in 1996. He is responsible for involving Bruce Springsteen in recording Pete Seeger's songs.

Near, Holly (b. 1949) Singer-songwriter Holly Near began singing while still in high school; she later attended the University of California, Los Angeles. She began her career as an actress, appearing in television shows, films, and on Broadway. Active in the antiwar movement during Vietnam, she went on to play a major role as a feminist and lesbian activist. Her numerous albums and outspoken feminism made her *Ms.* Woman of the Year in 1985.

Ochs, Phil (1940–1976) A topical songwriter whose work opposed war, racism, and poverty, Phil Ochs made seven albums, beginning with *All the News That's Fit to Sing* (1964) and culminating with *Rehearsals for Retirement* (1969), that galvanized the antiwar movement. In the 1970s, his music career slowed, and alcoholism and mental illness led to his suicide.

O'Reilly, Chris (b. 1989) Bagpiper and son of journalist David O'Reilly, Chris O'Reilly has crewed on the sloop *Clearwater* and was on board during the attacks on the World Trade Center of September 11, 2001

O'Reilly, David (b. 1948) Religion writer for the Philadelphia *Inquirer* and Pulitzer Prize–winning reporter David O'Reilly has written about folk music. He has crewed on the sloop *Clearwater* and was on board during the attacks on the World Trade Center of September 11, 2001.

Paull, Irene (1908–1981) A union organizer who later worked for civil rights, Irene Paull hosted Woody Guthrie and Pete Seeger when they traveled across the United States in the 1940s.

Primack, Eva Salina (b. 1984) International performer of Balkan folk songs Eva Salina Primack has studied this tradition since she was a girl. She holds a degree in ethnomusicology from the University of California, Los Angeles, and is a teacher at the Eastern European Folklife Center in Mendocino, California.

Radosh, Ronald (b. 1937) Author of numerous books related to the Cold War, historian Ron Radosh studied the banjo with Pete Seeger during the 1950s. A self-described "red-diaper baby," he turned to neoconservative politics, rejecting Seeger's (and others') identification with the Soviet Union.

Reagon, Bernice Johnson (b. 1942) Singer, composer, scholar, and social activist Bernice Johnson Reagon was once a Freedom Singer traveling with Martin Luther King, Jr. She founded the a cappella ensemble Sweet Honey in the Rock. She is currently professor emeritus of history at American University and curator emeritus at the Smithsonian Institution's National Museum of American History.

Reiser, Bob (b. 1941) A storyteller, educator, and children's book author, Bob Reiser is the coauthor with Pete Seeger of *Carry It On: The Story of America's Working People in Song and Picture* (1991) and *Everybody Says Freedom: The Civil Rights Movement in Words, Pictures, and Song* (1989).

Reynolds, Malvina (1900–1978) Folk and blues singer and prolific songwriter Malvina Reynolds earned a Ph.D. from the University of California, Berkeley, in medieval literature. She did not launch her musical career until she was in her late forties, when she met Earl Robinson, Pete Seeger, and others. In spite of her late start, next to Phil Ochs, Malvina Reynolds had more songs printed in *Broadside* than any other writer. Her most famous song, "Little Boxes," was Pete Seeger's only hit as a single; it has been revived as the theme for Showtime's *Weeds*.

Robinson, Earl H. (1910–1991) Raised in the Pacific Northwest, in 1934 Earl Robinson moved to New York City, where he joined the Communist Party and the Composers' Collective. He collaborated with Millard Lampell and Paul Robeson until McCarthy-era blacklisting brought an end to his film commissions. Robinson edited five books: *Young Folk Song Book* (1963), *Folk Guitar in Ten Sessions* (1966), *Songs of the Great American West* (1967), *The Brecht-Eisler Song Book* (1967), and *German Folk Songs* (1968). During the war in Vietnam he again became popular, having left the Communist Party. In 1969, his setting of Alfred Hayes's poem "I Dreamed I Saw Joe Hill Last Night" was sung by Joan Baez (as "Joe Hill") at the Woodstock Music and Art Fair in New York and became a popular success.

Seeger, Charles (1886–1979) An ethnomusicologist, composer, and professor, Charles Seeger attended Harvard University, conducted the Cologne Opera, and eventually became a professor of music at the University of California, Berkeley, until he was dismissed in 1916. He later taught at Juilliard before working for the WPA's Federal Music Project and the Pan-American Union. He then returned West to teach at the Institute of Ethnomusicology at the University of California, Los Angeles.

Seeger, Mike (1933–2009) Son of ethnomusicologist Charles Seeger and composer Ruth Crawford Seeger (the first female composer to be awarded a Guggenheim), brother to Peggy Seeger, and half-brother to Pete Seeger, Mike Seeger was a singer and multi-instrumentalist (autoharp, banjo, fiddle, dulcimer, guitar, mouth harp, and mandolin). He was a founding member, along with John Cohen and Tom Paley, of the old-time string band the New Lost City Ramblers. He was an ardent advocate for traditional music in America.

Seeger, Peggy (b. 1935) Folksinger and songwriter Peggy Seeger is half-sister to Pete Seeger and sister to Mike Seeger. Her American passport was revoked after she visited the USSR and China during the Cold War; after that, she resided primarily in Great Britain. She married Ewan MacColl, and the couple produced more than one hundred albums. Her feminist song "I Want to Be an Engineer" became an anthem for feminism in the United States and Britain.

Seeger, Pete (b. 1919) Folksinger, banjo player, activist, songwriter, and author Pete Seeger was a member of the Almanac Singers and later the Weavers. He is known for composing or setting to music and performing songs that include "Where Have All the Flowers Gone," "Waist Deep in the Big Muddy," and "Turn, Turn, Turn," among hundreds of others. A Harvard dropout and veteran of World War II, he was blacklisted, tried, and acquitted during the McCarthy era. Among the most recorded musicians in U.S. history, he is the recipient of two Grammies and a Kennedy Center Lifetime Achievement Award, and has been inducted into the Rock and Roll Hall of Fame.

Seeger, Toshi-Aline Ohta (c. 1922) Daughter of Greenwich Village radicals—her father was a Japanese exile of noble descent and her mother descended from slave-owning Southerners—activist Toshi Ohta Seeger married Pete Seeger in 1943. She was the manager for the Freedom Singers during the civil rights movement, and she was a founder-organizer of the *Clearwater* Festival Great Hudson River Revival. As a documentary filmmaker, Toshi Ohta Seeger has filmed folklore around the world—her oeuvre includes films of singing Ghanaian fishermen, a Yemenite village in Israel, Baul dancers in Calcutta, as well as folk song figures such as Lead Belly, Big Bill Broonzy, Odetta, and, of course, her husband, Pete Seeger. (These films are available through the American Folklife Center of the Library of Congress.)

Silber, Irwin (b. 1925) Journalist, editor, publisher, and political activist Irwin Silber was cofounder and editor of *Sing Out!* magazine and later became the cultural editor for the left-wing newsweekly the *Guardian* (U.S.). After a schism at the *Guardian*, Silber moved west to California with Barbara Dane (see her bio, and the pair established Paredon Records. His most recent book, *Press Box Red*, is a life of sports editor Lester Rodney, whose *Daily Worker* columns helped integrate major-league baseball.

Staninec, Annie (b. 1986) Award-winning fiddle player Annie Staninec grew up playing the violin and going to bluegrass and old-time festivals in California. She began performing when she was twelve, majored in violin at the School of the Arts in San Francisco, and now tours, competes, and teaches.

Starobin, Norma Rosen (c. 1920–1998) During the first folk revival, Norma Starobin was a folk dancer who organized Dance-Arounds in New York. She was a teacher of dance and music and an activist for social justice. Her husband, Joseph R. Starobin, was a professor and prominent Communist reporter, foreign editor of the *Daily Worker* from 1945 to 1954, and author of *American Communism in Crisis, 1943–1957* (1972). He was also in charge of the peace activities of the Communist Party USA.

Studer, Norman (1902–1978) Folklorist and progressive educator Norman Studer was a teacher at the progressive Little Red School House and founder of Elisabeth Irwin High School in 1941 before becoming the director of the Downtown Community School in lower Manhattan. He also founded Camp Woodland, a progressive summer camp that focused on folklore, which he directed until its closing in 1961. He coedited *Folk Songs of the Catskills* (1982) with Norman Cazden and Herbert Haufrecht.

Traum, Happy (b. 1938) Happy Traum was once a guitar student of folk and blues musician Brownie McGhee; he recorded with Pete Seeger, Bob Dylan, Phil Ochs, and the poet Allen Ginsberg, among others. During the folk boom, Traum was a member of the New World Singers.

Travers, Mary (1936–2009) Mary Travers came to Greenwich Village as a student at the Little Red School House; by 1961 she was part of the trio that would become one of the most successful folksinging groups of the 1960s, Peter, Paul and Mary. After the group disbanded, Travers produced five albums as a solo artist. Peter, Paul and Mary later returned to performing, including a 2005 performance at Carnegie Hall.

Young, Israel "Izzy" (b. 1928) Izzy Young founded the Folklore Center in Greenwich Village, New York, "a store for books and records and everything related to folk music." Bob Dylan remembers sitting in the back room listening to folk music records and reading books and even wrote a song about it, "Talking Folklore Center." For a decade, Young wrote "Fret and Frails," a column in *Sing Out!* Since 1973, he has owned and operated the Folklore Centrum in Stockholm, Sweden.

Notes

Introduction

1. Michael Scully, *The Never-Ending Revival: Rounder Records and the Folk Alliance* (Urbana: University of Illinois Press, 2008), 15.
2. Ronald D. Cohen, *Rainbow Quest: The Folk Music Revival and American Society 1940–1970* (Amherst: University of Massachusetts Press, 2002), 128.
3. Tristram Potter Coffin, "A Tentative Study of a Typical Folk Lyric: 'Green Grows the Laurel,'" *Journal of American Folklore* 65.258 (1952): 342.
4. David King Dunaway, "The Oral Biography," *Biography*, 14.3 (1982): 256–66.
5. David King Dunaway, Appendix to *Aldous Huxley Recollected: An Oral History* (New York: Rowman/Altamira, 1998).

Chapter 1

1. The epigraph from Joe Hickerson is quoted in *Wasn't That a Time! Firsthand Accounts of the Folk Music Revival*, ed. Ronald D. Cohen (Lanham, Md.: Scarecrow Press, 1995), 22–23.
2. September 7–8, 1978.
3. June 7, 2006.
4. May 16, 2006.
5. December 7, 1977.
6. June 7, 2006.
7. November 6, 1978.
8. Pete Seeger, *The Incompleat Folksinger* (New York: Simon and Schuster, 1972), 62.
9. John Cohen, in Cohen, *Wasn't That a Time*, 26.
10. Fannie Hardy Eckstorm, review of *Our Singing Country: A Second Volume of American Ballads and Folk Songs*, by John Lomax and Alan Lomax, *New England Quarterly* 15.3 (1942): 518.
11. John Avery Lomax, *Cowboy Songs and Other Frontier Ballads* (New York: Macmillan, 1918), xxi.
12. April 7, 1976.
13. November 6, 2007.
14. A topical song, one that takes on current events, is not necessarily sung in protest. Likewise, a protest song, one that seeks change, is not necessarily bound to a particular circumstance. ("Blowin' in the Wind," for example, or "We Shall Overcome," are protest songs that might be applied to multiple situations and are not defined by their topicality.)

15. May 23, 2006.
16. November 22, 1976.
17. May 26, 1977.
18. October 18, 2006.
19. Maud Karpeles, "Definition of Folk Music," *Journal of the International Folk Music Council* 7 (1955): 6.
20. Sam Hinton, "The Singer of Folk Songs and His Conscience," *Western Folklore* 14:3 (July 1965): 170.
21. KUSP interview, September 1978.
22. December 14, 1977.
23. June 5, 2006.
24. Ibid.
25. November 6, 2007.
26. July 24, 2007.
27. Pete Seeger quoted in Benjamin Filene, *Romancing the Folk: Public Memory and American Roots Music* (Chapel Hill: University of North Carolina Press, 2000), 194–95.
28. Gordon Friesen, "Introduction," *Broadside*, Vol. 1, ed. Sis Cunningham (New York: Broadside, 1964): 11.

Chapter 2

1. Shelly Romalis, *Pistol Packin' Mama: Aunt Molly Jackson and the Politics of Folksong* (Urbana: University of Illinois Press, 1998): 62.
2. Alan Lomax, Charles Seeger, and Ruth Crawford Seeger, *Folk Song USA* (New York: Signet, 1947): viii.
3. John Avery Lomax, *Cowboy Songs and Other Frontier Ballads* (New York: Macmillan, 1918): vii–viii.
4. June 17, 1976.
5. April 8, 1976.
6. Cecil J. Sharp, "Folk-song Collecting," *Musical Times*, January 1, 1907, 18.
7. August 8, 1978.
8. May 8, 1977.
9. Sharp, "Folk-song Collecting," 16.
10. As quoted in Richard Crawford, *America's Musical Life: A History* (New York: Norton, 2001), 610.
11. Louise Pound, review of *English Folk Songs from the Southern Appalachians*, by Cecil Sharp, Olive Dame Campbell, and Maud Karpeles, *Journal of American Folklore* 46:180 (April–June 1933): 200.
12. Dick Weissman, *Which Side Are You On? An Inside History of the Folk Music Revival in America* (New York: Continuum, 2006), 23.
13. David Dunaway, review of *Cecil Sharp*, by Maud Karpeles and A. H. Fox Strangways, *Ethnomusicology* 25 (May 1981): 327.
14. April 8, 1976.
15. December 14, 1977.
16. December 21, 1977.

17. April 7, 1976.
18. Weissman, 21.
19. Pete Seeger, *The Incompleat Folksinger,* 448–553.
20. April 8, 1976.
21. May 16, 2006.
22. April 8, 1976.
23. David King Dunaway, liner notes to *Pete Seeger, Live in Australia,* 1963 (Reelin' in the Years Productions, 2008).
24. July 24, 2000.
25. KUSP interview, September 1978.
26. November 10, 1976.
27. May 8, 1977.
28. May 6, 1977.
29. Gene Bluestein, *The Voice of the Folk* (Amherst: University of Massachusetts Press, 1972), 71.

Chapter 3

1. Andrew Fletcher, Political Works: Letter to the Marquis of Montrose, and Others (1703), 266.
2. Phillip Sheldon Foner, American Labor Songs of the Nineteenth Century (Urbana: University of Illinois Press, 1975), 18.
3. Some collectors did specialize in collecting these songs of discontent— among them Lawrence Gellert, who collected hundreds of African-American songs in the South, nearly half protest songs, but whose work was not well received (Gellert has been accused of making the songs up himself). Dick Weissman, *Which Side Are You On? An Inside History of the Folk Music Revival in America* (New York: Continuum, 2006), 27.
4. September 9, 2006.
5. Benjamin Filene, *Romancing the Folk: Public Memory and American Roots Music* (Chapel Hill: University of North Carolina Press, 2000), 48, 50.
6. June 17, 1976.
7. Aaron Copland, "Workers Sing!" in *Aaron Copland: A Reader: Selected Writings 1923–1972,* ed. Richard Kostelanetz (New York: Routledge, 2004), 88.
8. May 23, 2006.
9. March 18, 1976.
10. April 7, 1976.
11. April 15, 1976.
12. April 14, 1976.
13. March 18, 1976.
14. June 17, 1976.
15. April 15, 1976.
16. June 17, 1976.
17. March 18, 1976.
18. April 15, 1976.
19. April 6, 1976.

20. March 18, 1976.
21. April 6, 1976.
22. Bill Haywood, as quoted in Howard Zinn, *A People's History of the United States: 1492–present* (New York: HarperCollins, 2005), 329.
23. Cary Nelson, *Repression and Recovery: Modern American Poetry and the Politics of Cultural Memory, 1910–1945* (Madison: University of Wisconsin Press, 1992), 58.
24. Eileen Boris, "Great Depression and New Deal," in *Poverty in the United States: An Encyclopedia of History, Politics, and Policy*, ed. Gwendolyn Mink and Alice O'Connor (Santa Barbara, Calif.: ABC-CLIO, 2004), 25.
25. April 7, 1976.
26. May 6, 1977.
27. June 17, 1976.
28. May 23, 2006.
29. April 6, 1976.
30. May 6, 1977.
31. April 15, 1976.
32. May 6, 1977.
33. Neil V. Rosenberg and Alan Jabbour, *Transforming Tradition: Folk Music Revivals Examined* (Urbana: University of Illinois Press, 1993), 8.
34. As quoted in J. A. Williams, "Radicalism and Professionalism in Folklore Studies: A Comparative Perspective," *Journal of the Folklore Institute* 11.3 (March 1975): 213–34.
35. Shostakovich was denounced by the Communist Party at the beginning of the Great Terror under Stalin for his dissonant opera *Lady Macbeth of the Mtsensk District* (1934). The opera was consequently banned in the USSR until 1962.
36. Filene, *Romancing the Folk*, 41.
37. June 17, 1976.
38. August 8, 1978.
39. June 17, 1976.
40. March 18, 1976.
41. October 2000.
42. April 8, 1976.
43. April 14, 1976.
44. April 15, 1976.
45. April 7, 1976.
46. March 16, 2007.
47. June 17, 1976.
48. As quoted in Ronald D. Cohen, *Rainbow Quest: The Folk Music Revival and American Society 1940–1970* (Amherst: University of Massachusetts Press, 2002), 26.

Chapter 4

1. Ross Wetzsteon, *Republic of Dreams: Greenwich Village: The American Bohemia, 1910–1960* (New York: Simon and Schuster, 2003), 3.

2. Wetzsteon, *Republic of Dreams*, 89.

3. Wetzsteon, *Republic of Dreams*, 69.

4. As quoted in Wetzsteon, *Republic of Dreams*, 54.

5. March 15, 2008.

6. April 3, 1976.

7. As quoted in Ronald D. Cohen, *Rainbow Quest: The Folk Music Revival and American Society 1940–1970* (Amherst: University of Massachusetts Press, 2002), 27.

8. May 6, 1977.

9. May 25, 1977.

10. October 29, 1979.

11. April 16, 1976.

12. October 29, 1979.

13. April 8, 1976.

14. May 6, 1977.

15. March 15, 2008.

16. October 29, 1979.

17. March 18, 1976.

18. July 24, 2000.

19. March 15, 2008.

20. March 18, 1976.

21. Cohen, *Rainbow Quest*, 30–31.

22. November 22, 1976.

23. September 23, 1976.

24. May 6, 1977.

25. March 18, 1976

26. June 17, 1976.

27. May 26, 1977.

28. Alan Lomax, "Folksong Style," *American Anthropologist* 61 (1959): 11–12.

29. October 9, 1977.

30. May 6, 1977.

31. September 19, 2006.

32. April 16, 1976.

33. May 6, 1977.

34. September 26, 1976.

35. May 6, 1977.

36. Ibid.

37. May 8, 1977.

38. May 6, 1977.

39. April 16, 1976.

40. May 6, 1977.

41. October 29, 1979.

42. May 6, 1977.

43. April 16, 1976.

44. July 24, 2000.

45. April 15, 1976.

46. May 6, 1977.
47. November 6, 1978.
48. September 26, 1976.
49. People's Songs recruitment document, quoted in Robbie Lieberman, *My Song Is My Weapon: People's Songs, American Communism, and the Politics of Culture, 1930–1950* (Urbana: University of Illinois Press, 1995), 68.
50. Lieberman, *My Song Is My Weapon*, 70.
51. As quoted in Lieberman, *My Song Is My Weapon*, 72.
52. April 16, 1976.
53. September 26, 1976.
54. March 15, 2008.
55. January 19, 1977.
56. May 26, 1977.
57. September 26, 1976.
58. FBI memoranda on People's Songs, released under *Dunaway v. Kelley*, U.S. District Court, San Francisco (1976–81). Through the Freedom of Information Act, some six hundred documents on People's Songs have been released or declassified and deposited in the American Folklife Center.
59. FBI memoranda on People's Songs, released under *Dunaway v. Kelley*, U.S. District Court, San Francisco (1976–81).
60. January 19, 1977.
61. March 18, 1976.
62. Quoted in *Wasn't That a Time! Firsthand Accounts of the Folk Music Revival*, ed. Ronald D. Cohen (Lanham, Md.: Scarecrow Press, 1995), 100.
63. January 20, 1980.
64. November 22, 1976.

Chapter 5

1. "Barrel No. 2," *Time*, June 23, 1947.
2. March 6, 1977.
3. January 19, 1977.
4. March 6, 1977.
5. Ronald D. Cohen, *Wasn't That a Time!* (Lanham, Md.: Scarecrow Press, 1995), 99.
6. May 8, 1977.
7. April 14, 1976.
8. July 14, 1984.
9. March 24, 1980.
10. David A. Noebel, *Rhythm, Riots, and Revolution: An Analysis of the Communist Use of Music, the Communist Master Music Plan* (Tulsa: Christian Crusade, 1966), 9.
11. June 6, 1977.
12. April 8, 1976.
13. September 5, 1976.
14. May 26, 1977.
15. March 18, 1976.

16. August 8, 1978, and March 6, 1977.
17. Howard Zinn, *A People's History of the United States: 1492–Present* (New York: HarperCollins, 2005), 428–29.
18. William H. Chafe, *The Unfinished Journey: America since World War II* (New York: Oxford University Press, 2003), 104.
19. FBI documents released under *Dunaway v. Kelley*, U.S. District Court, San Francisco (1976–81).
20. May 23, 2006.
21. December 14, 1977.
22. April 8, 1976.
23. March 18, 1976.
24. March 15, 2008.
25. April 6, 1976.
26. March 15, 2008.
27. April 6, 1976.
28. August 29, 1977.
29. Pete Seeger, *The Incompleat Folksinger* (New York: Simon and Schuster, 1972), 49.
30. March 6, 1977.
31. August 29, 1977.
32. January 20, 1980.
33. November 22, 1976.
34. March 6, 1977.
35. Ibid.
36. May 26, 1977.
37. Ronald D. Cohen, *Rainbow Quest: The Folk Music Revival and American Society 1940–1970* (Amherst: University of Massachusetts Press, 2002), 69.
38. February 11, 1977.
39. January 19, 1977.
40. Robert A. Rosenstone, *Romantic Revolutionary: A Biography of John Reed* (New York: Knopf, 1975), 321.
41. Michael Barson and Steven Heller, *Red Scared: The Commie Menace in Propaganda and Popular Culture* (San Francisco: Chronicle Books, 2001), 90.
42. "Weighed in the Balance," *Time*, October 22, 1951.
43. Robert Cantwell, *When We Were Good* (Cambridge, Mass.: Harvard University Press, 1996), 159.
44. "Catholic War Vets and NY Journal Force Weavers' Cancellation," *Variety*, October 10, 1951.
45. November 10, 1976.
46. January 14, 1977.
47. June 7, 1977.
48. May 25, 1977.
49. November 10, 1976.
50. June 6, 1977.
51. FBI, National Office Memoranda, 1951, released under *Dunaway v. Kelley*, U.S. District Court, San Francisco (1976–81).

52. January 14, 1977.
53. August 8, 1978.
54. June 7, 1977.
55. March 18, 1976.
56. August 8, 1978.
57. September 26, 1978.
58. March 6, 1977.
59. January 14, 1977.
60. March 6, 1977.
61. Eric Bentley, ed., *Thirty Years of Treason: Excerpts from Hearings before the House Committee on Un-American Activities 1938–1968* (New York: Viking, 1971), 690.
62. March 15, 2008.
63. March 18, 1976.
64. December 7, 1977.
65. Harvey Matusow, *False Witness* (New York: Cameron and Kahn, 1955), 51.
66. March 15, 2008.
67. Lee Hays, interview of May 25, 1977.
68. Dick Weissman, *Which Side Are You On? An Inside History of the Folk Music Revival in America* (New York: Continuum, 2006), 70.
69. March 15, 2008.
70. March 6, 1977.
71. March 24, 1980.
72. March 18, 1976.
73. This concert is discussed in chapter 6.
74. January 14, 1977.

Chapter 6

1. As quoted in Ronald D. Cohen, *Rainbow Quest: The Folk Music Revival and American Society 1940–1970* (Amherst: University of Massachusetts Press, 2002), 101.
2. September 7–8, 1978.
3. September 5, 1976.
4. November 6, 1978.
5. Phil Ochs and Gordon Friesen, *Broadside, Vol. 11, Interviews with Phil Ochs,* recorded 1968, Folkways (1976) FW 05321.
6. June 7, 2006.
7. August 8, 1978.
8. July 14, 1984.
9. May 11, 1978.
10. May 19, 2006.
11. August 6, 2002.
12. November 6, 1978.
13. May 16, 2006.
14. Quoted in Neil V. Rosenberg and Alan Jabbour, *Transforming Tradition: Folk Music Revivals Examined* (Urbana: University of Illinois Press, 1993), 12.

15. Quoted in Rosenberg and Jabbour, *Transforming Tradition*, 13.
16. March 6, 1977, and October 9, 1977.
17. Cohen, *Rainbow Quest*, 130.
18. September 7-8, 1978.
19. Ochs and Friesen, *Broadside Vol. 11*.
20. Don McLean, interview of November 10, 1976.
21. July 16, 1984.
22. August 27, 1978.
23. Kenneth S. Goldstein, "A Future Folklorist in the Record Business," in Rosenberg and Jabbour, *Transforming Tradition*, 115.
24. Gordon Friesen, "Introduction to *Broadside* Vol. 1," *Broadside* 1 (1964): 6.
25. "Ban Is Put on Song about the Atom: Record Companies Withdraw Disk after Complaints It Follows Communist Line," *New York Times*, September 1, 1950, 4.
26. September 22, 1976.
27. September 5, 1976.
28. Friesen, "Introduction to *Broadside* Vol. 1," 6.
29. Bob Shelton, "Broadside Makes History," liner notes to *Best of Broadside 1962-1988: Anthems of the American Underground from the Pages of Broadside Magazine*, ed. Jeff Place and Ronald D. Cohen (Smithsonian Folkways, 2000).
30. Friesen, "Introduction to *Broadside* Vol. 1," 8.
31. April 14, 1976.
32. March 29, 2978.
33. May 19, 2006.
34. January 19, 1977.
35. August 8, 1978.
36. November 6, 1978.
37. July 15-17, 1984.
38. May 11, 1978.
39. July 15-17, 1984.
40. December 21, 1977.
41. July 15-17, 1984.
42. July 14, 1984.
43. December 21, 1977.
44. Ochs and Friesen, *Broadside Vol. 11*.
45. "Folk Frenzy," *Time*, July 11, 1960, 81.
46. September 4, 1976.
47. July 14, 1984.
48. August 8, 1978.
49. Russell Ames, *The Story of American Folk Song* (New York: Grosset and Dunlap, 1955), 276.
50. Ellen Stekert, "Cents and Nonsense in the Urban Folksong Movement: 1930-1966," in Rosenberg and Jabbour, *Transforming Tradition*, 86.
51. December 7, 1977.
52. October 18, 2006.
53. September 4, 1976.
54. October 18, 2006.

55. August 29, 1977.
56. April 8, 1976.
57. August 29, 1977.
58. May 16, 2006.
59. August 8, 1978.
60. November 6, 2007.
61. January 19, 1977.
62. July 24, 2000.
63. Sam Hinton, "The Singer of Folk Songs and His Conscience," *Western Folklore* 14:3 (July 1965): 170.
64. April 8, 1976.
65. January 19, 1977.
66. August 27, 1978.
67. December 30, 1977.
68. September 5, 1976.
69. Ochs and Friesen, *Broadside Vol. 11*.
70. July 14, 1984.
71. November 6, 1978.
72. April 6, 1976.
73. December 30, 1977.
74. Tom Lehrer, *Too Many Songs by Tom Lehrer* (New York: Pantheon, 1981), 96–97.

Chapter 7

1. July 10, 1978.
2. As quoted in Daniel J. Gonczy, "The Folk Music of the 1960s: Its Rise and Fall," in *The Dylan Companion*, ed. Elizabeth Thomson and David Gutman (London: Macmillan, 1990), 15.
3. Josh Dunson, *Freedom in the Air: Song Movements of the Sixties* (Westport, Conn.: Greenwood, 1980), 63.
4. December 7, 1977.
5. Bernice Reagon, "Let the Church Sing 'Freedom,'" *Black Music Research Journal* 7 (1987): 106.
6. December 15, 1977.
7. January 19, 1977.
8. Robert Shelton, "Rights Song Has Own History of Integration," *New York Times,* July 23, 1963, 21.
9. Hardeep Phull, *Story behind the Protest Song: A Reference Guide to the 50 Songs That Changed the Twentieth Century* (Westport, Conn.: Greenwood, 2008), 1.
10. June 27, 1978
11. December 7, 1977.
12. December 15, 1977.
13. Ibid.
14. January 19, 1977.
15. December 15, 1977.
16. April 14, 1976.

17. Fannie Lou Hamer, an organizer for SNCC, spoke before the 1964 Democratic Convention about the race situation in Mississippi, seriously jeopardizing Lyndon Johnson's nomination for president.
18. December 7, 1977.
19. Dunson, *Freedom in the Air*, 65.
20. Taylor Branch, *At Canaan's Edge: America in the King Years, 1965–1968* (New York: Simon and Schuster, 2006), 213.
21. September 7, 1976.
22. December 7, 1977.
23. As quoted in Howard Zinn, *A People's History of the United States: 1492–Present* (New York: HarperCollins, 2005), 459–60.
24. July 10, 1978.
25. June 27, 1983.
26. Hardeep Phull, *Story behind the Protest Song*, 4.
27. July 10, 1978.
28. KUSP interview, September 1978.
29. December 20, 2006.
30. Jerry Rodnitsky, "The Decline and Rebirth of Folk-protest Music," in *The Resisting Muse: Popular Music and Social Protest*, ed. Ian Peddie (Burlington, Vt.: Ashgate, 2006), 17.

Chapter 8

1. David Dunaway, *How Can I Keep from Singing: The Ballad of Pete Seeger* (New York: Random House, 2008), 304.
2. Paul Nelson, "Newport Folk Festival, 1965," *Sing Out!* 15:5 (November 1965), quoted in *The Pop, Rock, and Soul Reader: Histories and Debates*, ed. David Bracket (New York: Oxford University Press, 2005), 132.
3. Nelson, "Newport Folk Festival, 1965," 132.
4. Benjamin Filene, *Romancing the Folk: Public Memory and American Roots Music* (Chapel Hill: University of North Carolina Press, 2000), 213.
5. Bob Dylan, interview by Nora Ephron and Susan Edmiston, 1965, in *Bob Dylan: The Essential Interviews*, ed. Bob Dylan and Jonathan Cott (New York: Wenner, 2006), 50.
6. December 7, 1977.
7. August 27, 1978.
8. Phil Ochs and Gordon Friesen, *Broadside, Vol. 11: Interviews with Phil Ochs*, recorded 1968, Folkways (1976) FW 05321.
9. Bob Dylan, interview by Nora Ephron and Susan Edmiston, 1965, 52.
10. "Sibyl with Guitar," *Time*, November 23, 1962, 56.
11. D. K. Wilgus, "Folk Festivals," *Journal of American Folklore* 78:308 (April–June 1965): 190.
12. Ellen Stekert, "Cents and Nonsense in the Urban Folksong Movement: 1930–1960," in *Transforming Tradition: Folk Music Revivals Examined*, ed. Neil V. Rosenberg and Alan Jabbour (Urbana: University of Illinois Press, 1993), 84–107.

13. July 16, 1984.
14. Ronald D. Cohen, *Rainbow Quest: The Folk Music Revival and American Society 1940–1970* (Amherst: University of Massachusetts Press, 2002), 250.
15. The coining of the term "folk-rock," according to scholar Carl Belz, "served to make many students of contemporary music aware of the question of how folk and rock may in fact be related within the tradition of American music in general.... [that rock and roll] has assumed the character and function of the traditional folk sound." Carl I. Belz, "Popular Music and the Folk Tradition," *Journal of American Folklore* 80:316 (April–June, 1967): 130.
16. Belz, "Popular Music and the Folk Tradition," 130.
17. April 8, 1976.
18. Ochs and Friesen, *Broadside, Vol. 11.*
19. December 30, 1977.
20. March 24, 1980.
21. November 6, 1978.
22. "The Folk and the Rock," *Newsweek,* September 20, 1965, 88.
23. Quoted in Hardeep Phull, *Story behind the Protest Song: A Reference Guide to the 50 Songs That Changed the Twentieth Century* (Westport, Conn.: Greenwood, 2008), 103.
24. Daniel J. Gonczy, "The Folk Music of the 1960s: Its Rise and Fall," in *The Dylan Companion,* ed. Elizabeth Thomson and David Gutman (London: Macmillan, 1990), 16.
25. Ochs and Friesen, *Broadside, Vol. 11.*
26. KUSP interview, September 1978.
27. December 20, 2006.
28. March 30, 1978.
29. December 15, 1977.
30. June 5, 2006.
31. December 15, 1977.
32. March 30, 1978.
33. December 20, 2006.
34. December 21, 1977.
35. September 4, 1976.
36. June 7, 2006.
37. R. Serge Denisoff wrote anti-Stalinist critiques of Seeger, Guthrie, and friends in *Great Day Coming* (1971). Many in the folk music community rejected his analyses as cabalistic.
38. May 25, 1977.
39. December 20, 2006.
40. November 6, 2007.
41. April 28, 1977.
42. May 6, 1977.
43. March 18, 1976.
44. Bruce Jackson, "The Folksong Revival," in Rosenberg and Jabbour, *Transforming Tradition,* 77.

45. Michael Schumacher, *There But for Fortune: The Life of Phil Ochs* (New York: Hyperion, 1996), 354.
46. Jackson, "Folksong Revival," 73.
47. Charles Seeger, interview of April 8, 1976.
48. June 7, 2006.
49. November 6, 2007.
50. November 6, 1978.
51. Quoted in Rosenberg and Jabbour, *Transforming Tradition*, 80.

Chapter 9

1. Hardeep Phull, *Story behind the Protest Song: A Reference Guide to the 50 Songs That Changed the Twentieth Century* (Westport, Conn.: Greenwood, 2008), 200, 213.
2. Nicole Frehsee, "Music: Hot Trend—The YouTube Folk Revival," *Rolling Stone*, October 18, 2007, 71.
3. Ronald D. Cohen, *A History of Folk Music in the United States* (Lanham, Md.: Scarecrow Press, 2008), xi.
4. Simon Reynolds, "Music: Free Schtick—Freak-folk That Isn't Struggles with Meaning," *Village Voice*, November 2–8, 2005, C77.
5. According to *New York Times* critic Alan Light, "antifolkies" have "an unconventional, fearless approach to songwriting." Alan Light, "How Does It Feel, Antifolkies, to Have a Home, Not Be Unknown?" *New York Times*, August 11, 2006, 1.
6. Colin Irwin, "The New Folk Uprising," *Folk Roots* Issue 275 (May 2006): 25.
7. June 7, 2006.
8. July 14, 1984.
9. December 20, 2006.
10. June 4, 2006.
11. June 5, 2009.
12. Folk Alliance website, www.folkalliance.org.
13. "Mission Statement," Folk Alliance website, www.folkalliance.org.
14. Joel Okida, "Review of Opa Cupa!" *Folk Works: The Source for Folk/Traditional Music, Dance, Storytelling and Other Related Folk Arts in the Greater L.A. Area* (winter 2008–9), www.folkworks.org.
15. July 24, 2007.
16. Ibid.
17. February 19, 2009.
18. Ibid.
19. June 7, 2006.
20. June 27, 1983.
21. CD Baby website, http://cdbaby.com/about.
22. Frehsee, "Music: Hot Trend," 71.
23. Billy Bragg, "The Royalty Scam," *New York Times*, March 22, 2008, 13.
24. Quoted in Elizabeth Kinder, "Catching Up," *Folk Roots* Issue 275 (May 2006): 43.
25. September 4, 1976.
26. April 8, 1976.

27. June 5, 2009.
28. August 29, 1977.
29. June 5, 2009.
30. Ibid.
31. Ibid.
32. Riot Folk website, www.riotfolk.org.
33. May 23, 2006.
34. August 6, 2006.
35. June 5, 2006.
36. July 24, 2007.
37. June 5, 2009.
38. August 6, 2006.
39. December 20, 2006.
40. Thomas R. Gruning, *Millennium Folk: American Folk Music since the Sixties* (Athens: University of Georgia Press, 2006), 161.
41. July 24, 2007.
42. June 5, 2009.

Chapter 10

1. Stephen Spender, "Poetry and Revolution," in *The Thirties and After* (New York: Vintage, 1972), 32.
2. November 6, 1978.
3. May 23, 2006, and March 6, 1977.
4. December 20, 2006.
5. September 26, 1978.
6. T. S. Eliot, "Tradition and the Individual Talent," in *The Sacred Wood and Major Early Essays* (1920; reprint, Mineola, N.Y.: Dover, 1997), 28.
7. Phil Ochs and Gordon Friesen, *Broadside, Vol. 11: Interviews with Phil Ochs,* recorded 1968, Folkways (1976) FW 05321.
8. December 20, 2006.
9. June 5, 2009.
10. November 6, 1978.
11. December 7, 1977.
12. April 16, 1976.
13. June 27, 1983.
14. Oliver Sacks, *Musicophilia: Tales of Music and the Brain* (New York: Random House, 2008), xii.
15. December 20, 2006.
16. November 6, 1978.
17. December 20, 2006.
18. Pete Seeger, *The Incompleat Folksinger* (New York: Simon and Schuster, 1972), 271.
19. Charles Seeger, "The Music Process as a Function in a Context of Functions," *Anuario* 2 (1966): 3.
20. April 28, 1977.
21. May 19, 2006.

22. June 27, 1983.
23. May 19, 2006.
24. November 6, 2007.
25. November 10, 1976.
26. April 16, 1976.
27. June 5, 2009.
28. December 20, 2006.

Bibliography

Aaron, Daniel. *Men of Good Home: A Story of American Progressives*. New York: Oxford University Press, 1951.

Ames, Russell. *The Story of American Folk Song*. New York: Grosset and Dunlap, 1955.

Atkinson, David. "Folk Songs in Print: Text and Tradition." *Folk Music Journal* 8.4 (2004): 456–83.

Barrett, Edward L. *The Tenney Committee: Legislative Investigation of Subversive Activities in California*. Ithaca, N.Y.: Cornell University Press, 1951.

Barson, Michael, and Steven Heller. *Red Scared: The Commie Menace in Propaganda and Popular Culture*. San Francisco: Chronicle Books, 2001.

Belz, Carl I. "Popular Music and the Folk Tradition." *The Journal of American Folklore* 80, no. 316 (April–June, 1967): 130–42.

Bender, Thomas. *New York Intellect: A History of Intellectual Life in New York City, from 1750 to the Beginnings of Our Own Time*. New York: Knopf, 1987.

Bentley, Eric, ed. *Thirty Years of Treason: Excerpts from Hearings before the House Committee on Un-American Activities 1938–1968*. New York: Viking, 1971.

Blau, Joel, and Mimi Abramovitz. *The Dynamics of Social Welfare Policy*. New York: Oxford University Press, 2007.

Bluestein, Gene. "Songs of the Silent Generation." *New Republic* 144.11 (March 13, 1961).

——— . *The Voice of the Folk: Folklore and American Literary Theory*. Amherst: University of Massachusetts Press, 1972.

Boris, Eileen. "Great Depression and New Deal." In *Poverty in the United States: An Encyclopedia of History, Politics, and Policy*, ed. Gwendolyn Mink and Alice O'Connor. Santa Barbara, Calif.: ABC-CLIO, 2004.

Brackett, David. *The Pop, Rock, and Soul Reader: Histories and Debates*. New York: Oxford University Press, 2005.

Branch, Taylor. *At Canaan's Edge: America in the King Years, 1965–1968*. New York: Simon and Schuster, 2006.

Brown, Courtney. *Politics in Music*. Atlanta: Farsight Press, 2008.

Cantwell, Robert. *When We Were Good*. Cambridge, Mass.: Harvard University Press, 1996.

Carawan, Guy, and Candie Carawan. *Sing for Freedom: The Story of the Civil Rights Movement Through Its Songs*. Bethlehem, Pa.: Sing Out!, 1990.

Chafe, William H. *The Unfinished Journey: America Since World War II*. New York: Oxford University Press, 2003.

Chappell, William. *Popular Music of the Olden Times: A Collection of Ancient Songs, Ballads and Dance Tunes Illustrative of the National Music of England*. Whitefish, Mont.: Kessinger, 2004.

Coffin, Tristram Potter. "A Tentative Study of a Typical Folk Lyric: 'Green Grows the Laurel.'" *Journal of American Folklore* 65.258 (Oct.–Dec. 1952): 341–51.

Cohen, Ronald D. *Folk Music: The Basics*. New York: Routledge, 2006.

———. *A History of Folk Music Festivals in the United States*. Lanham, Md: Scarecrow Press, 2008.

———. *Rainbow Quest: The Folk Music Revival and American Society, 1940–1970*. Amherst: University of Massachusetts Press, 2002.

———, ed. *Wasn't That a Time!* Lanham, Md.: Scarecrow Press, 1995.

Crawford, Richard. *America's Musical Life: A History*. New York: Norton, 2001.

Dorson, Richard. *Folklore and Fakelore: Essays Toward a Discipline of Folk Studies*. Cambridge, Mass.: Harvard University Press, 1976.

Dunaway, David King. "American Political Song (1927–1957)." PhD diss., University of California, Berkeley, 1981.

———. *How Can I Keep From Singing: The Ballad of Pete Seeger*. New York: Random House, 2008.

———. "Music and Politics in the United States." *Folk Music Journal* 5.3 (1987): 268–94.

———. "Review of *Cecil Sharp*." *Ethnomusicology* 25 (May 1981): 327–28.

———. "Unsung Songs of Protest: The Composers Collective of New York." *New York Folklore* 5 (Summer 1979): 1–20.

Dunson, Josh. *Freedom in the Air: Song Movements of the Sixties*. Westport, Conn.: Greenwood, 1980.

Eckstorm, Fannie Hardy. "Review of: John Lomax and Alan Lomax's *Our Singing Country: A Second Volume of American Ballads and Folk Songs*." *New England Quarterly* (1942).

Ephron, Nora, and Susan Edmiston. "Bob Dylan Interview." In *Bob Dylan: The Essential Interviews*, ed. Bob Dylan and Jonathan Cott. New York: Wenner, 2006.

FBI documents released under *Dunaway v. Kelley*, U.S. District Court, San Francisco, and acquisitioned by the American Folk Life Center of the Library of Congress.

Filene, Benjamin. *Romancing the Folk: Public Memory and American Roots Music*. Chapel Hill: University of North Carolina Press, 2000.

"Folk Singing: Sibyl with Guitar." *Time* (November 23, 1962). www.time.com/time/magazine/article/0,9171,829501,00.html

Foner, Phillip. *American Labor Songs of the Nineteenth Century*. Urbana: University of Illinois Press, 1975.

Friesen, Gordon. "Introduction to *Broadside* Vol. 1." New York: Broadside, 1964.

Garofalo, Reebee. "Popular Music and the Civil Rights Movement." *Rockin' the Boat: Mass Music and Mass Movements*. Boston: South End Press, 1992.

Goldstein, Kenneth S. "A Future Folklorist in the Record Business." In Neil Rosenberg. *Transforming Traditions: Folk Music Revivals Examined*, 105–21. Urbana: University of Illinois Press, 1993

Gonczy, Daniel J. "The Folk Music of the 1960s: Its Rise and Fall." In *The Dylan Companion*, ed. Elizabeth Thomson and David Gutman. London: Macmillan, 1990.

Goodwin, Joanne L. "The Progressive Era." In *Poverty in the United States: An Encyclopedia of History, Politics, and Policy*, ed. Gwendolyn Mink and Alice O'Connor. Santa Barbara, Calif.: ABC-CLIO, 2004.

Greenway, John. *American Folksongs of Protest*. Philadelphia: University of Pennsylvania Press, 1953.

Gruning, Thomas R., *Millennium Folk*. Athens: University of Georgia Press, 2006.

Harris, Luther S. *Around Washington Square: An Illustrated History of Greenwich Village*. Baltimore: Johns Hopkins University Press, 2003.

Hinton, Sam. "The Singer of Folk Songs and His Conscience." *Western Folklore* 14.3 (July 1965): 170–73.

Irwin, Colin. "The New Folk Uprising." *Folk Roots*, Issue 275 (May 2006): 24–25, 27–29, 31.

Jones, John Bush. *The Songs That Fought the War: Popular Music and the Home Front, 1939–1945*. Waltham, Mass.: Brandeis University Press, 2006.

Kinder, Elizabeth. "Catching Up." *Folk Roots*, Issue 275 (May 2006): 43.

Lawless, Ray M. *Folksingers and Folksongs in America*. New York: Duell, Sloan and Pearce, 1960.

Lehrer, Tom. *Too Many Songs by Tom Lehrer*. New York: Pantheon, 1981.

Lichtman, Robert M., and Ronald D. Cohen. *Deadly Farce: Harvey Matusow and the Informer System in the McCarthy Era*. Urbana: University of Illinois Press, 2004.

Lieberman, Robbie. *My Song Is My Weapon: People's Songs, American Communism, and the Politics of Culture, 1930–1950*. Urbana: University of Illinois Press, 1995.

Lomax, Alan. *Folk Song Style and Culture*. Washington, D.C.: American Association for the Advancement of Science, 1968.

Lomax, Alan, et al. *Folk Song USA*. New York: Signet, 1947.

Lomax, John A., and Alan Lomax. *Folk Song: USA*. New York: Grosset & Dunlap, 1947.

Lomax, John Avery. *Cowboy Songs and Other Frontier Ballads*. New York: Macmillan, 1918.

Lyons, Peter. "The Ballad of Pete Seeger." In *The American Folk Scene: Dimensions in the Folksong Revival*, ed. David De Turk and A. Poulin. New York: Dell, 1967.

Matusow, Harvey. *False Witness*. New York: Cameron and Kahn, 1955.

Miller, Douglas T., and Marion Nowak. *The Fifties: The Way We Really Were*. New York: Doubleday, 1977.

Mitchell, Gillian. *The North American Folk Music Revival: Nation and Identity in the United States and Canada, 1945–1980*. Hampshire, England: Ashgate, 2007.

Mitsui, Toru, "The Reception of the Music of American Southern Whites in Japan." In Neil Rosenberg, *Transforming Traditions: Folk Music Revivals Examined*, 275–94. Urbana: University of Illinois, 1993.

Morris, Aldon D. "A Retrospective on the Civil Rights Movement: Political and Intellectual Landmarks." *Annual Review of Sociology* 25 (August 1999): 517–39.

Nelson, Cary. *Repression and Recovery, Modern American Poetry and the Politics of Cultural Memory, 1910–1945*. Madison: University of Wisconsin Press, 1992.

Nelson, Paul. "Newport Folk Festival, 1965." *Sing Out!* (November 1965). In *The Pop, Rock, and Soul Reader: Histories and Debates*, ed. David Bracket. New York: Oxford University Press, 2005.

Noebel, David A. *Rhythm, Riots, and Revolution: An Analysis of the Communist Use of Music, the Communist Master Music Plan*. City?: Christian Crusade Publications, 1966.

Olivier, Barry. "The University of California Folk Music Festival: This Year and Last." [1959]. In Ronald D. Cohen, *Rainbow Quest: The Folk Music Revival and American Society, 1940–1970*, 128. Amherst: University of Massachusetts Press, 2002.

Omond, G. W. Y. *Fletcher of Saltoun*. Edinburgh: Oliphant, Anderson, and Ferrier, 1897.

Percy, Thomas, Bishop of Dromore, *Reliques of Ancient English Poetry*, London: for J. Dodsley, 1765.

Phillips, Amy. "Folk the Pain Away." *The Village Voice*, 48:5 (January–February 2003): 97–98.

Phull, Hardeep. *Story Behind The Protest Song: A Reference Guide to the 50 Songs That Changed the 20th Century*. Westport, Conn.: Greenwood, 2008.

Pound, Louise. "Review of *English Folk Songs From the Southern Appalachians*." *Journal of American Folklore* 46.180 (April–June, 1933): 199–200.

Reagon, Bernice. "Let the Church Sing 'Freedom.'" *Black Music Research Journal*, 7 (1987): 105–118.

Rehder, John B. *Appalachian Folkways*. Baltimore: Johns Hopkins University Press, 2004.

Reuss, Richard. *American Folk Music and Left-Wing Politics, 1927–1957*. Lanham, Md.: Scarecrow Press, 2000.

Ritchie, Donald A. *Doing Oral History*. 2nd ed. New York: Oxford University Press, 2009.

Rodnitsky, Jerry. "The Decline and Rebirth of Folk-Protest Music." In *The Resisting Muse: Popular Music and Social Protest*, ed. Ian Peddie. Burlington, Vt: Ashgate, 2006.

Romalis, Shelly. *Pistol Packin' Mama: Aunt Molly Jackson and the Politics of Folksong*. Urbana: University of Illinois Press, 1998.

Rosenberg, Neil V. "'An Icy Mountain Brook': Revival, Aesthetics, and the 'Coal Creek March.'" *Journal of Folklore Research* 28.2/3 (1991): 221–40.

Rosenberg, Neil V., and Alan Jabbour. *Transforming Tradition: Folk Music Revivals Examined*. Urbana: University of Illinois Press, 1993.

Rosenstone, Robert A. *Romantic Revolutionary: A Biography of John Reed*. New York: Knopf, 1975.

Sacks, Oliver. *Musicophilia: Tales of Music and the Brain*. New York: Random House, 2008.

Schmidt, Eric Von, and Jim Rooney. *Baby, Let Me Follow You Down: The Illustrated Story of the Cambridge Folk Years*. Amherst: University of Massachusetts Press, 1994.

Schumacher, Michael. *There but for Fortune: The Life of Phil Ochs* (New York: Hyperion, 1996).

Scully, Michael F. *The Never-Ending Revival: Rounder Records and the Folk Alliance*. Urbana: University of Illinois Press, 2008.

Seeger, Charles. "The Music Process as a Function in a Context of Functions." *Anuario* 2 (1966): 1–42.

——— . *Studies in Musicology, 1935–1975*. Berkeley: University of California Press, 1977.

Seeger, Pete. *The Incompleat Folksinger*. Lincoln: University of Nebraska Press, 1992.

————. *Where Have All the Flowers Gone: A Singalong Memoir*. 3rd ed. Bethlehem, Pa.: Sing Out Publications, 2010.

Sharp, Cecil J. "Folk-song Collecting." *The Musical Times* (January 1, 1907): 16–18.

Shelton, Bob. "Broadside Makes History." Included in liner notes to *Best of Broadside 1962–1988: Anthems of the American Underground from the Pages of Broadside Magazine*. Produced by Jeff Place and Ronald D. Cohen. Smithsonian Folkways, 2000.

Shelton, Robert. "Rights Song Has Own History of Integration." *New York Times*, July 23, 1963.

Spender, Stephen. "Poetry and Revolution." In *The Thirties and After*. New York: Vintage, 1972.

Stekert, Ellen. "Cents and Nonsense in the Urban Folksong Movement: 1930–1960." In Neil Rosenberg, *Transforming Traditions: Folk Music Revivals Examined*. Urbana: University of Illinois, 1993.

Sterne, Jonathan. *The Audible Past: Cultural Origins of Sound Reproduction*. Durham, N.C.: Duke University Press, 2003.

Trager, Oliver. *Keys to the Rain: The Definitive Bob Dylan Encyclopedia*. New York: Billboard Books, 2004.

Vansina, Jan. *Oral Traditions*. Chicago: Aldine, 1965.

Wang, Betty. "Folksongs as Regulators of Politics." In *The Study of Folklore*, ed. Alan Dundes. Englewood Cliffs, N.J.: Prentice Hall, 1965.

"Weighed in the Balance." *Time*, October 22, 1951. www.time.com/time/magazine/article/0,9171,815585,00.html.

Weissman, Dick. *Which Side Are You On? An Inside History of the Folk Music Revival in America*. New York: Continuum, 2006.

Wetzsteon, Ross. *Republic of Dreams: Greenwich Village, the American Bohemia, 1910–1960*. New York: Simon and Schuster, 2003.

Wilgus, D. K. "Folk Festivals." *The Journal of American Folklore* 78.308 (April-June, 1965): 189–91.

Williams, J. A. "Radicalism and Professionalism in Folklore Studies: A Comparative Perspective." *Journal of the Folklore Institute*, Indiana University (1972).

Williams, Michael Ann. "The National Folk Festival." In *The Hayloft Gang: The Story of the National Barn Dance*, ed. Chad Berry (Urbana: University of Illinois Press, 2008): 187–97.

Wolfe, Charles, and Kip Lornell. *The Life and Legend of Leadbelly*. New York: DaCapo, 1999.

Zinn, Howard. *A People's History of the United States*. New York: HarperCollins, 2005.

Zinoviev, Grigorii. "Report to the 6th Plenum of the Enlarged Executive Committee of the Communist International, February 20, 1926." *International Press Correspondence* (Vienna, Austria) 6.18 (March 10, 1926).

Discography

This discography lists recordings of songs referenced in the text. When a particular performer or performance, recording, or arrangement of a song is referred to in the oral history, that specific version, or a near example, is listed here (a currently available issue, whenever possible). If a song is mentioned in the text without reference to a specific performer or recording, representative versions are listed (appropriate to the time and situation discussed in the oral history). For example, while numerous recordings exist of "We Shall Overcome," this discography does not attempt to list them all; rather, it lists the first recording of the song, which was made by the Freedom Singers at the Newport Folk Festival of 1963, and a recording by Pete Seeger—both recordings are mentioned in chapters 7 and 8—and a recording by Bruce Springsteen, which is mentioned in chapters 1 and 10.

"Ain't Gonna Let Nobody Turn Me Round"
Freedom Singers, *Voices of the Civil Rights Movement: Black American Freedom Songs 1960–1966*, 1997, Smithsonian Folkways SFW 40084

"Alice's Restaurant Massacree" (Arlo Guthrie)
Arlo Guthrie, *Alice's Restaurant*, 1967, Reprise Records K 44045

"All Mixed Up" (Pete Seeger)
Pete Seeger, *Pete*, 1996, Living Music Records LMUS 0032

"Appalachian Spring" (Aaron Copland)
Leonard Bernstein and New York Philharmonic, *Appalachian Spring Suite*, 1981, CBS MYK 37257

"Aunt Rhodie"/"Go Tell Aunt Rhody"/"Old Gray Goose" (traditional)
Woody Guthrie, "Go Tell Aunt Rhody," *The Asch Recordings*, Smithsonian Folkways SFW 40112

"Ballad for Americans" (music: Earl Robinson; lyrics: John La Touche)
Paul Robeson, *Paul Robeson: Songs for Free Men—1940–1945*, 1997, Pavilion Gemm 9264

"The Ballad of the Carpenter" (Ewan MacColl)

Ewan MacColl and Peggy Seeger, *New Briton Gazette, vol.* 1, 1960, Folkways FW 08732

Phil Ochs, *I Ain't Marching Anymore*, 1965, Elektra; rerelease, 2001, Elektra/Warner 73564

"Ballad of the Green Berets" (Barry Sadler)

Barry Sadler, *The Ballad of the Green Berets/Letter from Vietnam*, 1966, RCA Victor 47-8739

"Ballad of Harry Simms," "Death of Harry Simms" (traditional; lyrics: Jim Garland)

Molly Jackson and John Greenway, *The Songs and Stories of Aunt Molly Jackson*, 1961, Folkways FW 05457

"Ballad of the Student Sit-In" (traditional; lyrics: Guy Carawan, Eve Merriam, and Norma Curtis)

Sweet Honey in the Rock, *The Women Gather*, 2003, EarthBeat R2 73829

"The Battleship of Maine" (traditional)

New Lost City Ramblers, *The Early Years, 1958–1962*, 1991, Smithsonian Folkways SFW 40036

"Be Nobody's Darling but Mine" (Jimmie Davis)

Gene Autry, *Gene Autry Collection*, 1983, Murray Hill M 61072

"Biggest Thing Man Has Ever Done"/"The Great Historical Bum" (traditional; lyrics: Woody Guthrie)

Woody Guthrie, "Great Historical Bum," *Columbia River Collection*, 1987, Rounder ROUN 1036

"Blowin' in the Wind" (Bob Dylan)

New World Singers, *Broadside Ballads, vol.* 1, 1963, Folkways FW 05301

Bob Dylan, *Freewheelin' Bob Dylan*, 1963, Columbia CS 8786; rerelease, *Bob Dylan Collection 2*, 2005, Sony 75013

Peter, Paul and Mary, *In the Wind*, 1963, Warner Bros. WS 1570; rerelease, *Carry It On*, 2004, Rhino R2 73907

"Bombs over Baghdad" (John Trudell)

John Trudell, *AKA Graffiti Man*, 1992, Rykodisc RCD 10223

"Boomer's Story" (traditional)

Ry Cooder, *Boomer's Story*, 1972, Warner Bros. 26398-2

"Bonny Barbara Allan"/"Barbry Ellen"/"Barbara Ellen" (traditional)
Charles Seeger, *Versions and Variants of Barbara Allen*, 1964, Library of Congress, Division of Music, Recording Laboratory AAFS L54

"Bourgeois Blues" (Lead Belly)
Lead Belly, *Bourgeois Blues: Lead Belly Legacy*, vol. 2, 1997, Smithsonian Folkways SFW 40045

"Bring Them Home" (Pete Seeger)
Pete Seeger (with Billy Bragg, Ani DiFranco, and Steve Earle), *Seeds: The Songs of Pete Seeger*, vol. 3, 2003, Appleseed APR 1072

"The Candidate's a Dodger" (traditional)
Almanac Singers, *Their Complete General Recordings*, 1996, MCA MCAD 11499

"Casey Jones," "Casey Jones on the S.P. Line," "Casey Jones (the Union Scab)" (traditional; lyrics: Joe Hill)
"Casey Jones on the S.P. Line," Earl Robinson, *Strange Unusual Evening—A Santa Barbara Story*, 1970, UAW
"Casey Jones (the Union Scab)," Almanac Singers, *Talking Union and Other Union Songs*, 1955, Folkways FW05285

"Coal Creek March" (Pete Steele)
Pete Steele, *Banjo Tunes and Songs*, 1958, Folkways FW 3828

"Come All You Coal Miners" (traditional; lyrics: Sarah Ogan Gunning)
Sarah Ogan Gunning, *Harlan County, USA*, rerelease 2006, Rounder ROUN 4026

"Come and Go with Me to That Land" (traditional)
Guy Carawan, *Guy Carawan Sings Something Old, New, Borrowed and Blue*, vol. 2, 1959, Folkways FW 03548
Bernice Johnson Reagon, *Folk Songs: The South*, 1965, Folkways FW 02457

"Declaration of Independence" (music: Celius Dougherty; lyrics: Wolcott Gibbs)
Michael Cooney, *Pure Unsweetened: Live Family Concert*, 1982, Alliance WRC1-2310
Pete Seeger, *Young vs. Old*, 1971, Columbia CS 9873

"Desolation Row" (Bob Dylan)
Bob Dylan, *Highway 61 Revisited*, 1965, Columbia CS9189; rerelease, 2006, Columbia CK 92399

"Erie Canal" (traditional)
Pete Seeger, *American Favorite Ballads, vol. 4, Tunes and Songs*, 1963, Folkways FW 2323

Bruce Springsteen, *We Shall Overcome: The Seeger Sessions*, 2006, Sony 82876830742

"Eve of Destruction" (Barry McGuire)

Barry McGuire, *Eve of Destruction*, 1965, Dunhill D/DS 50003

"The Farmer Is the Man [Who Feeds Us All]" (traditional)

Pete Seeger *American Industrial Ballads*, 1992, Smithsonian Folkways SFW 40058

"Foggy Mountain Breakdown" (Earl Scruggs)

Flatt, Scruggs, and Foggy Mountain Boys, *Original Sound*, 1963, Mercury MG 20773

"Free and Equal Blues" (Earl Robinson)

Earl Robinson, *A Walk in the Sun and Other Songs and Ballads*, 1957, Folkway FW02324

"Get on Board Children" (traditional)

Paul Robeson, *Essential Paul Robeson*, 1958, Vanguard VSD 57/58

"Go Tell It on the Mountain" (traditional)

Peter, Paul and Mary, *In the Wind*, 1964, US 33
Fannie Lou Hamer, *Voices of the Civil Rights Movement: Black American Freedom Songs 1960–1966*, 1997, Smithsonian Folkways SFW 40084

"Go to Work on Monday" (Si Kahn)

Si Kahn, *Doing My Job*, 1982, Flying Fish FF 221; rerelease, *Thanksgiving*, 2007, Strictly Country SCR 63

"Goodnight Irene," "Irene" (Lead Belly)

Lead Belly, *Good Night, Irene*, 1939, Allegro LEG 9025
Weavers, *The Weavers at Carnegie Hall*, 1955, Vanguard VRS 9010
Ry Cooder, *Chicken Skin Music*, 1976, Reprise; rerelease, 1988, Reprise 2-2254

"Governor Pat Neff (Sweet Mary Blues)" (Lead Belly)

Lead Belly, *Shout On: Lead Belly Legacy*, vol. 3, 1998, Smithsonian Folkways SFW40105

"The Great Peace March" (Holly Near)

Holly Near, *And Still We Sing: The Outspoken Collection*, 2002, Calico Tracks Music CTM 0005

"Guantanamera" (José Martí)

Weavers, *Reunion at Carnegie Hall—1963*, Vanguard VSD 2150
Pete Seeger, *Headlines and Footnotes: A Collection of Topical Songs*, 1999, Smithsonian Folkways SFW 40111

"Highway 61 Revisited" (Bob Dylan)
> Bob Dylan, *Highway 61 Revisited*, 1965, Columbia CS9189; rerelease, 2006, Columbia CK 92399

"Home on the Range" (music: Daniel Kelley, David Guion; lyrics: Brewster Higley)
> Sons of the Pioneers, *Favorite Cowboy Songs*, 1956, RCA (Victor) LPM-1130
> Pete Seeger, *Cowboy Songs on Folkways*, 1991, Folkways SFW 40043

"The House Carpenter" (traditional)
> Texas Gladden, *Anglo American Ballads*, 1999, Rounder ROUN 1511

"The House I Live In" (Earl Robinson)
> Earl Robinson, *A Walk in the Sun and Other Songs and Ballads*, 1957, Folkways FW 02324

"I Am a Union Woman" (Aunt Molly Jackson)
> Molly Jackson and John Greenway, *The Songs and Stories of Aunt Molly Jackson*, 1961, Folkways FW 05457

"(I Can't Get No) Satisfaction" (Keith Richard and Mick Jagger)
> Rolling Stones, "(I Can't Get No) Satisfaction" [single], 1965, London 45-LON 9766 (USA)

"I Didn't Raise My Boy to Be a Soldier" (music: Al Piantadosi; lyrics: Alfred Bryan)
> Helen Clark, *I Didn't Raise My Boy to Be a Soldier*, 1915, Library of Congress, Edison Collection, Edison Blue Amberol 2580; Edison Record 3584

"I Don't Want Your Millions, Mister" (traditional; lyrics: Jim Garland)
> Almanac Singers, *Talking Union and Other Union Songs*, 1955, Folkways FW 05285
> Jim Garland, *Newport Broadside: Topical Songs at the Newport Folk Festival*, 1963, Vanguard VSD-79144

"I-Feel-Like-I'm-Fixin'-to-Die Rag (Vietnam Rag)" (Country Joe McDonald)
> Country Joe McDonald and the Fish, *I Feel Like I'm Fixin' To Die*, 1967, Vanguard VSD 79266; rerelease, 1987, Vanguard VMD-79266

"I Love Everybody" (traditional; lyrics: Southern Christian Leadership Conference [SCLC] Chorus)
> Freedom Voices with Pete Seeger, *WNEW's Story of Selma*, 1965, Folkways FW 05595

"I Wonder as I Wander" (traditional)
> John Jacob Niles, *John Jacob Niles Sings Folk Songs*, 1964, Folkways FW 02373

"If I Had a Hammer (Hammer Song)" (music: Pete Seeger; lyrics: Lee Hays)
Pete Seeger, *If I Had a Hammer: Songs of Hope and Struggle*, 1998, Smithsonian Folkways SFW 40096
Peter, Paul and Mary, *Peter, Paul and Mary*, 1962, Warner 1449; rerelease, *Carry It On*, 2004, Rhino R2 73907
Weavers, *Reunion at Carnegie Hall—1963*, 1963, Vanguard VSD 2150

"I'm a Rover [and Seldom Sober]" (traditional)
Watersons, *The Watersons*, 1966, Topic 12T142

"I'm Going to Say It Now" (Phil Ochs)
Phil Ochs, *In Concert*, 1966, Elektra EKL 310
Phil Ochs, *There but for the Fortune*, 1989, Elektra EKL 60832

"I'm on My Way (to Freedom Land)" (traditional)
Sweet Honey in the Rock, *Freedom Song*, 2000, Sony Classical SK 89147

"Indian Corn Song," "Corn Song" (music: Blackfire; lyrics: Woody Guthrie)
Blackfire, *Woody Guthrie Singles*, 2003, Woody Guthrie Archive CDWGS

"It Takes a Worried Man [To Sing a Worried Song]" (traditional)
Woody Guthrie, *Columbia River Collection*, 1987, Rounder ROUN 1036

"It's a Grand Old Flag" (George M. Cohan)
Billy Murray, "You're a Grand Old Rag," 1906, Library of Congress, Zon-o-phone Record, Zon-o-phone 425
Walter Huston, James Cagney, and Warner Bros. Chorus, "You're a Grand Old Flag," *Yankee Doodle Dandy*, 1942, Rhino 78210

"It's All Over Now, Baby Blue" (Bob Dylan)
Bob Dylan, *Bringing It All Back Home*, 1965, Columbia CL 2328
Bob Dylan, *The Other Side of the Mirror: Live at the Newport Folk Festival, 1963–1965*, 2007, Sony 714466

"Joe Hill"/"I Dreamed I Saw Joe Hill Last Night" (music: Earl Robinson; lyrics: Alfred Hayes)
Earl Robinson, *A Walk in the Sun and Other Songs and Ballads*, 1957, Folkways FW02324
Joan Baez, *Best of Woodstock*, 1995, Atlantic 82618
Joan Baez, *One Day at a Time*, 1970, Vanguard VSD 23010

"John Henry" (traditional)
Lead Belly, *Bourgeois Blues: Lead Belly Legacy*, vol. 2, 1997, Smithsonian Folkways SFW 40045
Woody Guthrie and Cisco Houston, *Classic Railroad Songs from Smithsonian Folkways*, 2006, Smithsonian Folkways SFW 40192

Bruce Springsteen, *We Shall Overcome: The Seeger Sessions*, 2006, Sony 82876830742

"Katie Cruel" (traditional)
Peggy Seeger, *Songs of Courting and Complaint*, 1955, Folkways FW 02049

"Kisses Sweeter Than Wine" (traditional; lyrics: Lead Belly)
Weavers, *The Weavers at Carnegie Hall*, 1955, Vanguard VRS 9010

"Lenin, Who's That Guy?" (Charles Seeger)
(never recorded)

"Lillibullero"/"Lilliburlero" (traditional)
Paul Clayton, *Folk Ballads of the English-speaking World*, 1956, Folkways FW 02310

"L'Internationale" (music: Pierre Degeyter; lyrics: Eugène Pottier)
Marc Blitzstein and New Singers, 1935, Timely 526, reissued on *Songs for Political Action*, 1996, Bear Family BCD 15720
Billy Bragg, *The Internationale*, 1990, Utility UTIL 11
Pete Seeger, *Songs of the Spanish Civil War*, vol. 1, *Songs of the Lincoln Brigade, Six Songs for Democracy*, 1961, Folkways FW 5436

"Little Boxes" (Malvina Reynolds)
Pete Seeger, *Broadside Ballads*, 1963, Folkways FW 05302
Malvina Reynolds, *Malvina Reynolds Sings the Truth*, 1967, Columbia CS 9413
Malvina Reynolds, *Ear to the Ground*, 2000, Smithsonian Folkways SFW 40124

"The Lonesome Death of Hattie Carroll" (Bob Dylan)
Bob Dylan, *The Times They Are A-Changin',* 1964, Columbia CL 2105/CS 8905

"Maggie's Farm" (Bob Dylan)
Bob Dylan, *Bringing It All Back Home*, 1965, Columbia Records CL 2328
Bob Dylan, *The Other Side of the Mirror: Live at the Newport Folk Festival, 1963–1965*, 2007, Sony 714466

"Michael Row Your Boat Ashore" (traditional)
Pete Seeger and Bernice Reagon, *Pete Seeger Now*, 1968, Columbia, CS 9717
Pete Seeger, *With Voices Together We Sing*, 1956, Folkways FW 02452

"Moving Day" (Harry Von Tilzer and Andrew Sterling)
Charlie Poole, *The Essential Charlie Poole*, 2009, Gum Tree Music GUM 7787

"Mr. Tambourine Man" (Bob Dylan)
Bob Dylan, *Bringing It All Back Home*, 1965, Columbia CL 2328

"MTA Song"/"Charlie on the MTA" (traditional; lyrics: Jacqueline Steiner and Bess Lomax Hawes)
Kingston Trio, *At Large*, 1959, Capitol T1199

"My Back Pages" (Bob Dylan)
Bob Dylan, *Another Side of Bob Dylan*, 1964, Columbia CS8993

"The 1913 Massacre" (Woody Guthrie)
Woody Guthrie, *Struggle*, 1990, Smithsonian Folkways SFW 40025

"Not in My Name" (John McCutcheon)
John McCutcheon, *Greatest Story Never Told*, 2002, Red House Records RHR 163

"Oh Freedom" (traditional; lyrics: SNCC)
Hollis Watkins, *Voices of the Civil Rights Movement: Black American Freedom Songs 1960–1966*, 1997, Smithsonian Folkways SFW 40084
Montgomery Gospel Trio, Nashville Quartet, and Guy Carawan, *We Shall Overcome: Songs of the Freedom Riders and the Sit-Ins*, 1961, Folkways 05591

"Oh Joy upon This Earth" (Charles Seeger and Fred Holland)
(never recorded)

"Oh the Girls They Go Wild, Simply Wild, Over Me" (Joe McCarthy and Fred Fischer)
Leake County Revelers, "They Go Wild, Simply Wild, Over Me," *Ragtime No. 2: The Country—Mandolins, Fiddles, and Guitars*, 1971, Folkways FW RBF18
Freedom Riders, "They Go Wild Over Me," *American History in Ballad and Song*, vol. 2, 1962, Folkways FW 05802

"Old Man Atom"/ "Talking Atomic Blues"/"Talking Atom" (Vern Partlow)
Sam Hinton, *Newport Broadside: Topical Songs at the Newport Folk Festival*, 1963, Vanguard VSD 79144

"On Account of That New Situation" (Woody Guthrie)
(never recorded)

"On Top of Old Smoky/Smokey" (traditional)
Roscoe Holcomb, *High Lonesome Sound*, 1998, Smithsonian Folkways SFW 40104
Burl Ives, *Wayfaring Stranger*, 1955/1964, Columbia CS 9041
Weavers, *Best of The Weavers*, 1959, Decca DL8893
Weavers, *Goodnight Irene, The Weavers 1949–1953*, 2000, Bear Family BCD 15930

"Only a Pawn in Their Game" (Bob Dylan)
Bob Dylan, *The Times They Are A-Changin,'* 1964, Columbia CL 2105/CS 8905

"Oxford Town" (Bob Dylan)
> Bob Dylan, *Freewheelin' Bob Dylan*, 1963, Columbia CS 8786; rerelease, *Bob Dylan Collection 2*, 2005, Sony 75013

"Poor Wayfaring Stranger" (traditional)
> Burl Ives, *Classic Folk Music from Smithsonian Folkways Recordings*, 2004, SFW 40110
> Roscoe Holcomb, *Mountain Music of Kentucky*, 1996, SFW 40077

"The Preacher and the Slave (Pie in the Sky)" (Joe Hill)
> Joe Glazer, *I Will Win: Songs of the Wobblies*, 1977, Collector COLL 01927

"The Range of the Buffalo" (traditional)
> Alan Lomax, *Songs of the Working People*, 1988, Flying Fish FF 483

"The Ringing of Revolution" (Phil Ochs)
> Phil Ochs, *Broadside Ballads*, vol. 10, *Phil Ochs Sings for Broadside*, 1974, Folkways FW 05320

"Roll the Union On" (traditional; lyrics: Almanac Singers)
> Almanac Singers, *Talking Union and Other Union Songs*, 1955, Folkways FW 05285
> Montgomery Gospel Trio, Nashville Quartet, and Guy Carawan, *We Shall Overcome*, 1961, Folkways FW 05591

"Round and Round Hitler's Grave" (traditional; lyrics: Almanac Singers)
> Almanac Singers, *That's Why We're Marching: World War II and the American Folksong Movement*, 1996, Smithsonian Folkways SFW 40021
> Almanac Singers, *Dear Mr. President*, 1942, Keynote K 306

"The Same Old Merry-Go-Round" (Ray Glasser and Bill Wolff)
> Michael Loring, *Songs for Political Action: Folk Music, Topical Songs, and the American Left*, 1996, Bear Family BCD 15720

"Schwab, Schwab, Charlie Schwab" (Charles Seeger)
> (never recorded)

"Scottsboro Boys" / "Scottsboro Boys Must Go Free" (Lead Belly)
> Lead Belly, *Lead Belly: The Library of Congress Recordings*, 1965, Elektra EKL 301/2

"So Long (It's Been Good to Know Yuh)" (Woody Guthrie)
> Weavers, *So Long/Lonesome Traveler*, 1950, Decca 27376
> Ramblin' Jack Elliottt, *Talking Woody Guthrie*, 1963, Topic 12T 93
> Woody Guthrie, *Dust Bowl Ballads*, 1964, Folkways FW 05212

"Solidarity Forever" (Ralph Chaplin)
Almanac Singers, *Talking Union and Other Union Songs*, 1955, Folkways FW 05285

"Somebody to Love" (Darby Slick)
Jefferson Airplane, *Surrealistic Pillow*, 1967, RCA Victor LPM 3766

"Sounds of Silence" (Paul Simon)
Simon and Garfunkel, *Sounds of Silence*, 1968, CBS Sony SOPM101

"Talking John Birch Paranoid Blues" (Bob Dylan)
Bob Dylan, *The Bootleg Series*, vols. 1–3, *Rare and Unreleased, 1961–1991*, 1991, Columbia C3T-47382
Bob Dylan, *The Bootleg Series*, vol. 6, *Live 1964—Concert at Philharmonic Hall*, 2004, Columbia/Sony CD 86882

"(Teacher) Uncle Ho" (Pete Seeger)
Pete Seeger, *Rainbow Race*, 1973, Columbia C 30739

"This Land Is Your Land" (Woody Guthrie)
Woody Guthrie, *Bound for Glory: Songs and Stories of Woody Guthrie*, 1956, Folkways FW 02481
Woody Guthrie, *This Land Is Your Land: The Asch Recordings*, vol. 1, 1997, Smithsonian Folkways SFW 40100

"This Little Light of Mine" (traditional)
Freedom Singers, *Voices of the Civil Rights Movement: Black American Freedom Songs 1960–1966*, 1997, Smithsonian Folkways, SFW 40084
Guy Carawan, *This Little Light of Mine*, 1959, Folkways FW 03552

"Tom Dooley" (traditional)
Kingston Trio, *Kingston Trio*, 1958, Capitol T 0996

"Tom Joad" (Woody Guthrie)
Woody Guthrie, *Dust Bowl Ballads*, 1964, Folkways FW 05212

"Too Much Love…" (no known source)
Not recorded.

"Tzena, Tzena, Tzena" (traditional; Hebrew lyrics by Issachar Miron)
Weavers, *Around the World/Tzena* (Hebrew), 1950, Decca 27053
Weavers, *Goodnight Irene/Tzena* (English), 1950, Decca 27077
Weavers, *Folksongs of America and Other Lands*, 1951, Decca DL 5285

"United Front Song"/"Einheitsfrontslied" (music: Hanns Eisler; lyrics: Bertolt Brecht)
Michael Loring, *Songs for Political Action: Folk Music, Topical Songs, and the American Left*, 1996, Bear Family BCD 15720.

Pete Seeger, *Songs of the Spanish Civil War*, vol. 1, *Songs of the Lincoln Brigade: Six Songs for Democracy*, 1961, Folkways FW 5436

"Universal Soldier" (Buffy Sainte-Marie)

"Waist Deep in the Big Muddy" (Pete Seeger)
Pete Seeger, *Waist Deep in the Big Muddy*, 1967, Columbia CL 2705/CS 9505
Pete Seeger, *The Best of Broadside, 1962–1988*, 2000, Smithsonian Folkways SFW 40130

"Wasn't That a Time?" (music: Pete Seeger; lyrics: Lee Hays)
Pete Seeger, *With Voices Together We Sing*, 1956, Folkways FW 02452

"We Shall Not Be Moved" (traditional)
Almanac Singers, *Talking Union and Other Union Songs*, 1955, Folkways FW 05285
Montgomery Gospel Trio, Nashville Quartet, and Guy Carawan, *We Shall Overcome*, 1961, Folkways FW 05591

"We Shall Overcome" (traditional; lyrics: Frank Hamilton, Guy Carawan, Bernice Johnson Reagon, Pete Seeger)
Freedom Singers, *We Shall Overcome*, 1963, Mercury MG 20879
Freedom Singers, *The Newport Folk Festival: The Evening Concerts 1963*, 1991, Vanguard VGDC 770022C
Pete Seeger, *Broadsides—Songs and Ballads*, 1964, Folkways FW 02456
Bruce Springsteen, *Where Have All The Flowers Gone? The Songs of Pete Seeger*, 1998, Appleseed 611587102423
Bruce Springsteen, *We Shall Overcome: The Seeger Sessions*, 2006, Sony 82876830742

"What's the Use of Wond'rin'" (music: Richard Rodgers; lyrics: Oscar Hammerstein II)
Carousel Original Cast, 1945, NAXOS MUSICALS 8.120780

"When You and I Were True" (traditional)
Bryan Bowers, *Bristlecone Pine*, 2006, Seattle Sounds CR0400-2

"Which Side Are You On?" (traditional; lyrics: Florence Patton Reece)
Florence Reece, *Coal Mining Women*, 1997, Rounder ROUN 4025
Florence Reece and Almanac Singers, *Classic Labor Songs*, 2006, Smithsonian Folkways SFW 40166
Almanac Singers, *Talking Union and Other Union Songs*, 1955, Folkways FW 05285

"White Rabbit" (Grace Slick)
Jefferson Airplane, *Surrealistic Pillow*, 1967, RCA Victor LPM 3766

"Who Killed Cock Robin?" (traditional)
John Jacob Niles, *John Jacob Niles Sings Folk Songs*, 1964, Folkways FW 02373

"Wimoweh"/"Mbube"/"The Lion Sleeps Tonight" (Solomon Linda)
Solomon Linda's Original Evening Birds, "Mbube," 1939, Gallo
Weavers, "Wimoweh," *The Weavers at Carnegie Hall*, 1955, Vanguard VSD 9010
Kingston Trio, "Wimoweh," *From the Hungry I*, 1959, Capitol T 1107
Miriam Makeba, "Mbube," *Miriam Makeba*, 1960, RCA Victor LPM 2267

"With a Pickax and a Stone" (Jimmy Collier)
Jimmy Collier, *Broadside Ballads,* vol. 5, *Time Is Running Out*, 1970, Folkways
FW 05312

"Woke Up This Morning with My Mind Set on Freedom" (traditional; lyrics:
Rev. Osby and Bob Zellner)
Freedom Singers, *Voices of the Civil Rights Movement: Black American Freedom
Songs 1960–1966*, 1997, Smithsonian Folkways SFW 40084

"The Yanks Will Never Come" (music: Arthur Lange; lyrics: Will Dixon)
Si Jenks and Victoria Allen, "The Germans Said, The Yanks Will Never Come,"
They'll Know We're Over! Bye and Bye, 1917, Joe Morris Music Co. (sheet music)

"You've Got to Be Carefully Taught" (music: Richard Rodgers; lyrics: Oscar
Hammerstein II)
South Pacific Soundtrack, 1958, RCA LSO 1032

Index

Adomian, Lan, 32
African-American singing tradition, 3,
    12, 19–21, 140
agitprop, 51, 59, 66
    See also protest songs
albums
    Alice's Restaurant (1967), 195, 206, 232
    All the News That's Fit to Sing (1964),
        208
    Buena Vista Social Club (1997), 204
    Bringing It All Back Home (1965), 134,
        237, 238
    Broadside (1963), 124
    Everybody's Got a Right to Live (1968),
        204
    Graceland (1985), 172
    [Silence] Is a Weapon (2007), 182
    Songs for John Doe (1941), 53
    Songs for Victory (1944), 64
    Southern Exposure (1941), 52
    Versions and Variants of "Barbara Allen"
        (1940), 15, 234
    Weavers at Carnegie Hall (1955), x, 110,
        235, 238, 243
Alice's Restaurant (film), 195, 206
Almanac House, 51–57, 65–66, 143
Almanac Singers, 2
    disbanding, 67–68
    members, 53–55, 65–66, 205–7, 210
    in New York City, 51–52; at Madison
        Square Garden, 57, 61; at the
        Rainbow Room, 66-67
    politics: pacifism, 53, 64; singing
        for the left, 59, 61, 66, 91, 95, 181;
        singing for unions, 52, 61, 65, 137;
        legacy, 192
    music: recording, 56, 64; songs, 234,
        236, 240–42; songwriting, 52,
        54–55, 143
American Square Dance Group, 121–22

Ames, Russell, 127
Andersen, Eric, 153
anti-communism, 67, 47
    blacklist, 3, 74–75, 80, 83, 93, 95; from
        television, 97–98; and the Weavers,
        95–102, 105, 110, 120, 163
    publications: *Counterattack*, 80, 102;
        Red Channels, 80, 86, 95–96, 102
    Red Scare (1919–1921), 38, 93
    Red Scare (1947–1957), 73–75, 76–106;
        McCarthyism, 93, 98, 101, 107, 114,
        118, 144
    riots, 76–79. *See also* Peekskill Riots
    targeting folksingers, 79–81, 104
    See also cold war; House Committee
        on Un-American Activities
        (HUAC)
Asch, Moses "Moe," 200, 202
    and Disc Records, 63
    and Folkways Records, 75, 125
    recording folk music, 20, 27, 56, 79,
        63–64, 123–24
    See also record companies: Folkways
        Records
Ashley, Clarence, 175
audiences, folk music
    college, 74, 114, 162
    live, 4, 62, 105, 186
    participation, 62, 71, 119, 130, 140, 159,
        165
    popular, 21, 115, 126
    urban, 2, 22, 28, 53, 132, 143
    virtual, 4
Autry, Gene, x, 233

Baez, Joan, 80, 110, 114, 237
    and civil rights, 144–45, 150
    and commercial success, 125, 132–33,
        135–36
    at Newport, 126–27, 144, 150

Balkan Music and Dance Workshops, 173
ballads, 5, 8–9, 15, 29, 117
  collected 8, 10, 13, 17–21, 24, 29, 170
  in protest, 29, 43, 129, 139, 143
  revived, 109, 116, 130, 169–70
Banhart, Devendra, 169
Bartók, Béla, ix, 1
Beatles, 8, 108, 149, 154, 169, 179
Belafonte, Harry, 104, 115, 203, 206
Benally, Clayson, 180, 191–92, 198, 200, 202
Benally, Jeneda, 14, 171, 182, 200, 202
Benally, Klee, 181–82, 183, 185, 187–88, 200, 202
Bernstein, Leonard, 95, 232
Bevel, James, 205
Bibb, Leon, 74, 90
Bikel, Theodore, 108, 144, 146
Blackfire, 168, 181, 183, 202, 237
Blitzstein, Marc, 32–33, 238
Blues Project, 207
Boggs, Dock, 175
Botkin, Benjamin, 42, 47, 167
Boulton, Laura, 20
Bound for Glory (1943), 53–54
Bowers, Bryan, 15, 242
Bowers, Pete. See Seeger, Pete
Boyd, Joe, 178
Bragg, Billy, 178, 184, 223, 234, 238
Brand, Oscar, 200, 202
  and the folk scene, 50, 54, 56, 71, 123
  and interrogation by the FBI and HUAC, 84–86, 100, 102–4
Brecht, Bertolt, 79, 191, 195, 209, 241
Bridges, Harry, 57
British Invasion, 108, 149
Broadway, 28, 56, 207
  See also music genres: show tunes
Broonzy, "Big" Bill, 9, 209
Brothers Four, 115, 131
Brown, James, 159
Burns, Robert, 18
Butterfield Blues Band, 151
Byrds, 156

California Labor School Chorus, 203
Camps, xi, 4, 107, 175, 176
  Camp Unity, 25–26
  Camp Woodland, 205, 209
Campbell, Olive Dame, 2, 17, 19–20, 187
Carawan, Guy, 107, 142, 200, 203–4
  and civil rights, 139, 141–42
  songs, 233–34, 239–42
Carnegie Hall, x, 8

folk music concerts, 8, 123, 203, 206, 211
  The Weavers' concerts, 105, 110, 206; recordings, 235, 237–38, 243
Carry It On (1991), 208
Carter Family, 55, 127
Carter, Maybelle, 101, 126
Casetta, Mario "Boots," 200, 203
  political folksinging, 62, 69, 84, 92, 200, 203; Peekskill, 77; People's Songs, 70–73; Wallace Campaign, 73
Cazden, Norman, 200, 203
  and the Composers' Collective, 31, 34
  on folk music, 43–47, 59
  and revolutionary music, 18, 35, 39
Central Intelligence Agency (CIA), 3, 83, 88,
Chandler, Len, 118, 204
Charles River Valley Boys, 169
Child, Francis James, ix, 8, 10, 18, 20, 22, 158, 170
Children's Music Network, 184
Christensen, Leo, 12, 57, 74, 200, 204
Chuck D, 170
civil rights movement, 136–51, 192–93, 202, 203–4, 205–6, 207, 208–9
  Albany Movement, 138–43
  March on Washington (1963), 112, 138, 144
  Nashville Sit-ins, 138–39, 142
  Poor People's Campaign, 192
  Selma, 137–38, 149, 157, 192, 236
  Southern Christian Leadership Conference (SCLC), 147, 236. See also civil rights performers: Freedom Singers; King, Martin Luther, Jr.
civil rights performers
  CORE Singers, 138–39
  Freedom Singers, 126, 138–39, 192; at Newport, 144, 150; songs, 232, 241–43
  Montgomery Gospel Trio, 138, 239–40, 242
  Nashville Quartet, 138, 239–40, 242
civil rights songs. See topical songs by subject
Claiborne, Bob, 72
Clancy Brothers, 206
Clearwater (sloop), 150, 160, 203, 207, 209
Clubs and coffeehouses, 3–4, 120, 137, 155
  Bitter End, 120
  Blue Angel, 155

Café Au Go Go, 206
Café Wha? 120
Club 47, 120
Gaslight Café, 75, 120
Gate of Horn, 3, 120–21
Gerdes Folk City, 75, 120, 122
hungry i, 104, 120, 243
Kettle of Fish, 153
McCabe's, 120
Purple Onion, 120
Unicorn, 120
Village Gate, 122
Village Vanguard, 66, 92
Coffin, Tristram Potter, 5
Cohen, John, 200, 203
    defining folk music, 8–9, 129
    traditional vs. revived folk music,
        23–24, 115, 122, 130–31
    and the New Lost City Ramblers, 13,
        112, 115, 122, 128
Cohen, Leonard, 204
cold war, 74–77, 83, 91, 93, 207, 209
    See also anti-communism;
        Communism; Red Scare
collectors, 7, 199
    anecdotes about, 23–24
    early collectors, 2, 7, 9–10, 13,
        17–28, 42–43
    New Deal collectors, 46–47
    See also Child, Francis James; ethno-
        musicology; Lomax, Alan; Lomax,
        John; Sharp, Cecil
Collier, Jimmy, 200, 203
    and civil rights music, 137, 146–47
    songs, 144, 243
Collins, Judy, 133, 136, 156, 164, 200,
    203
Cologne Opera, 30, 208
commercialization of folk music, 51,
    118
    debate over, 6, 9, 11, 127–36, 188
    during the folk boom, 107–9, 113, 122,
        125, 127–28, 169
    in the Internet age, 176–78
    "List of American Folk Songs on
        Commercial Records," 113
    See also Lomax, Alan
Commonwealth College, 52
Communism, 75, 83, 93
    Communist Manifesto, 29
    depression-era, 35, 37
    and folk music, 61, 79–80
    See also anti-communism; Red Scare
Communist Party USA, 38–39, 42–43,
    68, 75, 82–83, 93, 95
    and the Composers' Collective, 31, 36

and folk music, 13, 42–43, 57, 59, 79,
    95
    and People's Songs and Sing Out!
        73–74, 104
    Popular Front, 42, 50, 58, 75, 158
    Young Communist League, 59, 204
    See also anti-communism;
        Communism
Composers' Collective, 31–34, 37, 39–45,
    47, 49, 59, 81, 87
    and "Aunt" Molly Jackson, 40–41
Cooder, Ry, 26–27, 44, 161–62, 200,
    203
    songs, 44, 233, 235
Coon Creek Girls, 55
Cooney, Michael, 111, 121, 200, 203,
    234
Copland, Aaron, 32–34, 87, 232
copyrights, 22–24, 114, 141–42, 178
Cornett, "Banjo" Bill, 24
Corwin, Norman, 66
Counterattack, 80, 102
    See also anti-communism
Country Joe and the Fish, 158,
    206, 236
    See also McDonald, "Country" Joe
Cowboy Songs and Other Frontier Ballads
    (1910), 2, 17–18, 20
Cowell, Henry, 34
Cradle Will Rock (1937) (musical), 32
Crow Dog, Henry, 127, 148
Cunningham, Agnes "Sis," 53, 116, 118,
    204
Curran, Joe, 61
Curtis, Natalie, 20

Dane, Barbara, 82, 200, 203, 209
Davis, Rev. Gary, 122
DeCormier, Bob "Corman," 104
Degeyter, Pierre, 31, 238
    See also Pierre Degeyter Club
DeLacy, Hugh, 98–99, 190, 200, 204
Denisoff, R. Serge, 59, 162, 222
Denver, John, 128
depression. See Great Depression
des Volkes, 30, 191
DiFranco, Ani, 168, 234
Diggers, 29
Dixon, Dorsey, 126
Dorson, Richard, 154
Dos Passos, John, 40
Dreiser, Theodore, 40
Dunson, Josh, 138
Dust Bowl, 53, 135
    songs, 240–41
Dyer-Bennet, Richard 52, 108

Dylan, Bob, ix, 75, 112, 135, 152–53, 200, 205
  folk stardom, 124, 132, 156
  new aesthetic, 154, 156,
  at Newport Folk Festival, 126, 151–52, 154
  and protest songs, 144, 150–51
  rise, 117, 118, 122–24
  songs, 134, 150, 233–34, 236–41

Earle, Steve, 169–70, 234
Eastern European Folklife Center, 207
Eastman, Max, 49
Eisler, Hanns, 32–34, 39, 41, 195, 208, 241
Eliot, T.S., 191
Elliott, "Ramblin'" Jack, 75, 115, 133, 152, 200, 205, 240
English and Scottish Popular Ballads (1882), 10, 18
English Folk Songs from the Southern Appalachians (1917), 19, 43
Ephron, Nora, 199, 200
ethnomusicology, 5, 7, 13, 28, 154, 203, 208
Even Dozen Jug Band, 154
Everybody Says Freedom (1989), 207

False Witness (1955), 102
Federal Bureau of Investigations (FBI), 3–4, 57, 67, 75, 79, 83–84, 88, 216
  and Charles Seeger, 85, 87
  and NWA, 168
  and Oscar Brand, 84–86, 103
  and People's Songs, 71–73, 88
  and Pete Seeger, 80,
  and the Weavers, 96
  informants, 89–90, 102–4. *See also* Harvey Matusow.
festivals, 22, 48, 126–27, 144, 169, 175, 176, 196
  Antifolk Festival, 169
  Clearwater Festival Great Hudson River Revival, 209
  National Folk Festival (radio), 48
  Woodstock Festival, 158, 166
  Woody Guthrie Folk Festival, 187
  See also Newport Folk Festival
FitzGerald, Edward, xi
Flatt, Lester, 235
Fletcher, Andrew, 29
Folk Alliance, 3, 169, 172, 208
folk music, defining, 5, 7–16
  according to early collectors, 17, 19, 30, 42, 53, 172

  according to revivalists, 53, 113, 126–27, 132, 153
  as people's music, 30, 191
  International Folk Music Council, 13
  post-Newport 1965, 166, 169, 171–72, 176, 178, 188
folk music clubs, *see* clubs and coffeehouses
folk singers, 9, 16, 23–24, 53, 120–22, 127, 132, 153–54
  popularizers, 21, 23, 28, 115–16, 126, 128, 131–32
  singer-songwriters, 7, 11, 154, 167–69, 182; new aesthetic, 154
  singers of folksongs, 128, 132, 154; emulators, imitators, and interpreters, 128, 135, 154–55, 162, 175
  traditional, 8, 15, 42, 115–16, 122, 126–27, 154, 176; old-timey, 115, 128, 155; source singers, 22–24, 41–42, 52, 55, 115, 131. *See also* Guthrie, Woody; Jackson, "Aunt" Molly; music genres: traditional
  urban, 23–24; citybillies, 108, 126–27
folk process, 13–14, 22, 41, 116, 136, 141, 158
folk songs. *See* music genres; songs
folk-rock. *See* music genres
Folklore Center, 75, 120–21, 209
Folklore Centrum (Stockholm), 210
Frantz, Margaret Gelder, 165, 195, 200, 204
Free the Army Tour, 161
Friesen, Gordon, 16, 22, 200, 204
  and the Almanac Singers, 52–53, 61, 65, 67
  and *Broadside*, 112, 118
  on political song, 79, 118, 144, 193
  on folksingers, 122, 124, 162
  See also magazines, folk music: *Broadside*

Garland, Jim, 41–42, 52, 58, 233, 236
Gateway Singers, 114–15
Gellert, Lawrence, 20, 213
Genghis Blues (1999) (film), 203
Gibbs, Wolcott, 12, 234
Gilbert, Ronnie, 200, 204
  and the Weavers, 91, 97; blacklisted, 94, 97, 99, 105
  with Holly Near, 161, 163
Ginsberg, Allen, 209
Gladden, Texas, 164, 236
Glazer, Tom, 53

Golden Gate Quartet, 120
Goldstein, Kenneth, 115
Gooding, Cynthia, 108
Gottlieb, Lou, 114
Grammy Awards, 203, 208
Grand Old Opry, 55
Gray, Arvella, 123
Great Day Coming (1973), 59, 222
Great Depression, 24, 27, 35–38, 44,
   47–48, 51
Green, Archie, 126, 128, 162, 178, 201,
   204
   Only a Miner (1972), 204
Greenwich Village folk scene, 4
   1930s–1940s, 2, 34, 37, 49–75, 91
   1950s–1960s, 4, 86, 91–93, 100, 115,
   120–23, 154
   See also Washington Square Park
Grisman, David, 169
Grossman, Albert, 121, 123, 152
Gruning, Thomas, 187
Guard, Dave, 110, 114
   See also Kingston Trio
guerilla singing, 98
Gunning, Sarah Ogan, 52, 126, 234
Guthrie, Abe, 4
Guthrie, Arlo, 200, 205
   on folk music, 9, 109, 135, 157, 167,
      192; performing folk music, 111–12,
      196; on protest songs, 119–20, 189,
      194
   on Woody Guthrie, 69, 119, 189
   songs, 232
Guthrie, Sarah Lee, 4
Guthrie, Woody, 8, 27, 68, 108, 166, 171,
   187–88
   and the Almanac Singers, 2, 53–57,
      60, 65–66, 68
   and *Bound for Glory*, 53–54
   and People's Songs, 69–71
   and Pete Seeger, ix–x, 50, 130–31
   legacy, 8, 59–60, 135, 170, 184;
      "Woody's Children," 4, 14–15, 112,
      122, 161–62
   politics, 61, 69, 79, 119
   recording, 63–64
   songs, 14–15, 88, 118, 187, 189, 232–33,
      237–41
   songwriting, 54, 116–17

H.A.R.P., 205
Hamer, Fannie Lou, 144, 220–21, 235
   See also civil rights
Hamilton, Frank, 141–42, 242
Hammond, John, 157, 203

Harlan County, KY, 40, 50, 121, 234
   See also Jackson, Aunt Molly
Harper, Ben, 168
Harris, Rutha, 139
Harvard University, 10, 17–18, 30–31,
   54
Haufrecht, Herbert, 33, 45, 201, 205
Hawes, Bess Lomax, 201, 206
   and the Almanac Singers, 51, 53–54,
      58, 65–69
   on "Aunt" Molly Jackson, 40–42
   on Moses Asch, 63–64
   on topical song, 60–62, 165
   songs, 61, 239
Hawes, Pete "Butch," 53–54, 68, 206
Hayes, Alfred, 209, 237
Hays, Lee, 51, 69, 112, 189, 201, 205
   and the Almanac Singers, 53–54, 58,
      61–62
   and the Weavers, 91–92, 95, 100, 102,
      113
   and political song, 118–19, 162–63
   songs, 237, 242
Hellerman, Fred, 91, 105, 112, 201, 206
Herder, Johann Gottfried, 2, 18
Hestor, Carolyn, 121
Hickerson, Joe, 7
Highlander Folk School, 141–42, 202,
   205
Hill, Joe, 37, 52, 187
Hille, Waldemar, 58, 201, 205
Hinton, Sam, 14, 132
Holcomb, Roscoe, 176, 239–40
Holly, Buddy, 108–9, 134
Holzman, Jac, 123, 125
hootenanny, 105, 148
   Almanac hootenannies, 2, 51, 56–57
   People's Songs hootenannies, 70,
      74
   and the FBI, 3, 89
   antihoot, 169
Hoover, J. Edgar, 73, 80, 83, 96, 97
Horton, Zilphia, 141–42
House Committee on Un-American
   Activities (HUAC), 71, 74, 81, 91,
   93
   and folksingers, 79, 93–95, 100–103,
   110, 118
   See also anti-communism
Houston, Cisco, 27, 51, 237

Indigo Girls, 168
Industrial Workers of the World (IWW).
   See Wobblies
instruments, 170

instruments (*continued*)
  autoharp, 15, 154, 209
  banjo, 1, 43, 52, 79, 109, 127, 167,
    173; players, 24, 54–56, 110–11,
    157, 169
  dulcimer, 207, 209
  electric accompaniment, 130, 151,
    154–57, 169, 187
  fiddle, 10, 22, 79, 109, 164, 198; players,
    46, 169, 175, 197
  flute, 130
  guitar, 43, 52, 107, 115, 121, 126, 167,
    198; electric, 151, 181; players, 26, 45,
    151–53
  harmonica, 50, 65, 154, 177
  piano, 32–35, 39, 157
  violin, 30, 173, 210
International Folk Music Council, 13,
  23, 85
  See also Folk Alliance
Internet, 3, 11, 176, 177–78
  See also websites
Ives, Burl, 51–53, 59, 63–64, 108, 121, 128;
  songs, 239–40

Jackson, "Aunt" Molly, 6, 17, 50, 52, 58
  and the Composers' Collective,
    40–43
  songs, 8, 233, 236
Jefferson Airplane, 241–42
Jefferson, Blind Lemon, 55
Jenkins, Gordon, 91
John Birch Society, 79–81, 117, 160, 241
  See also Communism:
    anticommunism
Johnson, James, 18
Juilliard School, 31, 36

Kahn, Si, 201, 205
  on folk music, 11, 15, 131, 164, 166,
    196–97
  songs, 235
Kalb, Danny, 80, 157, 201, 205
Kallick, Kathy, 175
Kennedy Center Lifetime Achievement
  Award, 210
Kennedy, Stetson, 47, 201, 205
King, Charlie, 183–84
King, Martin Luther, Jr., 137–38
Kingston Trio, 108–16, 127–28, 164, 166
  songs, 109, 114, 116, 131, 241
Kirkpatrick, Frederick Douglass, 147,
  152, 203
Kittredge, George Lyman, 18
Korean War, 93, 100

labor movement, 29–30, 37, 44, 76, 112,
  141–42, 190
  See also topical songs by subject: union
    songs; unions
Ladysmith Black Mambazo, 172
LaFarge, Peter, 182, 203
Lampell, Millard, 51–57, 65–66, 201,
  205
  H. Partnow (pseudonym),
    206
Landau, Felix, 104
Lead Belly (Huddie Ledbetter), ix,
  23–27, 50, 68, 108, 120, 131
  and the Almanac Singers, 2, 52, 56–60
  and the Lomaxes, 24–25
  and the Weavers, 23, 26, 131
  legacy, 8, 168
  Negro Folk Songs as Sung by Lead Belly
    (1936), 25
  recording, 63–64
  songs, 23, 26, 234–40
Lehrer, Tom, 136
Lester, Julius, 146
Leventhal, Harold, 79–80, 95–98, 113,
  133, 201, 206
Lewis, John L, xi
Lewis, Laurie, 169
Library of Congress, 42
  American Folklife Center (formerly
    Archive of American Song),
    23–24, 45, 50, 161, 164, 199; David
    Dunaway Collection, 4, 199; and
    John and Alan Lomax, 24–25, 55,
    113, 120
  folk music recordings, 15, 164
Lieberman, Ernie "Sheldon," 104
Limeliters, 115, 128
Little Red School House, 53,
  122, 209
  Elisabeth Irwin High School, 209
Little Red Song Book (1909), 37, 166
  See also Wobblies
Lomax, Bess. *See* Hawes, Bess Lomax
Lomax, Alan, ix, 60, 108
  and "Aunt" Molly Jackson, 40,
    42, 58
  and politics, 47, 119–20
  collecting folk music, 8–9, 20, 23–25,
    58, 64
  performing, 53, 240
  promoting living folk music, 17,
    50–51, 63; during the folk boom,
    113–14
  See also songbooks: *Hard Hitting
    Songs for Hard Hit People*

Lomax, John Avery, 2, 10, 17–25, 55, 181, 187
  See also *Cowboy Songs and Other Frontier Ballads* (1910)
Lopez, Trini, 154
Lovin' Spoonful, 154
Lunsford, Bascom Lamar, 23–24

MacColl, Ewan, 180, 206, 208
  songs, 129–30, 233
Macon, "Uncle" Dave, 55
magazines, folk music
  Broadside, 117–18, 120–24, 144, 156, 193. *See also* Friesen, Gordon
  Caravan, 120
  Little Sandy Review, 120
  Musical Times, 19
  Folk Roots, 244
  People's Songs (bulletin), 58, 70, 72, 74, 206
  Sing Out! 73–74, 116, 118, 120–22, 128, 151, 155, 176; during the Red Scare, 73–74, 80. *See also* Moss, Mark; Silber, Irwin
  Urban Folk, 169
magazines, general
  New Masses, 49
  Newsweek, 138, 151, 157
  Redbook, 114
  Rolling Stone, 4, 169, 177
  Time, 132, 153
Magil, A. B., 50, 201, 206
Mammals, the, 184
Marley, Bob, 170
Marrs, Ernie, 116
Matusow, Harvey, 90–91, 102
McCarthy, Joseph, Senator, 80–81, 84, 93, 99, 114
McCutcheon, John, 112, 184, 186, 201, 206
  songs, 239
McDonald, Country Joe, 158–59, 161, 201, 206
  See also Country Joe and the Fish
McGhee, Brownie, 50, 52, 122
McGuire, Barry, 158, 235
McLean, Don, 26, 93, 96 114 197, 201, 206
Minstrelsy of the Scottish Border, 18
Mitchell, Joni, 127, 133, 168, 203
Moby, 169
Monroe, Bill, 162, 175
Moss, Mark D., 110, 162, 201, 206
  on folk music, 7–8, 166, 169, 176

Muddy Waters, 164
music genres, 3
  antifolk, 169
  Appalachian, 8, 43, 109, 129, 162, 169; collectors of, 19, 21, 24, 43
  Balkan, 15, 173–74, 185, 187
  blues, 24, 38, 58, 109, 112, 159, 169, 171–72; performers, 9, 45, 50, 55, 82, 131, 151, 159; songs, 26, 117, 151, 164, 234–35, 237, 239, 241
  bluegrass, 15, 155, 162, 169, 172, 175, 188; Dawg music and newgrass, 169; festivals, 175, 188, 197
  cajun, 7, 24
  calypso, 7, 38
  chain gang, 9, 21, 24–25, 52, 120, 141
  classical, x, 31, 34, 125, 130, 164, 169, 176
  country-western, 13, 24, 55, 67, 109, 135, 168; alternative country, 168–69; cowboy tunes, 10, 16–18, 20–21, 31, 42, 45, 58; hillbilly, 45, 47, 55, 67, 115–16, 135, 162
  disco, 9, 167
  folk (*see* folk music; folk singers)
  folk-rock, 134, 151, 153–57, 168, 222
  gospel, 137–39, 239–40, 242
  gypsy (Roma), 174
  hip-hop, 168, 170, 184–87
  jazz, 112–13, 176, 179
  Latin (salsa, *son*), 172
  Native American, 20, 181–82
  nu folk (folk noir, freak folk, naturalismo, psych-folk), 169
  punk, 14, 168–71, 180–88
  ragtime, 109, 179
  reggae, 170, 173
  rap, 7, 168, 170–71, 175, 185
  rhythm and blues, 107, 139
  rock and roll, 11, 107, 149, 153, 155–56, 167–70, 179, 184; rage-rock, 181, 202; rockabilly, 8, 151
  show tunes (Tin Pan Alley), 38, 44, 75, 166–67
  spirituals, 10, 19–20, 62, 137–40
  urban folk, 23, 50, 127, 137, 153, 170, 184
  zydeco, 7
  See also popular music
Musselman, Jim, 14, 184, 201, 206
  See also record companies: Appleseed Records

National Endowment for the Arts, 207
Near, Holly, 163, 170, 194, 198, 201, 206

Near, Holly (*continued*)
  on political music, 148, 159, 161, 186, 191
  songs, 194, 235
Neblett, Charles, 139
Nelson, Paul, 151
New Deal programs, 45, 76
  Farm Security Administration, 45–46
  Federal Music Project, 47, 209
  Federal Theater, 206
  Resettlement Administration, 45–47, 205
  Works Progress [Projects] Administration (WPA), 47, 208
New Lost City Ramblers, 13, 101, 112, 128, 162, 175
  old-time music, 115, 128
  songs, 13, 101, 233
  See also, Cohen, John; Seeger, Mike
Newport Folk Festival, 119, 125–27, 166–67
  Dylan goes electric (1965), 151–54, 158
  freedom sing (1963), 138, 144, 150
  recordings of, 236–39, 242
newspapers
  Daily Worker, 37, 56, 103, 206, 209
  Guardian, 210
  Mechanics Free Press, 29
  New York Times, 117, 129, 141, 155, 178, 197
  People's World, 74
  Philadelphia Inquirer, 207
  Village Voice, 121, 169
New World Singers, 124, 209, 233
Newman, Randy, 204
Niles, John Jacob, 108, 236, 243
Nilsen, Carl, 169
Nirvana, 168
North, Alex, 32

O'Reilly, Chris, 171, 201, 208
O'Reilly, David, 160, 201, 208
Ochs, Phil, ix, 75, 121, 166, 185, 201, 207
  and political music, 118, 144, 158–59, 191
  on Bob Dylan, 134, 153–54
  and record companies, 124–25
  on the rise of folk music, 109, 114, 154
Odetta, 210
Odum, Howard, 18, 20
Ohio State Fair, 96–97
Ohrlin, Glenn, 126
Old Left, 105, 165

oral history, 6, 21, 199–200, 231
oral tradition, 5, 18, 60, 140
oral transmission, 18, 53, 172
The Oysterband, 3

Paley, Tom, 101, 208
Pan-American Union (later UNESCO), 85
Partlow, Vern, 116, 239
Partnow, H. *See* Lampell, Millard
Paull, Irene, 145, 201, 207
Paxton, Tom, 121, 129, 132, 162, 204
Peekskill riots, 76–78
People's Artists, 73–74, 77–78, 88–91, 121
People's Music Network, 183–84
People's Songs, 58, 69–75, 183
  as a suspected Communist front, 88–91, 102, 120
  See also Hille, Waldemar; People's Artists
The People, Yes, 36
Percy, Thomas, Bishop, 18
Peter, Paul and Mary, 166
  and folk stardom, 75, 112, 126,
  singing for civil rights, 112, 119, 141, 144–46
  songs, 119, 124, 131, 141, 233, 235, 237
  See also Travers, Mary
Philips, Utah, 11
Pierre Degeyter Club, 31, 32, 34, 41, 59
  See also Degeyter, Pierre
Pins and Needles (1939) (musical), 59
political songs. *See* protest songs
Poole, Charlie, 166, 238
popular music, 17, 40, 59, 109–10, 115, 124, 133–34, 165
  pop charts, 79, 91, 114
  and folk, 11, 13–14, 81, 108–10, 126–28, 136, 153–55, 167–70;
  popularizers, 109, 114–15, 124, 129, 134
  and political song, 39, 59, 169
  songs, 38–39, 91, 109, 172
  See also music genres
Presley, Elvis, 109, 129
Primack, Eva Salina, 15, 173–76, 185, 187, 201, 207
Profitt, Frank, ii, 131
protest songs, 11–13, 156, 189–93, 211–12, 213
  the writing of, 32–33, 40–42, 116–18, 140; "We Shall Overcome," 141–43
  effectiveness, 12–13, 138, 192–93
  songs, 116, 139, 141, 144, 192

See also magazines: *Broadside, Sing Out!*; *topical songs by subject*
Progressive Party, 73–74
public domain. *See* copyrights
Public Enemy, 168

Quill, Mike, 61

radio, 11, 50–51, 72, 107, 109–10, 178
  and the blacklist, 80–81
  homogenizing music, 15, 113, 135
  role in folk music revivals, 107, 109–10, 115, 120
radio programs
  barn dances, 48
  National Folk Festival (1934), 48
  Oscar Brand's Folksong Festival, WNYC-AM, 202
  Social Security, 101–2
Radosh, Ronald, 104, 201, 207
Rage Against the Machine, 169
Rainbow Room, 66–67
Reagon, Bernice Johnson, 138–45, 152, 192–93, 201, 207
  songs, 234, 238, 242
  See also civil rights; Freedom Singers; Sweet Honey in the Rock
Reagon, Cordell, 138–39, 144
record companies, 23, 107, 124–25, 134, 168, 177
  [Asch-]Stinson Records, 63, 121, 164
  A & M Records, 125
  Alligator Records, 169
  Appleseed Records, 168, 184, 208, 234, 242
  Atlantic Records, 124
  Columbia Records, 64, 120–21, 124, 233–34, 236–42
  Decca Records, 67, 91, 239–41
  Disc Records (later Folkways), 63, 202
  Elektra Records, 120–21, 123–25, 233, 237, 240
  Folkways Records, 63–64, 75, 79, 120–25, 164, 177, 232–43
  Green Linnet Records, 168
  Rounder Records, 168, 233–34, 236–37, 242
  Shanachie Records, 168
  Smithsonian Folkways and Global Sound, 177, 232–35, 237–43
  Sugar Hill Records, 168
  Vanguard Records, 110, 120, 123, 125, 235–39, 242–43
  Waterbug Records, 168
Reece, Florence, 242
red-baiting. *See* anti-communism

Red Channels. See under anti-communism
Red Dust Players, 203
Red Scare. See under anti-communism
Reed, Susan, 108
Reiser, Bob, 84, 201, 207
Reliques of Ancient English Poetry (1765), 18
Reuss, Richard, 103
The Reviewers, 92
revivals, folk music, 4, 162, 166–67, 198
  first (1910–1953), 2, 20, 25, 28, 50, 55, 107, 166
  second, 3, 51, 92, 107–10, 113, 116–17, 127–28, 132; late revival, 155, 166
  third (1989-present), 3–4, 168, 172, 175, 177, 188–89. *See also* YouTube folk revival
revolutionary music. *See* protest songs
Reynolds, Malvina, 108, 134, 185, 201, 207
  and political music, 81, 116–18
  songs, 238
Reynolds, Nick, 114
  See also Kingston Trio
Rinzler, Ralph, 8, 101–102
Robeson, Paul, 73, 76, 78, 90, 232, 235
Robinson, Earl, 3, 84, 148, 201, 208
  on folk music, 7, 14, 25–26, 44, 108, 114
  on the Composers' Collective, 33–34, 44
  on Communism, 35–37, 82–83; and anti-communism, 100–101, 104
  and the Almanac Singers, 53–59
  and People's Songs, 69, 73
  on the politics of the sixties and seventies, 148, 159, 165
  songs, 165, 232, 234–37
Rodgers, Jimmie, 55
Rodriguez-Seeger, Tao, 4, 187
Rodgers (Richard) and Hammerstein (Oscar), 242–43
Rolling Stones, 108, 149, 171, 204, 236
Roosevelt, Theodore, President, 17–18, 20

Sacks, Oliver, 193
Sadler, Barry, 158, 233
Sainte-Marie, Buffy, 150, 206, 242
Saletan, Tony, x
Sanders, Betty, 118
Sandburg, Carl, 2, 19, 36, 43, 53
Sands, Carl. *See* Seeger, Charles
Schaefer, Jacob, 34, 59

Scherer, Gordon H., 100
School of the Arts (San Francisco, CA), 209
Scots Musical Museum (1787–1803), 18
Scott, Walter, Sir, 18
Scruggs, Earl, 131, 235
Seeger, Charles, ix, 5–6, 30–31, 36–37, 195, 199, 201, 208
  Carl Sands (pseudonym), 87
  with the Composers' Collective, 17, 31, 33, 38–39, 45
  on folk music, 10, 18, 21–25, 39–40, 45, 53, 130, 179; WPA, 45–47
  on the folk boom, 132–33, 135, 155, 166
  and the Red Scare, 81, 84–87
  songs, 234, 238–40
Seeger, Mike, 8, 100–101, 119, 122, 128, 201, 208
  and traditional performers, 115, 126
  legacy, 131, 161–62
  See also New Lost City Ramblers
Seeger, Peggy, 30, 87–89, 121, 129–30, 180, 201, 208
  songs, 233, 238
Seeger, Pete, 68, 129–30, 176, 196, 201, 208
  with the Almanac Singers, 53–57, 61–62, 67–68
  and the blacklist, 77, 80–81, 83–84, 86–87, 95–100, 104–5
  on the Composers' Collective, 34, 39, 41; on Charles Seeger, 30–31, 34–36
  and the folk boom, 107–8, 113, 122–23, 131–32; and folk-rock, 151–52, 155–57
  on folk music, 9, 14, 16, 19, 43; and folk music collection, 21, 24–25
  at the Newport Folk Festival, 126–27, 151–52
  legacy, 110–12, 161–62, 187, 193
  Pete Bowers (pseudonym), 53
  and People's Songs, 69–71
  politics and music, 46, 69, 73, 104, 119–20, 189–90; protest music, 12, 32–33, 60, 159–60, 183–84; and civil rights, 139–45, 147, 150
  recording, 64, 124, 169
  songs, 39, 62, 176, 232, 234–38, 241–42
  with the Weavers, 91, 95–97, 110
  and Woody Guthrie, ix–x, 50, 13
Seeger, Ruth Crawford, 39, 87, 208
Seeger, Toshi Ohta, 68, 92, 126, 138, 201, 208

  on FBI surveillance, 88, 90
Shane, Bob, 114
  See also Kingston Trio
Shankar, Ravi, 206
Sharp, Cecil, ix, 2, 17, 19–21, 43, 181, 187
Shelton, Robert, 117, 129, 155
Sherrod, Charles, 139
Shevchenko, Taras, ix
Siegmeister, Elie, 32, 47
Silber, Irwin, 59, 92, 103, 118, 152, 201, 209
  and People's Songs, 69–70, 72, 91
  and People's Artists, 74, 78, 90
  on political music, 13
  and *Sing Out!* 73–74, 118
Simon, Paul, 150, 154, 172, 241
Simon and Garfunkel, 241
Silverman, Jerry, 121
Silber, Marc, 154
Slave Songs of the United States (1867), x
Smithsonian Folkways. *See under* record companies
Smithsonian Institution, 206, 207
socialism, 31, 37–39, 43, 47, 49, 61, 79
Solomon brothers (Maynard and Seymour), 125
  See also record companies: Vanguard Records
song leading, 71, 142, 147, 202
songcatchers. *See* collectors
songs
  "1913 Massacre," 189, 238
  "Ain't Gonna Let Nobody Turn Me Round," 139, 231
  "Alice's Restaurant Massacree," 196, 206, 231
  "All Mixed Up," 177, 231
  "Appalachian Spring," 32, 231
  "Ballad for Americans," 165, 231
  "Ballad of the Carpenter," 129, 232
  "Ballad of the Green Berets," 158, 232
  "Ballad of the Student Sit-In," 139, 232
  "Barbara Allen," 15, 19, 233
  "Battleship of Maine," 13, 101, 232
  "Be Nobody's Darling but Mine," x, 232
  "Blowin' in the Wind," 119, 124, 211, 232
  "Bombs over Baghdad," 192, 232
  "Boomer's Story," 44, 232
  "Bourgeois Blues," 26, 233, 236
  "Bring 'Em Home," 160, 184, 233

"Candidate's a Dodger," 46, 233
"Casey Jones," 44, 58, 233
"Coal Creek March," 148, 233
"Come All You Coal Miners," 8, 233
"Come and Go with Me to That Land," 139, 233
"Death of Harry Simms," 40, 233
"Declaration of Independence," 12, 233
"Desolation Row," 134, 233
"Erie Canal," 233
"Eve of Destruction," 158–59, 234
"Farmer Is the Man [Who Feeds Us All]," 46, 234
"Foggy Mountain Breakdown," 132, 234
"Free and Equal Blues," 234
"Fret and Frails," 210
"Get on Board Children," 139, 234
"Go Tell Aunt Rhody," 155, 231
"Go Tell It on the Mountain," 141, 234
"Go to Work on Monday," 15, 234
"Goodnight Irene," 2, 13, 25–27, 57, 91, 98, 102, 117–18; recordings, 234, 238, 240
"Governor Pat Neff (Sweet Mary Blues)," 26, 234
"Great Historical Bum," 54, 232
"Great Peace March," 194, 234
"Guantanamera," 172, 234
"Highway 61 Revisited," 134, 233, 235
"Home on the Range," 23, 172, 235
"House Carpenter," 164, 235
"House I Live In," 165, 235
"I Am a Union Woman," 41, 235
"I Didn't Raise My Boy to Be a Soldier," 38, 235
"I Don't Want Your Millions, Mister," 41, 235
"I Love Everybody," 146, 235
"I Wonder as I Wander," 109, 235
"I-Feel-Like-I'm-Fixin'-To-Die Rag," 159, 235
"If I Had a Hammer (Hammer Song)," 8, 77, 92, 119, 131, 143, 236
"I'm a Rover [and Seldom Sober]," 130, 236
"I'm Going to Say It Now," 118, 236
"I'm on My Way (to Freedom Land)," 139, 236
"It Takes a Worried Man [To Sing a Worried Song]," 71, 236
"It's a Grand Old Flag," 38, 236
"It's All Over Now, Baby Blue," 151, 236
"Joe Hill"/"I Dreamed I Saw Joe Hill Last Night," 33, 236
"John Henry," 111, 121, 236
"Katie Cruel," 237
"Kisses Sweeter Than Wine," 53, 91, 237
"L'Internationale," 32–33, 195, 237
"Lenin, Who's That Guy?" 33, 237
"Lillibullero"/"Lilliburlero," xi, 29, 237
"The Lion Sleeps Tonight." See "Wimoweh"
"Little Boxes," 208, 237
"The Lonesome Death of Hattie Carroll," 159, 237
"Maggie's Farm," 151, 237
"Michael Row the Boat Ashore," x, 196, 237
"Moving Day," 167, 237
"Mr. Tambourine Man," 150, 237
"MTA Song"/"Charlie on the MTA," 61, 238
"My Back Pages," 150, 238
"Not in My Name," 186, 192, 238
"Oh Freedom," 139, 238
"Oh Joy Upon This Earth," 35, 238
"Oh The Girls They Go Wild, Simply Wild, Over Me," 39, 238
"Old Man Atom," 116, 238
"On Account Of That New Situation," 61, 238
"On Top Of Old Smoky/Smokey," 91, 238
"Only a Pawn in Their Game," 144, 238
"Oxford Town," 239
"Poor Wayfaring Stranger," 238, 239
"Preacher and the Slave (Pie in the Sky)," 37–38, 239
"Range of the Buffalo," 42, 239
"Ringing of Revolution," 144, 239
"Roll The Union On," 239
"Round and Round Hitler's Grave," 66, 239
"Same Old Merry-Go-Round," 73, 239
"(I Can't Get No) Satisfaction," 172, 235
"Schwab, Schwab, Charlie Schwab," 35, 239
"Scottsboro Boys" / "Scottsboro Boys Must Go Free," 26, 239
"So Long (It's Been Good to Know Yuh)," 2, 91, 118, 239

songs (*continued*)
  "Solidarity Forever," 62, 64, 240
  "Somebody to Love," 156, 240
  "Sounds of Silence," 140, 240
  "Talking Atomic Blues." *See* "Old
    Man Atom"
  "Talking Folklore Center," 210
  "Talking John Birch Paranoid Blues,"
    117, 240
  "This Land Is Your Land," 148, 187,
    240
  "This Little Light of Mine," 139, 240
  "Tom Dooley," 109, 114, 116, 131,
    240
  "Tom Joad," 117, 240
  "Too Much Love," 146, 240
  "Tzena, Tzena, Tzena," 91, 96, 172,
    240
  "(Teacher) Uncle Ho," 160, 240
  "United Front Song," 34, 195, 240
  "Universal Soldier," 150, 242
  "Waist Deep In The Big Muddy,"
    159–60, 210, 242
  "Wasn't That A Time?" 92, 241
  "We Shall Not Be Moved," 62, 139, 241
  "We Shall Overcome," 14, 139, 140–42,
    144, 147, 149, 170; recordings, 231,
    234, 237, 238, 239, 241
  "What's the Use of Wond'rin'," 195,
    241
  "When You and I Were True," 15, 241
  "Which Side Are You On?" 139, 213,
    218, 231, 241
  "White Rabbit," 156, 241
  "Who Killed Cock Robin?" 11, 242
  "Wimoweh," 92, 172, 242
  "With a Pickax and a Stone," 144,
    242
  "Woke Up This Morning With My
    Mind Set On Freedom," 139, 143,
    242
  "The Yanks Will Never Come," 57, 242
  "You've Got To Be Carefully Taught,"
    195, 242
songbooks, 4, 32–33, 121, 126
  American Songbag, 19, 28, 43
  Brecht-Eisler Song Book (1967), 208
  Folk Guitar in Ten Sessions (1966), 208
  Folk Songs of the Catskills (1982), 209
  German Folk Songs (1968), 208
  Hard Hitting Songs for Hard Hit People
    (1967), 66
  Lift Every Voice (1953), 90
  Our Singing Country (1941), 28
  The People's Songbook (1959), 142

  Songs of the Great American West
    (1967), 208
  Young Folk Song Book (1963), 208
  Little Red Song Book (1909), 37, 166
Songs about Work (1993), 205
Sosa, Mercedes, 206
Springsteen, Bruce, 14, 184, 187, 199
  songs, 231, 234, 237, 241
square dance, 45–46, 59–60, 89, 101
  See also American Square Dance
    Group
Staninec, Annie, 175–76, 201, 209
Starobin, Joseph R., 210
Starobin, Norma, 74, 89, 201, 210
Steele, Pete, 164, 234
Stekert, Ellen, 127, 154
Studer, Norman, 70, 197, 201, 210
Sturgill, Virgil, 23
Susskind, David, 97–98
Suzuki method, 175
Sweet Honey in the Rock, 208, 232, 236

television shows
  Hootenanny, 131
  Milton Berle Show, 97
  MTV, 170, 172
  Note of Triumph, 66
  Tonight Show, 97
  Today Show, 101
Terry, Sonny, 50, 52, 64, 122
Tharp, "Cowboy" Jack, 20
Tin Pan Alley. *See* music genres: show
  tunes
topical songs by subject, 149
  anti-globalization, 181, 186
  antiwar, 3, 12, 53, 150, 159, 181, 192
  civil rights, 3, 14, 119, 136–51. *See also*
    civil rights
  environmentalism, 12, 149–50, 181,
    183, 186
  feminism, 12, 161, 181
  union songs, xi, 37, 40, 64, 68, 112,
    169–70, 181; recordings, 233, 235,
    239, 240, 241
  See also protest songs
Traum, Happy, 79, 170, 201, 209
  on the folk boom, 110, 115, 124, 126,
    134, 154
Travers, Mary, 119, 131, 133, 141, 143, 201,
  209
  See also Peter, Paul and Mary
Turner, Gil, 122–24

Uncle Tupelo, 169
unions

American Federation of Labor (AFL), 37

American Federation of Musicians (802), 67, 83

International Longshore Workers Union (ILWU), 57

Industrial Workers of the World (IWW). *See* Wobblies

Congress of Industrial Organizations (CIO), 64

National Maritime Union, 57, 61, 68

Teachers Union, 89

Transport Workers Union, 57, 61

United Auto Workers (UAW), 61

United Brotherhood of Carpenters and Joiners of America, 204

Union Square (New York City), 36

University of California, Berkeley, 4–5, 17, 30, 155, 209

University of California, Los Angeles, 87, 207, 208

Institute of Ethnomusicology (UCLA), 87, 207, 208

University of California, Santa Barbara, 165, 233

Valens, Ritchie, 108

Vales, Dorothy, 139

Van Ronk, Dave, 114

Vietnam War, 12, 106, 108, 117, 145, 149–51, 157–60, 192; songs about, 232, 235

Villon, François, ix

Walker, Wyatt Tee, 141

Wallace, Henry, 2, 46, 73, 76, 91, 204

Ware, Charles Pickard, x

Warnow, Mark, 66

Warner, Anne, ii

Washington Square Park, 3, 49, 63, 100, 105, 120, 132, 154

See also Greenwich Village

Watson, Doc, 8, 126

The Weavers, x, 2, 102, 113, 127–28
    popularity, 91–93, 110, 125, 131
    blacklisting, 93–100, 102, 105, 163
    legacy, 110, 112, 115, 131, 186
    songs, 23, 25–27, 91–92, 172, 118, 235, 236, 237, 238, 239, 240, 241, 242

Websites
    Bebo, 178
    CD Baby, 177
    Mudcat, 177
    Music Genome Project, 177
    MySpace, 4
    Pandora, 177
    YouTube. *See* YouTube folk revival

Weisberg, Eric, 132

White, Josh, 8, 51–52, 103, 108, 120

Wiggins, Ella Mae, 43

Wilco, 168, 184

Williams, Robert Pete, 126

Wobblies, 30, 32, 36–39, 44, 49, 60, 166, 239
    See also unions; *Little Red Song Book*

Woodstock Festival, 158, 166

Workers' Song Book, 32–33, 39
    See also Composers' Collective

Works Progress Administration. *See* New Deal programs

World Festival of Youth and Students, Moscow (1957), 88, 202

World War II, 63, 69, 71, 76, 82, 181

War on Terror, 181

Young, Israel "Izzy," 75, 120–21, 123, 154–55, 201, 209

Young, Andrew, 139

Young, Neil, 154, 168

Youngbloods, 155

YouTube folk revival, 4, 169, 177

THE OXFORD ORAL HISTORY SERIES

J. TODD MOYE (University of North Texas), KATHRYN NASSTROM (University of San Francisco), and ROBERT PERKS (The British Library Sound Archive), *Series Editors* DONALD A. RITCHIE, *Senior Advisor*

Doing Oral History, Second Edition *Donald A. Ritchie*

Approaching an Auschwitz Survivor: Holocaust Testimony and its Transformations *Edited by Jürgen Matthäus*

A Guide to Oral History and the Law *John A. Neuenschwander*

Freedom Flyers: The Tuskegee Airmen of World War II *J. Todd Moye*